TOWN GARDENING

A PLANNING AND PLANTING GUIDE

TOWN GARDENING

A planning and planting guide

PETER STAGG M HORT(RHS), FI HORT
Foreword: PERCY THROWER MBE, VMH, AHRHS, NDH

MILDMAY BOOKS

LONDON

trees, the weeping willow or the solitary *Cupressocypris ley-landii*, which has been grossly overplanted in recent years, as your focal point.

Beginning with the rear garden, leave the foreground (as viewed from the house) clear, either as an expanse of grass or as a paved area, to give an illusion of distance. Have the main borders facing south or west, that is, in the sunniest position, and put paths, if you want them, on the shady side. Never put a path down the middle, as this would make the garden appear much smaller. All borders, whether they are for roses, shrubs or herbaceous plants, should run *down* the garden, never across it. The framework and background of trees and shrubs should be in proportion with the house. Arrange them to give contrast – plan rounded against columnar shapes, consider different shades of foliage and flower, and endeavour to achieve a balanced, harmonious overall effect. Do not plant too close to boundaries, for your neighbours can cut back any encroachment. Place trees or arboreal shrubs in positions where they will screen unsightly views, provide some privacy, or soften an adjoining building.

Avoid the temptation to include cheap, fast-growing plants in your designs. Quality is vital. Space in a small garden is too valuable for any but the best of its kind – so allocate places only to those plants that give you the most pleasure and that you know will thrive in your garden's conditions. Do not plant those which are likely to outgrow their positions, unless you intend them simply to act as temporary 'fillers'. It is worth getting to know as many plants as possible. They are the paint on the canvas. A wide variety of well-chosen plants will give more enjoyment than a solid mass of colour. A select list of plants should be carefully compiled and borne in mind. This will probably necessitate the occasional polite refusal of neighbours' surplus plants! Above all, do not buy any plant until you have acquainted yourself with all the details of it, have seen some good specimens of it, have noted where they are growing, and are satisfied that it is of proven garden merit, hardy, and likely to flourish in the conditions you can provide.

Rich colouring in flowers is a particular asset in town gardening, and for this reason seasonal bedding plants are important, although a considerable period of the year can be covered by a careful selection of trees and shrubs. While to confine the garden to roses, alpines or herbaceous plants will give an abundance of colour at a particular time of the year, this can be uninteresting once the flowers are over. In the very large garden this difficulty does not arise because, collectively, these specialized areas and features will give an all-year-round interest. In the small garden a wide variety of distinctive plants will give the year-round interest.

Heathers are the exception to this general rule. Different species and varieties flower throughout the year; furthermore they range in height from low-growing forms to tree heathers. They also associate well with other shrubs and conifers, but they are unfortunately not happy in industrial areas or sites exposed to heavy traffic, and only a few species are tolerant of chalk.

Up to 50 per cent of the total planting should, in my view, be evergreens. These provide contrast, are a good background for other shrubs and flowers, and effectively soften hard materials such as concrete, stone and brick. They also give valuable shelter to birds during the harsh winter months, and provide them with ideal nesting sites in the spring. Excellent value can be had from those plants that give a double display. *Rhododendron luteum*, the fragrant yellow azalea, flowers in the spring, and its leaves turn to rich shades of crimson in the autumn. The many *Camellia japonica* varieties give a wonderful show of flowers in the spring, and magnificent shining evergreen leaves as a bonus for the rest of the year. These are particularly suited to town gardens: in the City of London gardens over 40 varieties of *Camellia japonica* flourish. *Rosa rugosa* 'Frau Dagmar Hastrup' has good foliage, fine flowers in the summer, and large, beautiful, rich crimson hips in the autumn. These are only a few examples of the many good dual-purpose shrubs.

Unfortunately, only those evergreens with leathery leaves will survive in polluted industrial areas. All conifers, other than the deciduous species, should be excluded in these conditions. Rain and overhead watering clean and reduce clogging of pores in the leaves of evergreens, but regrettably do not have the same effect on conifers. Leaves are the plant's food factory, and must be kept in good condition. This is why the control of pests and diseases is so important. Healthy leaves mean a thriving plant.

Pollution of the atmosphere over a long period affects the soil by a build-up of poisonous deposits. In severe cases, replacement of the top 12 inches (at least) with fresh soil is the only remedy. In certain circumstances, the excavated soil could be used to create different levels, giving the illusion of additional space. This also applies where an informal layout includes a pond with a rock garden. By using the excavated soil in a similar way, provided the top 12 inches are reserved for good imported topsoil, attractive features are achieved with the minimum effort and cost. When altering levels, remember that the damp-proof course of the house or outbuilding must not be covered.

Where appreciably different levels exist, a terraced garden can be very attractive (see drawing on page 45). A simple rule to observe is that horizontals should be wider and verticals shorter with each successive lower terrace, the idea being to give a concave effect when the garden is viewed from the top. This can be accentuated by planting taller plants on the upper levels and lower plants on the bottom terraces. As Capability Brown said, 'Plant the hill-tops and flood the valleys.'

Walls, as we know, were invented for supporting plants on the outside and books on the inside. To have a house well clothed with choice climbing plants is the best way of merging it with the garden. Furthermore, the plants will protect the fabric of the house from the weather. Where garden walls exist, they can be exploited by planting a wide variety of climbing plants. Whatever is finally planted in your garden, corms, tubers and bulbs will make a splendid addition, with different species flowering in each month of the year. Many of them are not grown as profusely as their charm and beauty merit. I have described some favourites later in this book.

You probably want a garden shed. This need not be a plain box, but can take the form of a summerhouse hung with shingle tiles, or made of plain timber with a thatched roof. If this is too costly, an ordinary basic shed could be completely covered with attractive climbing plants. *Hedera canariensis, Hedera colchica, Celastrus orbiculatus, Clematis montana* 'Grandiflora' and *Clematis montana* 'Elizabeth' are only a few.

A series of rectangular gardens with identical fences or walls, row after row, is the standard pattern in towns. If you have one of these gardens, try to make it different by *not* having a central lawn surrounded by flower borders! Different levels, an archway, a pergola, hedges, a dry wall and decorative paving are some features which will help to overcome the all-too-familiar layout. A particularly exciting way to add interest is to have water, in a formal or informal pool, with or without a fountain or waterfall. This gives you an excellent opportunity to introduce aquatic plants, and perhaps a few fish. Or consider covering your path with a pergola. The pillars should be of stone or brick. The overhead timbers are best in oak, but secondhand softwood will do just as well if vigorous climbers are planted – they will, surprisingly, keep the timbers dry and help to preserve them. By including some feature or combination of features of this type, interest and variety have been achieved. You have established the main subject of your picture, and the background and framework will fall into place around it as you place your carefully selected trees, shrubs and other plants.

Once you have made your general design, and decided upon your main features, you can begin the all-important task of planting – putting the paint on the canvas! Select your key trees and shrubs, site these in their permanent positions, and fill in with fast-growing shrubs that will be discarded as the key plants develop. Planting reasonably close ensures that the plants give each other some measure of shade and shelter, which is vital to allow them to grow away without any undue check. The key plants will vary from 6 feet to 30 feet apart; the temporary, fast-growing shrubs can be scattered between them about 5 feet apart. Moving any key plants is, of course, best avoided, but it may be that some will need to be transplanted at a later date. This should always be done in autumn.

Open-planned front gardens are unfortunately prone to abuse by dogs, which can cause considerable damage to choice plants. Where there is this trouble, a fence, wall or protective hedge is usually the only solution. *Berberis gagnepainii* or *Poncirus trifoliata*, both impenetrable, make very attractive hedges and require clipping only once a year. A fine garden with good-quality plants is no place for cats or dogs, and if you are not prepared to exclude them, my immediate reaction would be to advise you to concrete the area over. Of course you are free to find your own compromise, but you are likely to lose many charming plants!

Plant names, to many people, are difficult to understand. There are normally two names given to a plant. The first is the generic, or group name, and the second the specific, or species name. Usually there are many species belonging to the same genus. Plants of garden origin have a third name, which denotes the variety, or cultivar. An example of such a plant is *Campanula* (generic) *rotundifolia* (specific) *alba* (varietal). *Campanula* means 'little bell', *rotundifolia*, 'round-leaved', *alba*, 'white'. Knowing the translation of the Greek or Latin names can often assist in the memorizing or the identification of a certain plant. Where this might be helpful, I have given the translation of the generic names in the text. Specific names, which in many cases are common to several plants, appear in the glossary of the end of the book, to avoid unnecessary repetition.

There are various ways in which the enjoyable challenge of planning a garden might be approached. The plans on the following pages are intended simply as suggestions.

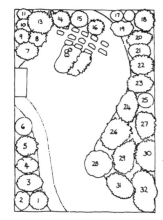

1. Rhododendron 'Praecox'
2. Hamamelis mollis
3. Abelia grandiflora
4. Cytisus × praecox
5. Magnolia × soulangiana 'Brozzonii'
6. Chamaecyparis lawsoniana 'Fletcheri'
7. Prunus incisa
8. Viburnum plicatum 'Mariesii'
9. Syringa × josiflexa 'Bellicent'
10. Rosa rugosa 'Roseraie de l'Hay'
11. Cotoneaster rothschildianus
12. Aesculus parviflora
13. Prunus subhirtella 'Autumnalis'
14. Arundinaria nitida
15. Thujopsis dolabrata
16. Phyllostachys nigra
17. Juniperus 'Sky Rocket'
18. Magnolia × loebneri 'Leonard Messel'
19. Berberis thunbergii 'Atropurpurea'
20. Elaeagnus pungens 'Maculata'
21. Berberis darwinii
22. Sambucus racemosa 'Plumosa Aurea'
23. Camellia japonica 'Giulio Nuccio'
24. Rosa moyesii 'Nevada'
25. Chamaecyparis lawsoniana 'Pottenii'
26. Romneya coulteri
27. Cotinus coggygria 'Royal Purple'
28. Juniperus × media 'Pfitzerana Aurea'
29. Cotoneaster rotundifolius
30. Abutilon vitifolium
31. Rhododendron vaseyi
32. Ceanothus 'Cascade'

Underplant bulbs in variety

17

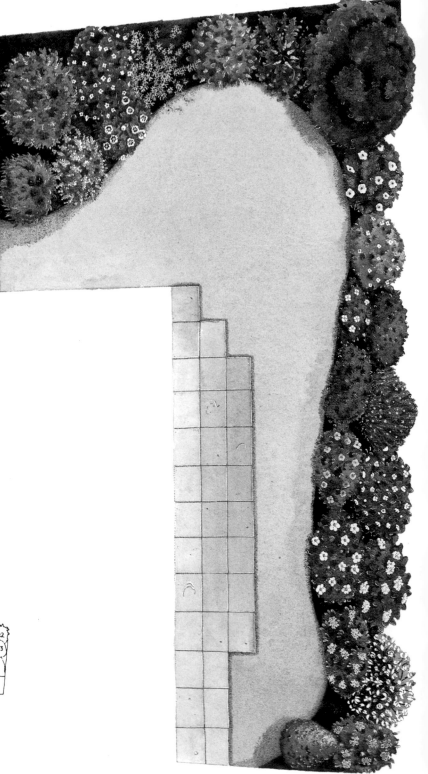

1. *Phyllostachys flexuosa*
2. *Kolkwitzia amabilis*
3. *Prunus lusitanica*
4. *Rubus × tridel*
5. *Paeonia suffruticosa* 'Renkaku'
6. *Hamamelis mollis*
7. *Syringa microphylla* 'Superba'
8. *Mahonia japonica*
9. *Acer nikoense*
10. *Rosa moyesii* 'Nevada'
11. *Poncirus trifoliata*
12. *Euonymus yedoensis*
13. *Cistus × corbariensis*
14. *Fuchsia* 'Mrs Popple'
15. *Erica arborea* 'Alpina'
16. *Philadelphus* 'Beauclerk'
17. *Rosa rugosa* 'Frau Dagmar Hastrup'
18. *Viburnum dilatatum*
19. *Romneya coulteri*
20. *Magnolia × soulangiana* 'Brozzonii'
21. *Rhododendron luteum*
22. *Rhododendron vaseyi*
23. *Juniperus × media* 'Pfitzerana Aurea'

Underplant bulbs in variety

Hedge: *Fagus sylvatica*

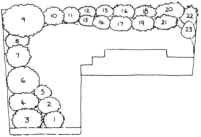

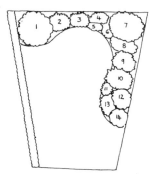

Hedge: *Ilex aquifolium*

1. *Gleditsia triacanthos* 'Sunburst', underplanted with *Daphne laureola* and *Sarcococca hookerana didyma*
2. *Rosa spinosissima* 'Frühlingsgold'
3. *Camellia* 'Magnoliaeflora'
4. *Ceanothus arboreus* 'Trewithen Blue'
5. *Rhododendron yunnanense*
6. *Pieris formosa forrestii* 'Wakehurst Form'
7. *Magnolia denudata*
8. *Rosa bourbon* 'Boule de Neige'
9. *Hibiscus syriacus* 'Blue Bird'
10. *Syringa × chinensis*, underplanted with *Erica × darleyensis*
11. *Hypericum* 'Rowallane'
12. *Philadelphus* 'Belle Etoile'
13. *Viburnum carlesii* 'Diana'
14. *Cornus mas*, underplanted with *Iris stylosa*

Underplant bulbs in variety

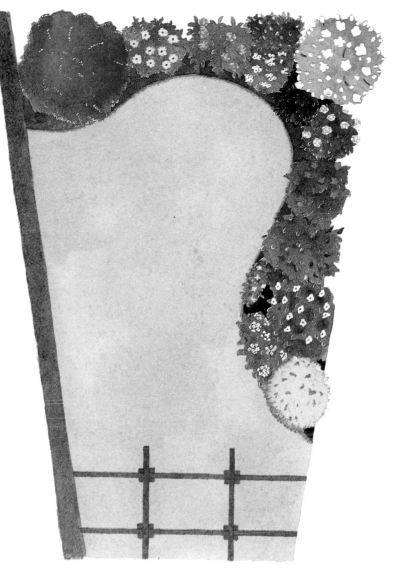

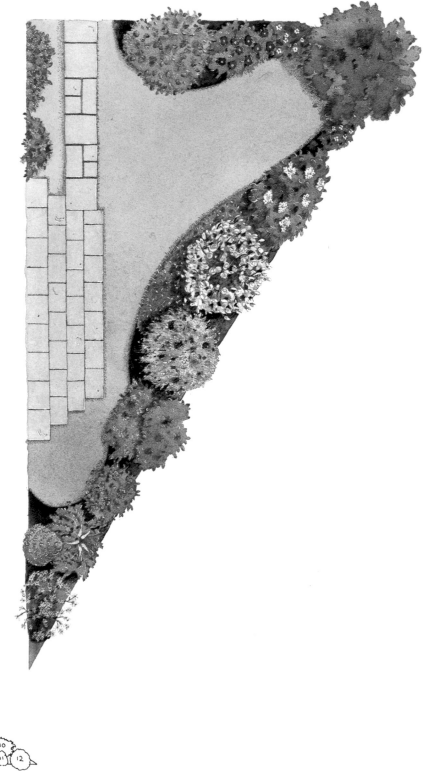

1. *Ceanothus* × *lobbianus*
2. *Rosa moyesii* 'Nevada'
3. *Morus nigra*,
    underplanted with
    Rubus tricolor
4. *Viburnum plicatum*
    'Mariesii'
5. *Magnolia alba* 'Superba',
    underplanted with
    Muscari comosum
    'Monstrosum'
6. *Corylopsis willmottiae*
7. *Parrotia persica*
8. *Rhododendron* 'Tessa'
9. *Rhododendron* 'Augfast'
10. *Mahonia japonica*
11. *Thuja occidentalis*
    'Rheingold'
12. *Hamamelis mollis*
13. *Clematis* 'Mrs
    Cholmondeley'
14. *Solanum crispum*
    'Glasnevin'

Underplant bulbs in variety

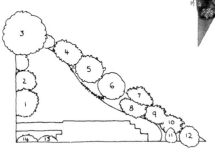

Hamamelis mollis
Camellia japonica
'Adolphe Audusson'
Abelia grandiflora
Berberis linearifolia
Ceanothus 'Delight'
Rosa spinosissima
'Frühlingsmorgen'
Syringa × josiflexa
'Bellicent'
Aesculus parviflora
Garrya elliptica
Chusquea couleou
Ceanothus gloriosus
Poncirus trifoliata
Mahonia japonica
Camellia japonica 'Mrs D.
W. Davis'
Abutilon vitifolium
Drimys winteri
Hedera helix 'Goldheart'
Actinidia kolomikta
Rosa 'Handel' with
Clematis macropetala
Campsis radicans
Magnolia × loebneri
'Leonard Messel'
Halesia carolina
Hemerocallis 'Hyperion'
Ligularia clivorum
Primula pulverulenta
'Bartley Strain'
Primula florindae
Osmunda regalis
Hosta glauca
Iris kaempferi
Primula helodoxa
Lysichitum camtschatcense
Kirengeshoma palmata
Caltha palustris 'Flore Pleno'

Pool:

Nymphaea 'James Brydon'
Nymphaea 'Chromatella'
Butomus umbellatus
Pontederia cordata

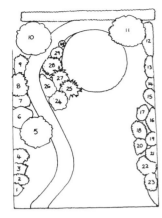

1. *Viburnum × bodnantense*
2. *Rhododendron Mucronulatum*
3. *Rhododendron augustinii*
4. *Rhododendron* 'Dairymaid'
5. *Acer pseudoplatanus* 'Brilliantissimum'
6. *Berberis darwinii*
7. *Eucryphia glutinosa*
8. *Camellia japonica* 'Mathotiana'
9. *Paeonia suffruticosa*
10. *Acer griseum* underplanted with *Rhododendron orbiculare*
11. *Prunus subhirtella* underplanted with *Erica carnea* 'Springwood White' and *Erica × darleyensis*
12. *Erica mediterranea* 'Superba'
13. *Kalmia latifolia*
14. *Osmanthus delavayi*
15. *Rhododendron yunnanense*
16. *Rhododendron* 'Matador'
17. *Rhododendron race mosum*
18. *Pieris formosa forrestii* 'Wakehurst Form'
19. *Rosa alba* 'Belle Amour'
20. *Rosa rugosa* 'Frau Dagmar Hastrup'
21. *Berberis linearifolia*
22. *Hamamelis mollis*
23. *Romneya coulteri*
24. *Helleborus orientalis*
25. *Kniphofia galpinii*
26. *Perovskia atriplicifolia*
27. *Iris sibirica*
28. *Arundinaria auricoma* (brilliant golden yellow variegated bamboo)
29. *Euphorbia wulfenii*
30. *Agapanthus* 'Headbourne Hybrids'

Hedge: *Taxus baccata* (yew)

Bulbs in Lawn: *Narcissus cyclamineus* 'Peeping Tom' and *Crocus tomasinianus*.

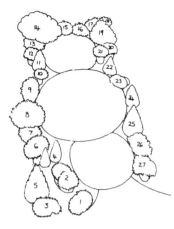

1. *Arundinaria fortunei*
2. *Phyllostachys viridi-Glaucescens*
3. *Cortaderia selloana* 'Sunningdale Silver'
4. *Juniperus × media* 'Pfitzerana Aurea'
5. *Chamaecyparis lawsoniana* 'Pottenii'
6. *Arundinaria nitida*
7. *Rhododendron* 'Temple Bell'
8. *Magnolia × loebneri* 'Neil McEacharn'
9. *Camellia japonica*
10. *Arundinaria auricoma*
11. *Chamaecyparis lawsoniana* 'Fletcheri'
12. *Phyllostachys nigra*
13. *Rhododendron* 'Blue Bird'
14. *Arbutus × andrachnoides*
15. *Phyllostachys nigra*
16. *Camellia japonica*
17. *Rhododendron* 'Humming Bird'
18. *Rhododendron* 'Elizabeth'
19. *Cornus nuttallii*
20. *Chusquea couleou*
21. *Arundinaria fastuosa*
22. *Cryptomeria japonica* 'Elegans'
23. *Phyllostachys nigra* 'boryana'
24. *Chamaecyparis pisifera* 'Filifera Aurea'
25. *Thujopsis dolabrata*
26. *Abutilon vitifolium*
27. *Arundinaria murielae*

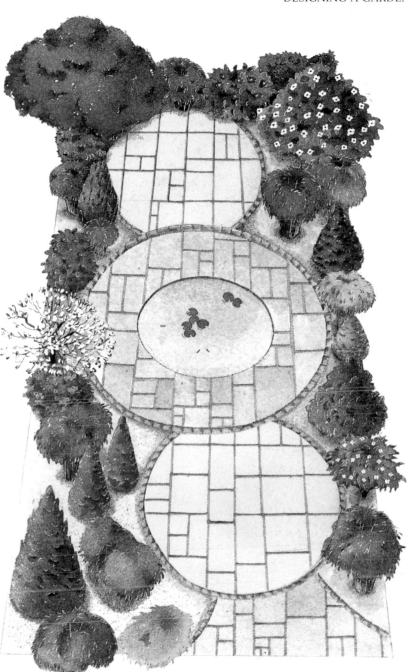

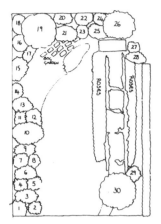

1. *Mahonia japonica*
2. *Hypericum* 'Rowallane'
3. *Hibiscus syriacus* 'Blue Bird'
4. *Choisya ternata*
5. *Cistus* × *corbariensis*
6. *Syringa microphylla* 'Superba'
7. *Philadelphus* 'Belle Etoile'
8. *Berberis thunbergii*
9. *Camellia japonica* 'Purity'
10. *Magnolia denudata*,
    underplanted with
    Erica carnea 'Vivellii'
11. *Elaeagnus pungens* 'Maculata'
12. *Romneya coulteri*
13. *Rosa rugosa* 'Roseraie de
    l'Hay'
14. *Ceanothus* 'Cascade'
15. *Rubus* × *tridel*
16. *Philadelphus* 'Burfordensis'
17. *Ceanothus divergens*
18. *Cotoneaster exburiensis*
19. *Laburnum anagyroides*
    'Aureum', underplanted
    with *Erica* × *darleyensis*
20. *Rhododendron augustinii*
21. *Azalea mollis*
22. *Azalea* 'Exbury Hybrid'
23. *Azalea kaempferi*
24. *Rhododendron yunnanense*
25. *Rhododendron* 'Tessa'
26. *Acer nikoense*, underplanted
    with *Erica carnea* 'King
    George' and 'Springwood
    White'
27. *Rhododendron* 'Naomi Glow'
28. *Rhododendron* 'Matador'
29. *Rhododendron* 'Damaris'
30. *Hamamelis mollis*,
    underplanted with *Erica
    carnea* 'Ruby Glow'

    Rose borders: Hybrid Tea
    and Floribunda roses

    Pergola: climbing roses with
    clematis

    Hedge: *Thuja plicata*

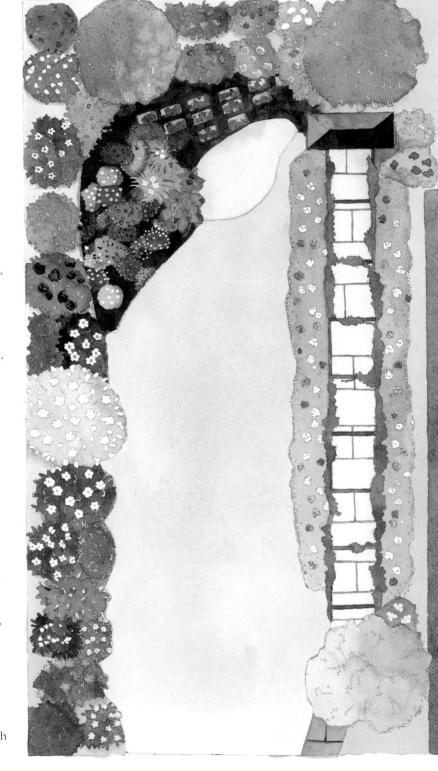

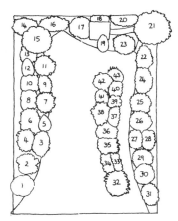

1. *Cornus mas*
2. *Viburnum × bodnantense*
3. *Azalea 'Exbury Hybrid'*
4. *Camellia japonica 'Jupiter'*
5. *Juniperus × media*
   'Pfitzerana Aurea'
6. *Ceanothus 'Cascade'*
7. *Magnolia stellata*
8. *Poncirus trifoliata*
9. *Rosa moyesii 'Nevada'*
10. *Philadelphus 'Burfordensis'*
11. *Syringa × prestoniae 'Isabella'*
12. *Juniperus communis 'Hibernica'*
13. *Rhododendron 'Tessa'*
14. *Rhododendron 'Temple Bell'*
15. *Gleditsia triacanthos 'Sunburst'*
16. *Rhododendron 'Augfast'*
17. *Osmanthus delavayi*
18. *Corylopsis willmottiae*
19. *Drimys winteri*
20. *Hibiscus syriacus 'Blue Bird'*
21. *Prunus lusitanica*
22. *Rosa moyesii 'Geranium'*
23. *Morus nigra*
24. *Rubus × tridel*
25. *Viburnum dilatatum*
26. *Magnolia × soulangiana 'Lennei'*
27. *Agapanthus umbellatus*
28. *Phyllostachys nigra*
29. *Rosa rugosa 'Roseraie de l'Hay'*
30. *Garrya elliptica*
31. *Rhododendron luteum*
32. *Agapanthus*
    'Headbourne Hybrids'
33. *Euphorbia characias*
34. *Malva alcea*
35. *Alstroemeria 'Ligtu Hybrids'*
36. *Sidalcea 'Sussex Beauty'*
37. *Echinops ritro*
38. *Romneya coulteri*
39. *Campanula lactiflora*
40. *Solidago 'Golden Falls'*
41. *Aruncus sylvester*
42. *Monarda 'Mrs Perry'*
43. *Salvia superba*

25

A simple, informal design which disguises rectangular boundaries. A, B and C are trees, and the path takes a curve towards the shadier side of the garden before leading towards the pergola in the far corner. Glimpsed through the foliage of tree C, the pergola subtly suggests that the garden is longer and wider than it really is. You could put tubs on the patio.

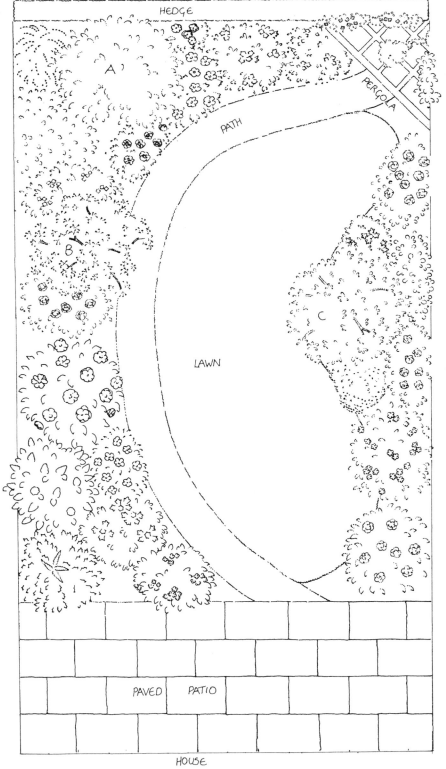

This is a formal terraced garden, sloping away from a paved patio. Steps descend from both retaining walls. A garden that slopes away from the house can offer a succession of pleasant surprises: the first terrace conceals a semi-circle of herbaceous plants; the second terrace a small, central pool and symmetrically curving steps. By planting 'tall' on the upper terrace (the small trees A, B, C, D, E and F) and planting 'low' on the lower the slope of the garden can be excitingly emphasized.

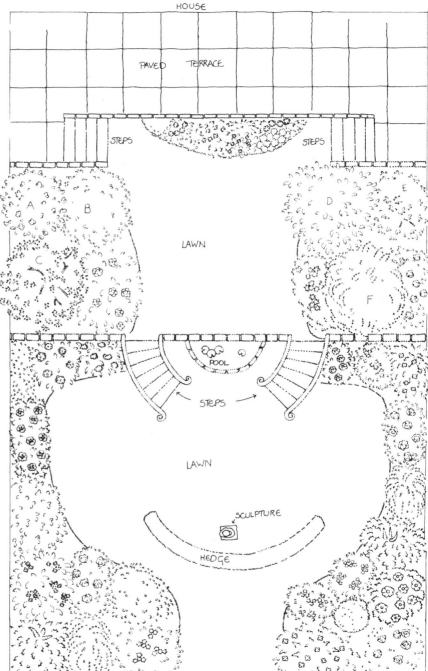

Curving borders and islands of low-growing shrubs lead the eye to the pergola in the far corner of this garden. No pools, no walls, no terraces – just the sweep of a well-groomed lawn and shrubs and herbaceous plants chosen for their form and colour. The two trees, A and B, give height and movement.

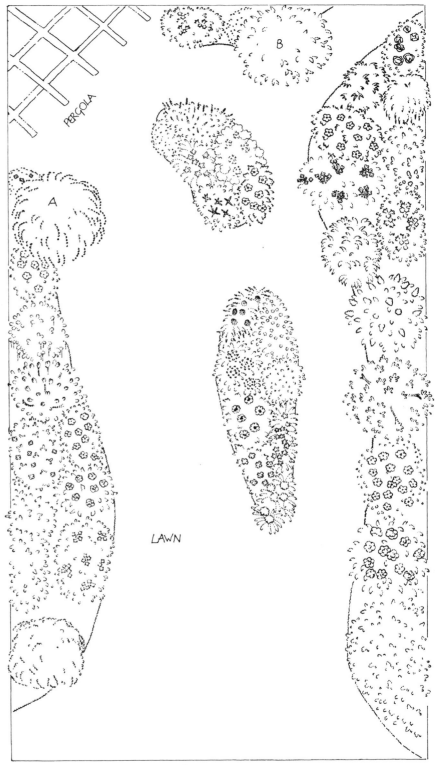

PERGOLA

B

A

LAWN

HOUSE

A design like this is choc-a-bloc with interest. A most rewarding variety of plants can be grown when you have a pergola-covered path, a summer house, herbaceous borders, several ponds *and* a bog garden! The three linked ponds, on different levels, are really the focus of the design. The bog garden on the far side has stepping stones set into it. Five trees, A, B, C, D and E, complete the picture.

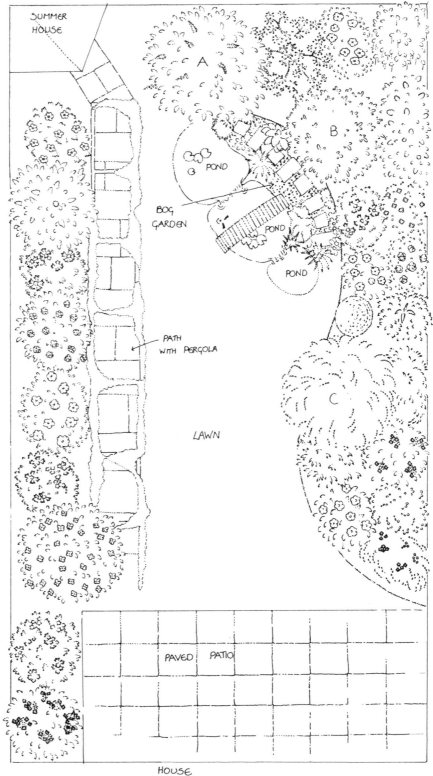

SUMMER HOUSE

A

B

POND

BOG GARDEN

POND

PATH WITH PERGOLA

POND

LAWN

C

PAVED PATIO

HOUSE

Yet another rectangle which has been given the 'gentle curve' treatment. Enclosed on two sides by an evergreen hedge, it has four trees, A, B, C and D, for interest and privacy. Banks of shrubs, small conifers and hardy perennials fill the borders. The side lawn contains spring bulbs.

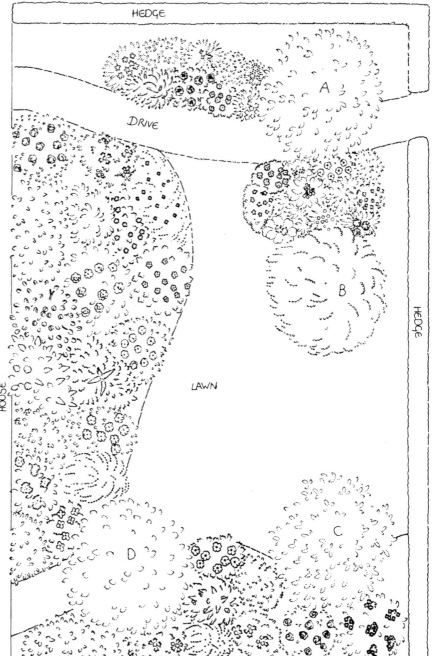

Framed by the loggia – always a pleasing transition between house and garden – the view from this house is of a formal garden planned around a large, paved, rectangular pool, with herbaceous and shrub borders raised behind low retaining stone walls. Trees A, B and C close the vista from the house, creating a backdrop for all the other plants in the garden.

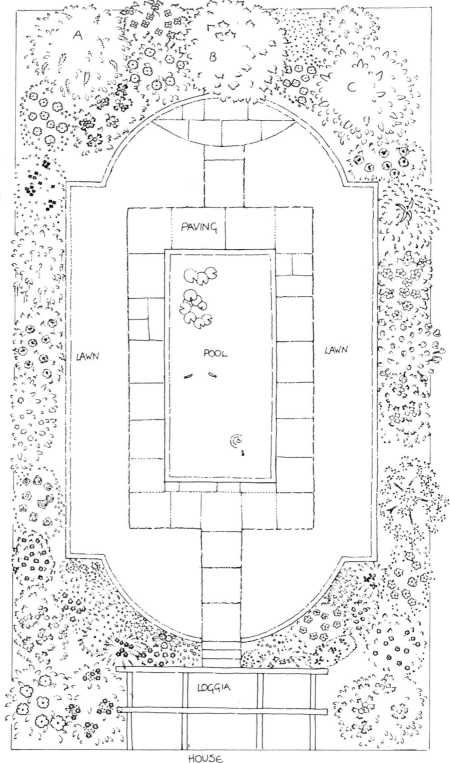

PAVING

LAWN

POOL

LAWN

LOGGIA

HOUSE

CHAPTER 2

Soil and drainage

Moving house can be a great pleasure, though nobody would deny that it can cause a certain amount of anxiety. Moving garden usually brings just as many problems. Very rarely is the ideal garden inherited with a suitable house. The model garden is one with a gently sloping, south or south-west aspect, sheltered from north and east winds, with a well-drained, fibrous loam soil, cultivated over many years, which has the right mixture of sand, silt and clay combined with plenty of humus. A pH reading (see below) of between 5.0 and 6.0 opens the door to the joy of cultivating the vast Ericaceous tribe which includes rhododendrons, azaleas, pieris, vaccineums, pernettyas, cassiopes and the numerous other calcifuge plants that have made such an immense contribution to many fine English gardens. However, whatever type of garden is acquired, new or old, the initial clearance of weeds is generally a 'must', and in an old-established garden some judicious pruning is inevitable. For those acquiring a new house and garden, thorough preparation for planting is paramount if disappointments and regrets are to be avoided. There are simply no short cuts.

Dealing with weeds

Weeds can be tackled in a variety of ways. Try bastard digging, that is, incorporating about 2 hundredweight or one good 4-cubic-foot barrowload of compost, well-rotted farmyard manure or spent mushroom manure to 10 square yards, and as work proceeds removing as many weed roots as possible. By leaving the land fallow until the following autumn, subsequent weed growth can be effectively dealt with by digging out, hoeing and using herbicides. In areas where trees and shrubs are already established and are to be retained, clear the surface of all weed growth, then lay down sheets of black polythene,

Opposite:
No substitute for spade power!

33

anchored with stones. Make small slits every 4 square feet for rainwater to drain away, and leave this sheeting in position for about 12 months. All persistent weeds, such as bramble, bindweed and ground elder, will die out. This method looks unsightly, but it does work. Digging and breaking the feeding roots of trees and shrubs is detrimental, and best avoided. For this reason, established shrub borders and rose beds should never be dug, only top dressed annually with compost, farm-yard manure, spent mushroom manure or leaf mould.

It is worth noting the species of weeds that are flourishing, because weeds do adapt themselves to particular soil conditions, and may indicate what those conditions are. For example, the healthy growth of spurrey, sorrel, heartsease and plantain denotes certain acidity. The presence of bracken, foxgloves, gorse, daisies and heather may also suggest acidity. Clover is very intolerant of acid conditions and favours a chalky soil. Wild clematis (old man's beard, or traveller's joy), birds-foot trefoil, scabious, ladies' fingers (*Anthyllis vulneraria*), kidney vetch, bladder campion and chicory all thrive on an alkaline soil. Loamy soils in good condition produce an abun-dance of groundsel, chickweed, fat hen and sow thistle. Soils which are wet and badly drained are strongholds for sedges, rushes, flags, mare's tail and meadow-sweet. Common moss is associated with starvation and poor aeration. Regular feeding and aeration is the only remedy for moss in lawns.

Chemical weedkillers are an extremely effective method of weed control if prudently applied. Contact herbicides, such as Paraquat, kill only the plants they touch, and leave the soil uncontaminated. Alternatively systemic weedkillers, namely 245T, a brushwood killer, and those containing 24D, are absorbed by plants via the cell sap and translocated throughout the whole plant system, stimulating growth; the plant quickly becomes twisted, distorted and a sickly yellow, and eventually dies. There are many herbicides applied to the soil which kill a considerable number of different species and suppress further growth. These persistent soil herbicides must be used with extreme care, for overdoing can cause soil sterility for years. Simazine, Kerb and Round-up fall into this group. The manu-facturers' instructions must be strictly observed.

Soil types

Fertile soils contain all the ingredients for healthy plant growth, and by careful management fertility will be not only maintained but improved. A fertile soil is an amalgamation of clay, sand and humus, a mixture which contains not only a number of chemicals, but hoards of bacteria, insects, earthworms and fungi. Without the bacteria, in particular, the soil would quickly become inert and infertile. Good management encourages these beneficial bacteria to increase; to survive they must have oxygen, moisture and food. Their function breaks down complex substances into simple plant foods which are easily absorbed. There are harmful bacteria, but these thrive in badly drained and poorly aerated soils.

There are four main types of soil: clay, chalk, sand and peat, the type being determined by whichever of these substances is present in the largest proportion. Soil is made up of various-sized particles. In a clay soil very small particles predominate, in a sandy one larger ones predominate. Small particles lie closely together, restricting water movement and aeration, which is why clay soils are cold and wet, making cultivation difficult. When the space between particles is small, air penetration is limited, to the detriment of beneficial soil bacteria and plant roots. Both need plenty of oxygen to flourish. The stickiness of clay is also caused by the collodial properties of the clay particle, which has the ability to hold plant foods and act as a storehouse.

The compost heap

A clay soil, well cultivated and regularly supplied with organic material, becomes friable and crumb-like. The problem for most people is how to get sufficient organic material to do any good. Compost heaps have been recommended in countless books, with full construction details, yet surprisingly few are made. Good compost is beyond price, because it will immeasurably improve the structure, aeration and retention of moisture of all types of soil. Used as a mulch, it will suppress weeds and provide a cool root run, which so many plants enjoy. It is an excellent material with which to line planting holes, for it will encourage a vigorous root system during a plant's first year. It is a well-balanced source of plant foods, and regular applications will dramatically improve fertility.

Making a compost heap is quite a simple job. It is much easier than making a bonfire! Leaves, grass-mowings, kitchen waste, soft hedge-clippings, herbaceous border stems and other organic material will readily rot down if given the right conditions. The process of decomposition is brought about by bacteria, oxygen and moisture. Small heaps made in the open rarely decay because they do not generate sufficient heat. An ideal size for a compost heap in the average garden is about 5 feet wide by 6 feet long by 3 feet high. A sheltered position at the bottom of the garden is suitable, and there should be enough space to have two heaps, the new one being made while the old is rotting down. If the compost is kept well watered, decomposition will be more successful. If the outside does not rot down, either the heap can be turned edges to middle, top to bottom, with copious watering as the work proceeds, or the outside layer can be used to form a base for a new heap. There is no excuse for discarding any organic material. This includes plane leaves, which are difficult to rot down unless mixed with other organic material and well watered.

Unfortunately, in town or country, rats are attracted to the kitchen waste and the snug warmth which a compost heap generates. The centre of a heap, properly made, will heat up to 160°F; it should in any case be above 120°F to get optimum decomposition. The problem of vermin is easily solved by laying a ½-inch-mesh chicken wire on the ground where the heap is to be built, driving in an angle-iron or post vertically at each corner, wrapping chicken wire around to form four sides, and lacing the bottom wire mesh to the lower edges of the side wire; a simple wooden frame with a ½-inch mesh wire forms the lid. Subsequently, if rats are seen, bait in a land drain kept topped up will quickly eliminate them. Once the heap has been started, and material is being added, cover it with old sacks, carpet or similar materials to keep in the heat. A timber container made with old railway sleepers is ideal, for heat is retained and vermin easily excluded. The timber should be painted with a bituminous paint to prevent decay.

Once the container is made, with either chicken wire or timber, the making of the compost heap itself is simple. Put in a 10-to-12-inch layer of organic waste, then add a 1-inch layer of soil to introduce soil bacteria and a dusting of lime at about half a pound per square yard. Add another 10-inch layer of organic material, a layer of soil and dusting of lime and continue adding to the heap in this way. The material will begin to sink as decomposition gets under way. When the container is full, begin another heap. Urine is an excellent activator, and should be added daily to the heap; it is also very high in potassium. When the heap goes cold the compost will be a dark brown or black crumbly material, full of worms and very similar to well-rotted farmyard manure. It is then ready for use.

If a quantity of leaves is available, a leaf pen is advised; a

off the weeds and put them into the bottom, except for the pernicious weeds such as couch, docks, thistle, bindweed and mare's tail – shake these out and leave them on the surface to dry out. Turn the next trench over into the first, fork over the bottom to a spit deep, add compost or manure and proceed until the border is completed by replacing the excavated soil from the first trench into the last.

Waterlogged soil

The ground may, unfortunately, be waterlogged. This could be caused by compression of the soil, which is known as 'panning'. In this case the ground is described as 'hidebound'. Once the soil is cultivated, however, the water will probably drain away. If it does not, then it may be necessary to install a drainage system. Where the ground is low-lying, especially in relation to local streams and rivers, this will override any drainage systems when they flood, and in these circumstances it is pointless to plant trees and shrubs which will not tolerate waterlogged conditions. But this provides an excellent opportunity to lay out a water garden, and plant aquatics and bog plants. The cutting of a few large ditches, the raising of some planting islands to give extra soil depth, and the creation of a pool or pools, with associated bog garden and primula ditch, will immediately provide a most interesting and attractive solution to an otherwise difficult site problem. If you suspect there is a drainage problem, it is quite easy to confirm it by digging several holes about 30 inches deep, at random throughout the garden, and checking the water table. This should be done in the winter, when the water table rises to its highest level. If the holes fill with water quickly, or fill 12 inches or more with water which remains static in the holes, a drainage system is needed.

It is important to realize that a drainage system should exist only to prevent a rapid rise of the water table through the soil. It should not be made in order to allow rain-water to pass through the soil more quickly, or to drain surface water. Rain is aerated, and very beneficial to plant growth, and one of the reasons for applying organic materials to soil is to improve its water-holding capacity, which is a very important factor in periods of drought. Drainage water is quite different. This water rises from below. It is therefore unaerated and generally sour, and when it floods fertile soils it is most harmful, killing the roots of trees, shrubs and plants as well as beneficial soil bacteria, because of a lack of oxygen.

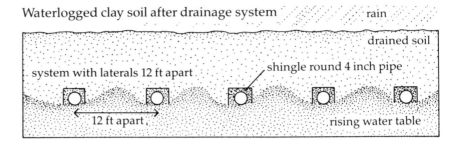

Waterlogged clay soil after drainage system

System with laterals 24 ft apart

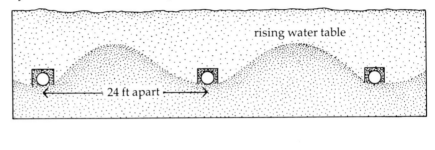

Laterals 48 ft apart

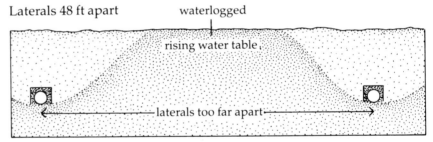

Installing an efficient drainage system is not difficult provided there is a suitable outlet, in the form of a ditch, stream or pond. In many books the reader is advised to dig one or several soakaways, that is, large holes filled with hardcore. This is a satisfactory method for the drainage of house gutters through a freely draining soil, but is most unsuitable for any land drainage scheme. A drainage system is only as good as its outlet. If there is no satisfactory outlet, do not waste time and money on soakaways, because, as the water rises and the soakaways fill up, the water will back up through the entire pipe system and the soil will be as it was before the installation of any drains.

For the reader who has a waterlogged soil and a suitable outlet, the task of laying drains can be made easier by hiring a specialist contractor, who, with a small machine, will cut the

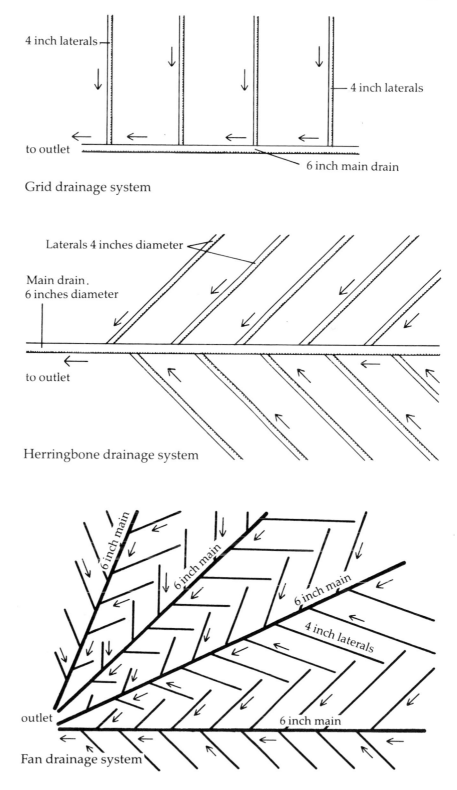

4 inch laterals

4 inch laterals

to outlet

6 inch main drain

Grid drainage system

Laterals 4 inches diameter

Main drain,
6 inches diameter

to outlet

Herringbone drainage system

6 inch main

6 inch main

6 inch main

4 inch laterals

6 inch main

outlet

Fan drainage system

drainage trenches 4 to 6 inches wide without causing too much disturbance. If this work is done in late spring or summer, it is surprising how little disturbance and mess is caused. Lay the main drain or drains from the outlet first; this should be 30 or 36 inches deep. The system can be in a grid, herringbone or fan arrangement as shown in the preceding diagrams. Main drains should be about 40 to 50 yards apart, and laterals on clay 12 feet apart, because drainage water does not move laterally through the soil. Lay all drains to a gradual fall of about 1 in 100 to 1 in 150. To get an efficient system, it is most important that the bottom of the trench is firm with a running level. With laterals 4 inches in diameter and mains 6 inches in diameter, and inspection chambers every 100 to 150 feet, the subsequent task of rodding to clear roots and silt is made much easier. By backfilling a 6-inch layer of shingle around the pipes, silting is kept to a minimum.

Ideally, a drainage scheme should be installed before any garden layout is undertaken. If this is not possible, laterals and mains will have to be laid through established planting, but this will not be a common occurrence because the survival rate on waterlogged soils will be minimal. Drains can either be round clay tiles or continuous perforated plastic.

'Dirt' or poor soil

One of the reasons why so many older town gardens are disappointing is that the soil is lifeless and inert after many years of severe atmospheric pollution. The 1965 Clean Air Act has reduced this hazard to some extent, but traffic fumes remain a problem. Nevertheless, it is now possible to cultivate a wide range of plants, indeed there is almost no limit provided basic requirements are met. When the soil is completely inert, the only solution is to change the top 12 inches – this is a discouraging prospect, particularly where access is difficult, but the results will make the effort worth while. The hard work in exchanging topsoil can be reduced by using some of the old soil to create different levels in a new layout of the garden before the new imported topsoil is placed. If the soil is not 'dirt' (lifeless) but only poor, applications of organic material – spent mushroom manure, compost, farmyard manure or leaf mould – will work wonders provided enough is applied. If liberal annual dressings are given, a good, deep, fertile soil can be achieved within a few years. To supplement these organic bulky materials, apply organic fertilizers, that is, 2 ounces of dried blood per square yard in spring or summer, and 4 ounces of bonemeal per square yard in autumn or winter.

A profile of attractive terracing (see text, page 15).

Correct terracing

horizontals wider and verticals shorter with each successive lower terrace

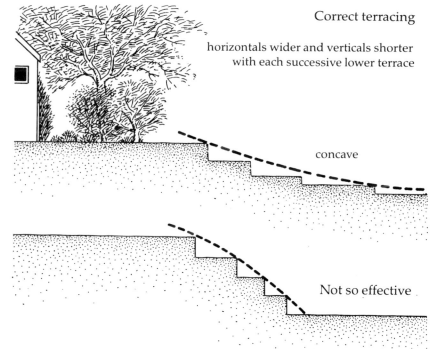

concave

Not so effective

CHAPTER 3

Shrubs

Shrubs are an essential part of any garden. The evergreens provide privacy and winter interest, and, along with the trees, form the garden's backbone. The deciduous shrubs give the necessary relief and contrast. The smaller the garden, the more difficult it is to plan, and the more restraint is needed to avoid overcrowding. It takes some imagination and skill to choose, from the immense reservoir of shrubs, a diverse collection to give fragrance, shape, colour and texture of foliage, flower, fruit and bark all the year round.

Devotees of herbaceous and seasonal bedding plants will say they prefer flowers to shrubs or a 'shrubbery'. The best gardens, however, embrace trees, shrubs, herbaceous plants, alpines, aquatics and seasonal bedding. The main requirements for a good shrub garden are proper drainage and well-dug soil, bastard trenched (see the chapter on soil) and, if heavy, plenty of grit or sand worked in. A quantity of manure, compost, spent mushroom manure or rotted straw should also be dug in. The old adage, 'spend 19s. 6d. on the preparation and 6d. on the shrub' is a wise pronouncement indeed.

Beginners should not be too alarmed by the number of shrubs available. Time and enthusiasm will resolve most of the doubts. I have endeavoured to select some of the best of their kind from an enormous pool.

Abelia × grandiflora. Named after Dr Clarke Abel, physician and author on China, who discovered *Abelia chinensis* while attached to Lord Amherst's embassy to China in 1816–17. This is a semi-evergreen hybrid between *A. chinensis* and *A. uniflora*. It is much hardier and more vigorous than either parent, and grows to about 5 feet high and 5 feet wide. Slightly fragrant, ¾-inch-long, tubular, white tinged pink flowers, up to four to a stalk, appear between July and October. Attractive, late-flowering shrubs are especially useful in the garden. *Abelia*

Opposite:
A shrub garden illustrating contrasting foliage colours, textures and shapes.

grandiflora is suited to chalky and heavy clay soils, provided a good start is given by adequate preparation of the planting position. It thrives in towns, but is not for cold exposed gardens or the northern regions. Award of Garden Merit 1962.

Abeliophyllum distichum. A lovely deciduous February-flowering shrub introduced from Korea in 1924. A well-drained, sunny position is best. The, sweet, fragrant, white flowers, tinged with pink, are produced in profusion on leafless stems. When trained on to a wall it is a delightful sight on a cold winter's day. It grows to about 4 feet high. Immediately after flowering, cut back flowering shoots to promote new growth for the following year's blossoms. This is an excellent town garden plant which merits wider cultivation. Award of Merit 1937, First Class Certificate 1944.

Abutilon vitifolium is a handsome shrub for the sunny sheltered garden.

Abutilon vitifolium. This fine, soft-wooded shrub is very tolerant of industrial and town pollution provided that it has a sunny, sheltered position. It is a native of Chile and was first raised from seed in Dublin by Captain Cottingham, an amateur gardener, in 1836. Unfortunately it is not a long-lived plant, but because it is so easy to replace from seed this should not be a deterrent. The flowers vary from pale to purplish blue, but there is also a white form, *A.v.* 'Album', which received an Award of Merit in 1961. The 3-inches-across, saucer-shaped flowers of rare beauty appear between May and July. It grows to about 15 feet high by 8 feet wide. It does not withstand heavy frost and is not for cold northern gardens, but is suited to mild coastal and sheltered areas. It thrives on chalk and is happy on most well-drained soils.

Aesculus parviflora. *Aesculus*, Latin name for an oak or mast-bearing trees. This deciduous flowering shrub is easy to cultivate and transplants well in any reasonably fertile soil, including chalk and clay. It grows to some 10 feet high and 15 feet wide. The 8- to 12-inch erect panicles of white flowers with red anthers are produced in great profusion in late July-August, when few other shrubs are in flower. Tolerant of the most exposed cold gardens, it excels in urban polluted atmospheres. It is generally an extremely useful and attractive shrub. The large compound leaves of about five leaflets turn a warm, golden colour in the autumn. It was introduced from the south-eastern United States by John Fraser in 1785. Award of Merit 1966, Award of Garden Merit 1969.

Berberis. This genus of some 70 evergreen and deciduous species and hybrids is very easy to cultivate in any well-drained fertile soil. *B. vulgaris*, the common barberry, is a native of the British Isles, but is not much grown because it is a host for wheat rust. Dr Nicholas Culpeper, the early seventeenth-century astrologer-physician who, after a short apprenticeship to an apothecary in St Helen's Bishopsgate set up his own practice in Red Lion Square, Spitalfields, in 1640, wrote about *B. vulgaris*, 'Mars owns the shrub, and presents it to the use of my countrymen to purge their bodies of cholera.' Notwithstanding these medicinal remedies and attributes, some of the barberries are superb garden plants, and those I particularly favour are:

B. darwinii. An attractive evergreen with lovely, deep-orange flowers appearing in April-May, followed by a large crop of blue berries in the autumn. The latter are particular favourites of blackbirds. It has fine foliage but is a little gaunt in habit; however, a little pruning to retain its shape is all that is necessary. It will grow 12 feet high, with a 12-foot spread. Award of Garden Merit 1930.

B. linearifolia. A native of Chile and Argentina. Introduced to Britain in 1927, it is an attractive evergreen which bears deep orange and red flowers in the spring. The habit is somewhat leggy and gaunt, but it can be used advantageously in a position where it does not take up much space. It grows 10 feet high and about 4 feet wide. First Class Certificate 1931.

B. × lologensis. A natural hybrid of *B. darwinii* and *B. linearifolia*, this is a most attractive flowering evergreen shrub. It grows to about 8 feet high and 6 feet wide and has apricot-yellow flowers against small, dark green, glossy leaves, making a splendid splash of colour in May. A good crop of purple fruits follows in the autumn. Award of Merit 1931.

B. × rubrostilla. Probably the finest of all fruiting barberries, this grows to about 3 feet high and 3 feet wide. The deciduous foliage is beautifully coloured in the autumn, and this, together with an abundance of large, translucent, amber red berries, highlights this shrub as a 'must' for the small garden. First Class Certificate 1916, Award of Garden Merit 1969.

B. × stenophylla. An attractive evergreen growing to about 10 feet high and 9 feet wide. It appeared as a hybrid in Handsworth, near Sheffield, in about 1860. It has a profusion of golden yellow flowers on arching stems in

April-May. It does throw up suckers, and can be somewhat invasive. It needs to be contained by cultivating the area around it; however it does require some space to develop its natural beauty. First Class Certificate 1864, Award of Garden Merit 1923.

B. thunbergii. Particularly suited to the small garden because of its compact growth – 4 feet high and 3 feet wide. Its magnificent vivid-red-tinted autumn foliage is unsurpassed. The first European botanist to notice this barberry was Thunberg, in Japan, in 1784. Surprisingly it did not arrive here until some 90 years later. Award of Garden Merit 1927, First Class Certificate in 1890. There is an excellent purple-leaved variety, B.t. 'Atropurpurea', which received an Award of Merit 1926 and an Award of Garden Merit 1932.

B. wilsoniae. An extraordinarily fine small shrub which was discovered and introduced from China in about 1904 by Mr Ernest H. Wilson, after whose wife the plant is named. It grows to about 3 feet high and 3 feet wide, and has an abundance of lovely coral berries with exceptionally fine coloured foliage in the autumn. First Class Certificate 1907, Award of Garden Merit 1969.

Camellia japonica. This impressive hardy evergreen is ideal for the sheltered, shady town garden with an acid soil. Should the soil be alkaline, grow these splendid shrubs in containers (as recommended in the chapter on tubs). There are hundreds of named varieties ranging from single, semi-double and double, with various habits from erect to spreading. Although they are slow-growing – about 6 inches per year at most – they eventually grow to a height of 20 feet plus. Because they resent disturbance intensely, and rarely survive transplanting, give them plenty of space to develop. They are key plants, so infill with temporary plants to be removed later as the camellias mature. Buy container-grown plants, but ensure they are not pot-bound.

For those growing camellias for the first time, I recommend tried and trusted varieties, as follows:

C.j. 'Adolphe Audusson'. Blood-red spotted white, semi-double. Very dependable. Award of Merit 1934, Award of Garden Merit 1969.

C.j. 'Betty Sheffield'. White variegated red and pink, semi-double. Medium compact growth. The sports 'Blush Sheffield' and 'Betty Sheffield Supreme' are both excellent and reliable.

Camellia japonica
'Donckelarii'.

C.j. 'Daikagura'. Bright rose-pink, splotched white. Large, peony-form flower. Slow, compact growth, very hardy and free-blooming. Many excellent sports.

C.j. 'Debutante'. Light pink, free-flowering. Medium to large peony-form flower. Quite vigorous, upright growth. Once established, it likes the sun.

C.j. 'Donckelarii'. Red marbled white, large, semi-double flowers. Slow, bushy growth, hardy. An excellent flowering evergreen. Award of Merit 1960, Award of Garden Merit 1969.

C.j. 'Dr Tinsley'. Very pale pink, shading to deeper pink, semi-double flowers, Compact, upright growth; hardy.

C.j. 'Elegans' (Chandler) Var. Rose-pink and white, very large anemone-form, slow spreading growth. A good wall plant. Award of Merit 1953, First Class Certificate 1958, Award of Garden Merit 1969.

C.j. 'Giulio Nuccio'. Coral-rose, very large, semi-double flowers with irregular petals. Vigorous, upright growth; a magnificent plant. Award of Merit 1962.

C.j. 'Magnoliaeflora'. Blush-pink, medium, semi-double flowers which resemble magnolia flowers. Very free-flowering. Compact growth, hardy. A fine shrub both in and out of flower. Award of Merit 1953.

C.j. 'Mathotiana Supreme'. A deep-red sport of 'Mathotiana'. Very large, semi-double flowers. Vigorous, compact, upright growth.

C.j. 'Mrs D. W. Davis'. Blush-pink, very large, semi-double flowers. Vigorous, compact, upright growth. Award of Merit 1960.

C.j. 'Purity'. White rose form to formal double flowers. Vigorous, upright growth.

C.j. 'Tomorrow'. Strawberry-red, semi-double flowers. Vigorous, open, and slightly pendulous growth. Award of Merit 1960.

Calluna vulgaris (Scotch heather or ling). Also known as *Erica vulgaris*. *Calluna* is from the Greek *kalluno*, to cleanse, referring to the use of this heather in the besom or broom. By careful selection from among the vast range of *Calluna* and *Erica* species and varieties it is possible to ensure flowers all the year round. The genus *Calluna* differs from the genus *Erica* only in so far as the colour is in the calyx, that is, the outer part of the flower known as the sepals. In the genus *Erica* the colour is confined to the corolla, or the petals. In good fertile soils both *Calluna* and *Erica* species are relatively short-lived, because they grow too quickly. They are semi-xerophytes, that is, their foliage is especially adapted to cope with irregular water supplies and where atmospheric conditions, such as wind, favour a high rate of transpiration. Plants in these situations have an obvious need to economize as far as their water supply is concerned. The foliage of callunas and ericas reflect those conditions.

Readers will no doubt know of splendid heather displays on roundabouts and similar roadside planting schemes; but these are in rural districts or coastal areas. Polluted industrial areas and atmospheres laden with traffic fumes such as are found in many cities and towns are definitely not suitable. A well-drained, lime-free soil is essential. An abundance of sunshine and a clean atmosphere are the only other requirements. Remove the flowering shoots immediately after flowering.

Varieties range in height from 3 feet high down to a few inches; their foliage varies from green and silver to gold and bronze. Flowers can be single or double, white, pink, purple or crimson. Callunas are best planted in groups or drifts of one variety together with groups of ericas and daboecias. The choice conifer or shrub – and there are many which associate well with heathers – helps to give a pleasing harmonous layout when carefully sited against a background of larger conifers, rhododendrons, acers, magnolias and the like. These are the ingredients for an attractive heather garden. It is extremely easy to press certain views too hard, but the accepted practice of group planting, in scale with the whole, rather than a host of solitary plants of many varieties, is in my view the right one. Naturally it is interesting to have as many varieties as one can afford, but there is the danger of having too many in an allotted space. There are a considerable number of varieties which merit a place in every suitable garden, but it is only possible here to comment on a few which are among the best:

C.v. 'Alba Plena'. White double flowers. An outstanding heather with pale foliage, and flower spikes up to 10 inches long. Flowers in September-October, 12 inches high. Award of Merit 1938, Award of Merit after Wisley trial 1960, Award of Garden Merit 1969.

C.v. 'Alportii'. Deep crimson flowers, olive-green foliage. Erect growth. Plant 18 inches apart. Flowers in August-September. 24 inches high. Award of Merit and Award of Garden Merit 1947.

C.v. 'County Wicklow', or 'Camla'. Double flowers, shell pink, cut back after flowering. Semi-prostrate, becoming

Calluna vulgaris 'Gold Haze', a particularly fine Scotch heather which received a First Class Certificate for its foliage and an Award of Merit for its flowers. Must have full sun.

brittle with age. Plant 18 inches apart. Flowers in August-September, 9 inches high. Award of Merit after trial 1960, First Class Certificate after trial 1961, Award of Garden Merit 1969.

C.v. 'Gold Haze'. Bright golden foliage with sprays of white flowers. Plant 18 inches apart. Flowers in August-September. 24 inches high. Award of Merit after trial 1961, First Class Certificate after trial 1963, Award of Garden Merit 1969.

C.v. 'H.E. Beale'. A fine plant with 12-inch spikes of double, silver-pink flowers, and easy to grow in a lime-free soil. Plant 18 inches apart. Flowers in September-November. 24 inches high. Award of Garden Merit 1942, First Class Certificate 1943.

C.v. 'J.H. Hamilton'. Double flowers of rose pink, very free, on short spikes. Plant 18 inches apart. Flowers in August-September. 9 inches high. Award of Merit 1935, Award of Merit after Trial 1960, First Class Certificate after trial 1961, Award of Garden Merit 1962.

C.v. 'Mair's Variety'. Spikes up to 12 inches long of pure white flowers. This variety forms a splendid pyramidal shrub. Plant 18 inches apart. Flowers in August-September. 3 feet high. Award of Merit after trial 1961, First Class Certificate after trial 1963.

C.v. 'Peter Sparkes'. Double, deep pink flowers similar to those of 'H.E. Beale', and more vigorous, but not so tall. Plant 18 inches apart. Flowers in August-October. 18 inches high. Award of Merit 1958. First Class Certificate after trial 1962. Award of Garden Merit 1969.

C.v. 'Ruth Sparkes'. Golden foliage with double white flowers, but is inclined to revert. The green shoots should be pinched out. Plant 18 inches apart. Flowers in September-October. 9 inches high.

C.v. 'Tib'. Fully double, crimson flowers, produced on slender spikes. Plant 18 inches apart. Flowers in July-September. 15 inches high. Award of Merit after trial 1960, First Class Certificate after trial 1962.

Caryopteris × clandonensis. *Caryopteris* from Greek *karnon*, a nut, and *pteron*, a wing (the fruits are winged.) This deciduous shrub was introduced in 1844 by Robert Fortune, a native of Berwickshire and one of the greatest of all plant collectors. In 1841 he left the Edinburgh Botanical Gardens to take up the position of Superintendent of the Horticultural Society's hothouses at Chiswick. Two years later the Society sent him

Caryopteris × *clandonensis* 'Ferndown' is a deciduous shrub and produces its feathery, tubular flowers in late summer and early autumn.

to the East to collect rare and new plants. In 1844 he visited the district of Ningpo and was responsible for the introduction of many beautiful hardy and tender plants. He became curator of Chelsea Physic Garden but resigned and went again to China in 1848, remaining essentially a plant collector. The shrub, a native of China and Japan, was subsequently reintroduced by Charles Maries in 1880. With its blue flowers appearing in October, it is a useful addition to the garden. It is not completely hardy, and not a shrub for the cold northern areas, often being cut to the ground in severe winters. It grows to about 4 feet high, and should be pruned in March, all the previous year's wood being cut back to within two or three buds of the old wood. It is ideal in a sunny, sheltered position at the front of a shrub border or against a wall. The varieties 'Arthur Simmonds' (Award of Merit 1933, Award of Garden Merit 1942) and 'Ferndown' (Award of Merit 1953) both produce beautifully bright blue flowers in abundance, and are worth cultivating although they are somewhat tender.

Ceanothus (Californian lilac). A lovely genus of blue flowering evergreen and deciduous plants, which range from prostrate shrubs to small trees. Hard winters unfortunately cause havoc, particularly with the evergreen varieties, which I prefer, because they are tender. In sheltered town gardens they excel, however, and in cold districts they are worth trying against a sunny, sheltered wall. A well-drained, fertile soil is required, and while very chalky soils are not to their liking, polluted industrial atmospheres cause no concern. The following, most of which will grow to between 6 and 10 feet, are recommended:

C. arboreus 'Trewithen Blue'. (See also in chapter on ornamental trees). This magnificent arboreal shrub, or small tree, is the best of a fine genus. It can grow to about 18 feet, is evergreen and flowers in June. Award of Merit 1967.
C. 'Cascade'. When grown on a wall this has a lovely, weeping habit, and reaches a height of about 8 feet. Rather hardier than most, this showy evergreen hybrid is one of the best with its numerous very large clusters of bright blue flowers in the spring. Award of Merit 1946.
C. 'Delight'. A fine evergreen hybrid, one of the best, and hardier than many. It flowers in the spring with long panicles of blue flowers. Award of Merit 1933, Award of Garden Merit 1957.
C. divergens. A particularly attractive, semi-prostrate plant

which will cascade over walls and is useful for paved areas, banks or ground cover. It is evergreen, with deep blue flowers in the spring.

C. 'Gloire de Versailles'. This is a deciduous shrub, particularly useful because it flowers in July and August when very few other shrubs flower. It should be pruned in March, the previous season's growth being cut back to about four buds of the old wood. The large panicles of powder-blue flowers are produced on the current wood. First Class Certificate 1872, Award of Garden Merit 1925.

C. gloriosus. A fine, prostrate, evergreen shrub, ideal for banks, paved terraces, the front of shrub borders, and ground cover. It has lavender-blue flowers in April and May, and is a particular favourite. It requires plenty of space to spread.

Ceanothus gloriosus.

C. 'Henri Defosse'. This variety is similar to 'Gloire de Versailles' and also needs to be pruned in March. It, too has flowers in July and August, but they are deep blue. Award of Merit 1926.

C. × lobbianus. An excellent, large-growing, evergreen hybrid, flowering in May and June. One of the best, and excellent on a sheltered, south-facing wall. Award of Garden Merit 1969.

C. prostratus (squaw carpet). A creeping evergreen plant, very useful for banks, terraces and ground cover and to give the contrast so important in planting schemes. Award of Merit 1935.

C. thyrsiflorus 'Repens' **(creeping blue blossom).** A vigorous, hardy, mound-forming, evergreen shrub with Cambridge blue flowers. It is an excellent plant for the small garden, and is useful on banks, terraces and retaining walls and as ground cover.

C. 'Topaz'. Similar to 'Gloire de Versailles', it also requires pruning in March to produce, on the current season's growth, light indigo blue panicles of flowers in July and August. Award of Merit 1961, Award of Garden Merit 1969.

C. × veitchianus. Where there is unrestricted space of up to 10 feet high and about 10 feet wide, this evergreen, with its vivid blue flowers borne in great abundance in March and April, merits a place. It is one of the hardiest of the ceanothus tribe, but in colder areas it needs a sunny, sheltered, south wall. Award of Garden Merit 1925.

Ceratostigma willmottianum. From Greek *keras*, a horn, and *stigma*, alluding to the horn-like branches of the stigma;

willmottianum after the garden designer Miss Willmott. This is a charming, dainty shrub, with vivid blue flowers in autumn reaching a height and width of about 3 feet. It should be pruned each spring, the previous season's growth being cut back to about two buds. In a hard winter it will be cut to the ground, but will grow away from the roots in the spring. It prefers the sun. Provided that the soil is not waterlogged during the winter, it will flourish in clay soil. A very useful autumn-flowering shrub for the small garden. It is very good in association with the primrose yellow, bell-shaped *Clematis rehderana*; both excel in chalky soils. Introduced from western China in 1908. Award of Merit 1917, Award of Garden Merit 1928.

Cistus. Greek, rock rose. Peacham referred in 1634 to a rock rose, 'sistus that beareth that excellent gumme ladanum'. This is a genus of many species found in the Mediterranean region and particularly in Spain and Portugal. Most species of the genus are tender, the older plants being much more susceptible than the younger ones. They are short-lived in any event, but I have included them because they are excellent for infilling new borders, surviving until key shrubs are established. They are particularly useful on dry, sunny banks, and excel in chalky soils and coastal areas. Because they resent disturbance, container-grown plants are necessary. Unfortunately this lovely genus of plants, with their individual flowers lasting only a day, is not for cold exposed gardens or northern areas.

The following are recommended:

Cistus laurifolius produces papery white flowers in April, May and June.

C. × corbariensis. An evergreen shrub of Corbières, in southern France, this is one of the hardiest and best. It grows to about 3 feet high by 3 feet wide. The crimson tinted buds, opening to white flowers, are produced in June and continue to flower into August. The shrub has attractive reddish young growth.

C. laurifolius (laurel-leaved cistus). This is an attractive evergreen growing to about 6 feet high, with an erect habit. On a hot, sunny day the 3-inch-long, dark, glaucous-green leaves give off a pleasant, faint fragrance. The flowers, about 3 inches across, are white with yellow centres, and are produced from June into August. It is hardier than *C. cyprius* and *C. ladaniferus*, which are both very similar. In *C. cyprius* the white flowers are in clusters, and in *C. ladaniferus* they are solitary; both have a crimson blotch at the base of the petal, while *C. laurifolius* has pure white flowers borne in erect panicles. Award of Garden Merit 1969.

C. populifolius. This evergreen is a native of south-west Europe and has been cultivated since 1656. Quite distinctive, having larger leaves and longer stalks, it is hardier than most other species. It grows up to 7 feet high. The white flowers, 2 inches across, have a yellow stain at the base of each petal. Award of Merit 1930.

Clethra alnifolia (sweet pepper bush). From Greek *klethra*, an alder, which some species resemble. *Clethra* is a member of the Ericaceae family, and dislikes chalky soils. A deciduous shrub from North America, it grows to about 8 feet high, producing fragrant white flowers in August and September. It loves a moist, peaty soil, is very hardy, and is ideal for cold gardens and northern areas. Flowers are produced at the end of the current season's growth. Pruning in March, cutting back the previous year's wood to within three buds, will ensure a maximum crop of flowers of good quality. Award of Garden Merit 1969.

Cotoneaster. From Latin *cotoneus*, quince, and probably a corruption of *adinstar*, likeness, i.e. quince-like. The large genus contains many fine deciduous and evergreen species, varying in habit from prostrate to tree-like. Grown mainly for autumn colour, they also have an irresistible appeal to the apiarist because of the profusion of small white or pink flowers which bees adore. Cotoneasters are most accommodating shrubs, thriving on hot poor soils, excelling in chalk and clay, and extremely tolerant of coastal, salt-laden air and industrial atmospheric pollution. They are all exceptionally hardy. Some make fine windbreaks, admirable for cold exposed gardens and northern areas. They do, however, resent root disturbance, and rarely survive transplanting. Container-grown plants are essential. It would be impossible to grow all the cotoneasters of merit other than in the largest of gardens.

The following are recommended:

C. adpressus 'Praecox'. This deciduous shrub, 3 feet high by 6 feet wide, has arching branches with extra-large, orange-red fruit, and fine red foliage in autumn.

C. exburiensis. A useful large evergreen with lovely yellow fruit. It is very tough and makes a good windbreak for the exposed cold garden. It grows to about 12–15 feet high, and has spreading branches extending to about 10 feet. Award of Garden Merit 1969.

C. horizontalis. An accommodating plant with a horizontal habit of growth, frequently used to cover ugly stonework, brickwork, manholes and other intrusive objects. It grows to about 2 feet high with a 6–7-foot spread. It makes a beautiful wall plant, and is particularly useful on a north-facing wall. Award of Garden Merit 1925. It has unfortunately, in my view, been overplanted by landscape architects, who seem to delight in planting huge drifts of up to 70 yards and more of one shrub. Notwithstanding the merits of the shrub, how very boring this is! Variety, contrast and year-round interest should be the objective.

C. microphyllus. An evergreen of low, prostrate habit, excellent on banks and cascading over retaining walls; it makes good ground cover and prevents weeds from becoming established. However, beware of overplanting this accommodating shrub.

C. rotundifolius. A semi-evergreen, about 5 feet high, introduced in 1825. This native of the Himalayas is, in my view, one of the best. It has large red fruit which the birds seem to ignore, attractive, round-leaved foliage, and a habit ideal for the small garden. Award of Merit 1927.

Cytisus × praecox (Warminster broom). From Greek *kytisos*, trefoil leaves. Brooms are immensely useful because of the rapidity of their growth. As infillers in the shrub border while key plants are developing they are unsurpassed. The genus as a whole is relatively short-lived. *Praecox* is one of the best of many hybrids. It first appeared in the nursery of Messrs Wheeler of Warminster about 1867. It is one of the first to flower, doing so in early May. The striking, cream-coloured, pea-shaped flowers are produced in great abundance. Height and spread 5–6 feet. Some people do not like its distinctive odour, but I do not think it unpleasant. This is an extremely hardy shrub which excels on well-drained clay, sandy and limy soils, in a hot, sunny position. It is not suitable for thin soil over chalk, however, because it becomes chlorotic, that is, it suffers from an iron and magnesium deficiency. The previous season's growth (the old flowering wood) should be cut back immediately after flowering to prevent the shrub from getting too 'leggy' and gaunt. Never cut into the older wood of any broom. Award of Merit 1933.

Daboecia cantabrica (Connemara heath). This plant was first found in Connemara about 1699. It grows to about 2 feet high and 2 feet across. The urn-shaped, rosy-purple flowers appear

Daboecia cantabrica
'Atropurpurea' flowers
throughout the summer.

in May and continue until October. It is a natural bog plant, which must be kept moist with plenty of top dressing of peat.

The following varieties are recommended:

> *D.c.* 'Alba'. Snow-white flowers, 18 inches high. Award of Garden Merit 1969.
> *D.c.* 'Atropurpurea'. Deep purple flowers, 18 inches high. Award of Garden Merit 1969.
> *D.c.* 'Bicolor'. A purple flower with a dash of white, half white, or all white, 18 inches high. Award of Garden Merit 1969.

Daphne. Daphne was the Greek name for *Laurus nobilis*, named after the river god's daughter in Greek mythology who, on being pursued by Apollo, prayed for aid and was transformed into a laurel tree. A sandy or limy soil suits most daphnes, although a well-drained clay is acceptable. A moist, cool root run provided by a 3-inch mulch of spent mushroom manure, peat or compost is very much to their liking. *Daphne laureola* (spurge laurel), a fragrant native of Britain, requires shady woodland conditions; the others flourish in a sunny position. None require any pruning. They all dislike root disturbance and rarely survive transplanting. Pot-grown plants are essential; small seedlings generally found at the base of established plants must be potted early if a successful increase is to be achieved. All daphnes are superbly scented. Unfortunately, for no apparent reason, fine plants suddenly die; but this should not deter the reader from cultivating them because they are easily raised from seed or layers. Several are hardy and most suitable for northern areas and exposed gardens.

> **D. × burkwoodii** (synonymous with 'Somerset'). This daphne grows rapidly up to 3 feet high. Rose-pink flowers, sweetly scented, appear in May and June. Award of Merit 1935.
> **D. mezereum.** *Mezereum* from the old Persian name *madzaryon*, deadly, the destroyer of life, because all parts of the shrub are poisonous. John Gerard, the herbalist, remarks '. . . if a drunkard do eat one grain or berry of this plant, he cannot be allured to drink any drink at that time, such will be the heat in his mouth and choking in the throat'. There have been various cases of death of both man and beast caused by this plant. Culpeper comments in his *Complete Herbal*, 'The whole plant has an exceeding acrid biting taste and is very corrosive.' He goes on to remark that

'the bark of the root, or the inner bark of the branches is to be used, but it requires caution in the administration, and must only be given to people of robust constitutions and very sparingly even to those.' *D. mezereum* is a deciduous shrub, flowering in February and March. Its purple-reddish flowers are sweetly scented, appearing before the leaves, densely clothed on the previous year's shoots. Height and spread 4 feet. Award of Garden Merit 1929. There is a pure white form, *D.m.* 'Alba', which has translucent yellow berries.

D. odora 'Aureomarginata'. A fine, exquisitely fragrant winter- and spring-flowering shrub, growing to about 4 feet high. It is fairly hardy, although a sheltered position is recommended in the interest of the flowers. An ideal shrub to have near the house.

Daphne odora 'Aureomarginata' is one of the most popular of the daphnes.

Elaeagnus × ebbingei. This shrub has attractive, pale silver foliage, and the white flowers appearing in August are sweetly scented. It makes a fine windbreak and is tolerant of all soils, including chalk, as well as salt-laden winds and industrial, polluted atmospheres. A large shrub, up to 12 feet high by 10 feet wide. Award of Garden Merit 1969.

Elaeagnus pungens 'Maculata'. A finely coloured variegated shrub which thrives in any soil, including chalk and clay, and is extremely tolerant of industrial pollution. It is quite hardy. This is a striking plant and ideal for lighting up a dark corner. It grows 6 feet high and 6 feet wide. First Class Certificate 1891, Award of Garden Merit 1969.

Erica (heather). A garden that is too big or too demanding is, sooner or later, going to be neglected. Fortunately, much of the work can be reduced by a sympathetic design which includes a carefully considered planting scheme. An informal layout is very much easier to look after, and happily significantly increases the opportunities to use a very much wider choice of plants. Heathers, conifers, shrubs and bamboos are all labour-saving and offer an immense reservoir to choose from. A specialized group of plants, namely heathers, complemented with selected specimens of conifers, rhododendrons and other associated shrubs, is aesthetically most acceptable, creating a tranquillity difficult to equal. These plants provide colour and interest throughout the year, and range in height from a few inches to several feet, thereby achieving contrast and scale. In short, a heather garden has considerable merit, and in many situations is a wise choice.

Regrettably, heathers will not survive in polluted industrial atmospheres, or in cities and towns with a heavy traffic-fume problem. They prefer the sun and clean air, but will, however, withstand cold winds and salt-laden air in coastal districts. Sandy or peaty soils suit them best, but clay, provided that it is drained and improved with sedge peat or sphagnum moss peat, is acceptable. Limy soils are no good for any heathers except *E. carnea, E. terminalis, E. mediterranea* and *E. darleyensis,* which are all lime-tolerant except on very shallow chalk soils. *E. australis* and E. *vagans* are less tolerant, but are worth trying on a deeper soil over chalk.

Maintenance consists of weeding until they are well established and, as and when necessary thereafter, pruning or cutting back flowering spikes after flowering, watering as they form flower spikes and flower buds and top dressing of peat annually. Plant between September and April, but the earlier the better, to take advantage of the summer warmth in the soil, for establishing the plants before the winter. As with *Calluna vulgaris,* planting in groups or drifts is advisable for the best effect.

I have selected some of the best from a very large range.

Erica arborea 'Alpina' is a hardy tree heather.

E. arborea. The tree heather from Southern Europe, North Africa and the Caucasus, where it grows to a height of 20 feet. In this country it grows to about 8 feet high. White blossoms, hawthorn-scented, February to April.

E.a. 'Alpina'. This variety is rather smaller, and flowers a little later. It will withstand the cold better than the type plant. Award of Garden Merit 1933, Award of Merit 1962.

E. australis (Spanish heath). Olive green foliage with pink flowers, April to May. 6 feet high. A native of Spain and Portugal and introduced to Britain in 1769. Award of Merit 1935, First Class Certificate 1962, Award of Garden Merit 1969.

E. carnea (mountain heath). From the central European Alps, a very hardy winter-flowering shrub. The following are recommended varieties:

E.c. 'Eileen Porter'. Low-growing carmine red flowers, October-April. Plant about 18 inches apart. Award of Merit 1956. *E.c.* 'King George V'. Deep rose flowers, February-April. Forms a neat bush 9–12 inches high. Plant 18 inches apart. Award of Merit 1922, Award of Garden Merit 1927.

Erica carnea 'Springwood White' is a very hardy excellent carpeter for banks and underplanting shrubs.

E.c. 'Loughrigg'. Blue-green foliage with light green turning to bronze at the tips, reddish purple flowers, February-March, 9–12 inches high. Plant 18 inches apart. Award of Merit after trial 1966.

E.c. 'Praecox Rubra'. Deep rose-red flowers, December-January. Prostrate habit. Plant 18 inches apart. Award of Merit after trial 1966, First Class Certificate after trial 1968.

E.c. 'Springwood White'. Large, white flowers with brown anthers, January-April, 9 inches high. Very rampant. Plant 2 feet apart. Award of Merit 1930, Award of Garden Merit 1940, First Class Certificate after trial 1964.

E.c. 'Springwood Pink'. Rose-pink flowers, February-April, 9 inches high. Not so rampant as 'Springwood White', and foliage a deeper green. Plant 18 inches apart. Award of Merit after trial 1964, Award of Garden Merit 1969.

E.c. 'Vivellii'. Bronze foliage with deep carmine flowers, February-April. Close, bushy habit. Plant 15 inches apart. Award of Merit after trial 1964, First Class Certificate after trial 1965, Award of Garden Merit 1969.

E. ciliaris (Dorset heath). *Ciliaris* means fringed with hair, and refers to the leaves. This heather is found in western France, Spain, Portugal, Dorset and Cornwall. It is more tender than other heathers and will not withstand drought conditions so well. All varieties flower from July to October.

E.c. 'Maweana'. Rosy-red flowers, 18 inches high. A vigorous upright variety. Plant 18 inches apart.

E.c. 'Mrs C. H. Gill'. Red flowers with dark green foliage, 12 inches high. Plant 12 inches apart.

E.c. 'Stoborough'. White flowers and apple-green foliage, 24 inches high. Plant 18 inches apart.

E. cinerea (bell heather). Native from Southern Spain to Norway, including Britain and Ireland. *Cinerea*, grey or ashen, refers to the underparts of the leaves. This is the most calcifuge (lime-hating) of all heathers. It prefers dry, sandy soils and plenty of sunshine. Most flower during August and September, but some flower in June and July.

E.c. 'Coccinea'. Blood-red flowers with deep green foliage, June-July. 4 inches high. Plant 12 inches apart.

E.c. 'Domino'. White flowers with ebony-coloured calices, deep green foliage. Bushy habit. 9 inches high. Plant 15 inches apart.

E.c. 'Eden Valley'. Rosy-lilac flowers paling to white at the calyx. Prostrate habit. Plant 12 inches apart.

E.c. 'Golden Drop'. During the summer and autumn the foliage is golden, and during the winter this slowly turns to red. The flowers are pinkish purple but there are very few. Essentially a foliage plant. 6 inches high.

E.c. 'P.S. Patrick'. Deep purple flowers, 15 inches high. Award of Merit after trial 1967, Award of Garden Merit 1969.

E. × darleyensis. *Darleyensis* refers to the place of origin, the Darley Dale nurseries of Messrs James Smith and Sons, at the beginning of the century. Also known as *Erica × darleyensis* 'Darley Dale'. Hybrid between *E. carnea* and *E. mediterranea*. It is lime-tolerant. Flowers October to May. 2 feet high. Award of Merit 1905, Award of Garden Merit 1924.

E. × d. 'Arthur Johnson'. Magenta flowers, November-May. 24 inches high. Award of Merit 1952, Award of Garden Merit 1969.

E. × d. 'George Rendall'. Pink flowers, December-May. 18 inches high. Award of Garden Merit 1969.

E. × d. 'Silberschmelze'. A lovely white heather. Award of Merit after trial 1968, Award of Garden Merit 1969.

E. lusitanica. Similar to *E. arborea*. White tinged pink flowers, December to April. Comes from southern Europe. Grows to about 8 feet high in Britain.

E. mediterranea. Indigenous to Portugal and north-west Spain, this erica has an upright, bushy habit, dark green foliage and pink flowers from late February to May. It grows up to 5 feet in this country and is tolerant of limy soils. The wild Irish form *E.m. hibernica* is no different from the continental form.

Recommended varieties are as follows:

E.m. 'Coccinea'. Deep pink flowers, deepening to red, March-May. 2 feet high. Plant 2 feet apart.

E.m. 'Superba'. Pinkish purple flowers better than the type plant, March-May. Up to 5 feet high. Plant 3 feet apart.

E.m. 'W. T. Rackliff'. White flowers with brown anthers, March-May. Up to 3 feet high. Plant 3 feet apart.

E. tetralix (cross-leaved heather). Common in south-west Europe, Sweden, Germany and Great Britain. Flowers from June until October.

E.t. 'Alba Mollis'. White and silver foliage, 9 inches high. Plant 12 inches apart. Award of Merit 1927.

E.t. 'Con Underwood'. Crimson bells and silvery foliage, 9 inches high. Plant 12 inches apart.

E. vagans (Cornish heath). From Asia, Egypt and Europe, never far from the coast. It flowers from July to October. The faded flowers become a russet-brown, and are most attractive throughout the winter. They should be pruned in early spring.

E.v. 'Lyonesse'. The best of the white varieties, 30 inches high. Plant 24 inches apart. Award of Merit 1928, Award of Garden Merit 1969.
E.v. 'Mrs D. F. Maxwell'. An outstanding variety with deep cerise flowers, 4 feet high. Plant 24 inches apart. Found near Mullion in the 1920s and introduced in 1925. Award of Merit 1925, Award of Garden Merit 1969, First Class Certificate after trial 1970.
E.v. 'St Keverne'. Bright rose pink, a lovely heather. Plant 24 inches apart. Award of Merit 1914, Award of Garden Merit 1927.

Eucryphia glutinosa. This is a very desirable shrub, although it is difficult to establish because it resents root disturbance. It has large, white, rose-like flowers with lovely yellow stamens in July and August, and splendid autumn foliage. It is only for the sheltered garden with a lime-free, moist, peaty soil, where it will grow to 10 feet or more. First Class Certificate 1880, Award of Garden Merit 1935.

Eucryphia × nymansay. This is hardy, and is more lime-tolerant than *E. glutinosa*. It is a hybrid between the tender, lime-tolerant *E. cordifolia* and the acid-loving *E. glutinosa*. It was first raised at Nymans in about 1915 by Mr James Comber, head gardener to the late L. C. R. Messel. Height 15 feet or more. Award of Merit 1924, First Class Certificate 1926.

Euonymus alatus. *Euonymus* named after Euonyme, the mother of the Furies in Greek mythology, or from the Greek *euonymos*; *eu*, beautiful or good, *onoma*, a name. A native of China and Japan (the world's storehouse of exquisite plants), *E. alatus* justifies a place in the garden for its beautiful display of fruit and scarlet leaves in the autumn. This deciduous shrub is quite hardy. It grows to 8 feet high, and is extremely tolerant of town and industrial polluted atmospheres and salt-laden coastal regions. The branches have distinctive corky wings. It is not fussy about soil, provided it is not waterlogged, and excels on chalk. No pruning is required. It is frequently attacked by caterpillars, but these are easily controlled by spraying an insecticide. Plant in a sunny position. Award of Garden Merit 1932.

Euonymus yedoensis. A first-class deciduous shrub, grown for its autumn colour. A native of Japan, this shrub grows to about 8 feet high and bears lovely delicate pink fruits in the autumn, when its foliage turns yellow and scarlet. It is perfectly hardy and is not particular about soils – it likes chalk – or polluted atmospheres. It must have the sun to give a good account in the autumn. No pruning is required. Award of Merit 1924, Award of Garden Merit 1969.

Fothergilla major. Commemorating Dr John Fothergill, who in the eighteenth century developed a garden – second only to Kew Gardens – now known as West Ham Park, in the London Borough of Newham. This park and several other large open spaces outside the City have been maintained by the Corporation of the City of London out of their private funds for over a hundred years. *F. major*, which comes from North America, excels in the peaty soil beloved by rhododendrons. Not for a limy soil. It is a fine shrub which grows 6 feet high and has magnificent autumn foliage. Its fragrant, bottlebrush-like flowers, 2 inches long, appear before the leaves in spring. No pruning is required. Award of Merit 1927, Award of Garden Merit 1946, First Class Certificate 1969.

Fuchsia 'Mrs Popple'.

Fuchsia 'Mrs Popple'. *Fuchsia* is named after Leonhard Fuchs, a sixteenth-century German botanist. There are several fuchsias which, although cut to the ground by frost, spurt into growth in the spring and produce an excellent display of foliage and flower from July to September each year. 'Mrs Popple' is a hardy, reliable, dwarf shrub with large flowers and good habit. A fine plant for the discerning. Award of Merit 1934, Award of Garden Merit 1958, Award of Merit after trial at Wisley 1962.

Garrya elliptica 'James Roof'. *Garrya* was named by the Scot David Douglas in honour of Mr Garry of the Hudson Bay Company who assisted him in his plant-collecting expeditions in North-west America; *elliptica* refers to the ellipse-shaped leaves. This valuable hardy evergreen thrives in all types of soil. It is quite at home in towns, industrial areas and salt-laden coastal regions. In northern or colder gardens a sheltered position suits it, indeed it makes a fine wall plant. There are male and female garryas, the male being preferable. 'James Roof' is a male clone with extra long catkins which appear

January-February. Pruning is only necessary to keep it within reasonable bounds; allow sufficient space when planting. It grows to about 10 feet high and 8 feet wide.

Hamamelis mollis which produces scented frost-proof flowers during the winter.

Hamamelis mollis (witch hazel). From Greek *hama*, together, and *mela*, fruit; flowers and fruit are borne on the shrub at the same time. This native of China is the best of the witch hazels, and immeasurably enhances every garden which has one. Although it is not particular about soil, it does not do well on chalk. It is slow-growing, but eventually, after some 20 years plus, develops into quite a large shrub, 8 feet high by 8 feet wide. It flowers very freely when only 2 feet high. The exquisite, sweet-smelling, rich golden yellow flowers, prolifically produced from December to February, remain undamaged even in the harshest winter. It thrives in a sunny position and makes an excellent specimen plant. Ideally it should be near the house, where its blossom and fragrance can be enjoyed in the depth of winter. It is extremely tolerant of polluted atmosphere – a fine town shrub. Plant October-November. No pruning is required; the flowers are produced on the previous year's wood. Mulch every year because it prefers a moist soil with plenty of humus. First Class Certificate 1918, Award of Garden Merit 1922.

Hibiscus syriacus 'Blue Bird' (tree hollyhock). *Hibiscus* is a name of ancient origin, used by Virgil for mallow-like plants; *syriacus* refers to Syria – Linnaeus suggests that it was from Syria, but it has been found in the wild only in India and China. John Gerard mentioned its cultivation in Britain in the sixteenth century. This shrub thrives in towns and polluted atmospheres, and flourishes on chalk. The only requirement is sunshine. It is particularly useful, because it flowers from August to October when very few others are in flower. It is exceptionally hardy and will grow to a height of 6–10 feet. No pruning is necessary, and indeed very little attention is required once it is established. Award of Merit 1965, Award of Garden Merit 1969.

The violet-blue flowering tree hollyhock *Hibiscus syriacus* 'Blue Bird' is an excellent town shrub.

Hypericum patulum 'Hidcote'. Most species of *Hypericum* are tolerant of shade and are extremely useful on that account. The variety 'Hidcote' is a handsome late-summer-flowering shrub; lovely yellow flowers over 2 inches in diameter appear from July to October. It is best grown in the sun, but will still give a good display in shade. It grows up to 4 feet high and can spread up to 6 feet. An invaluable shrub for the small garden, ideal for a bank, happy on all soils, especially chalk, and tolerant of town and industrial atmospheres. Award of Merit 1954, Award of Garden Merit 1954.

Hypericum 'Rowallane'. A remarkably fine shrub, although a little tender and needing a sheltered, south-facing wall position. It is unquestionably the best of the genus, and bears exquisite large golden yellow flowers from July to October. Award of Merit 1943.

Indigofera pseudotinctoria. Indigoferas are a late-flowering genus; *pseudotinctoria* has splendid foliage and pink, pea-shaped flowers from July to October. It revels in the sunshine and is not fussy about the type of soil, provided it is well drained. Invariably it is cut to the ground each winter unless planted by a sheltered, south-facing wall, but when in the open and cut by frost it springs from the root with vigour as soon as the weather improves. An admirable shrub for the small garden; height about 6 feet. Award of Merit 1965.

Kalmia latifolia. Named by Linnaeus in honour of Peter Kalm, one of his pupils and author of a famous eighteenth-century book about North American travel. All the species of the genus enjoy the same cool, moist, acid, peaty soils favoured by rhododendrons. *K. latifolia* is a hardy evergreen from eastern North America, a choice shrub which has lovely pink flowers in June. It grows up to 8 feet high if conditions suit it. The foliage is poisonous to animals. If grown in a container in a limy district it must be watered not with tap-water, but with rain-water. Award of Garden Merit 1948.

Kolkwitzia amabilis (beauty bush). A native of China and introduced by Ernest Wilson for Messrs Veitch in 1901, this shrub grows up to 6 feet high and 6 feet wide. Its beauty merits wider cultivation. It is very free-flowering provided it is not grown on too rich a soil. Pale pink, trumpet-like flowers with a yellow throat are produced in May and June. Not particular about soil, it grows well on chalk. Plenty of sunshine is essential for it to flower well, but it is tolerant of polluted atmospheres and salt-laden winds. An accommodating shrub excellent for any garden. Prune immediately after flowering by cutting the old flowering wood back to new growth. Award of Merit 1923.

Magnolia. See the chapter on ornamental trees.

Mahonia japonica. Introduced from China in 1845 by Robert Fortune, this is a superb member of the barberry family. An evergreen shrub of stately habit, it grows in excess of 6 feet high by 6 feet wide. It resents root disturbance, and is most unlikely to survive transplanting. Therefore only purchase container-grown plants. In February it produces long racemes of very fragrant yellow flowers. Its shiny leaves repel dirt, making it an admirable town shrub. It is not particular about soil, being quite happy on chalk and clay. An excellent shrub for all gardens, it is best situated near the house so that its perfume and flowers may be enjoyed in the depth of winter. Award of Merit 1916, Award of Garden Merit 1962.

Osmanthus delavayi. From Greek *osme*, perfume, and anthos, a flower – sweet-scented flowers; *delavayi* after Abbé Delavay who sent seed to Maurice de Vilmorin in 1890 (it is said that only one germinated). A particularly fine evergreen with small dark leaves and very fragrant, white, tubular flowers in April. Excellent on all types of soil, it is very tolerant of industrial pollution and salt-laden winds. A native of China, it is in my view much superior to × *Osmarea burkwoodii*, a bi-generic hybrid between *Osmanthus delavayi* and *Phillyrea decora*. *O. delavayi* resents root disturbance, and although quite hardy is not vigorous in cold regions. It is relatively slow-growing, but is worth waiting for. Height and spread 6–8 feet. Award of Merit 1914, Award of Garden Merit 1923, First Class Certificate 1931.

Paeonia suffruticosa (**moutan peony** or **tree peony**). *Paeonia* after Paeon, a physician of ancient Greece who first used the plant medicinally. 'Moutan' is a Japanese name derived from Men-tang, the King of Flowers in Chinese mythology. *P. suffruticosa* and its many named varieties are in my view the best tree peonies and rank among the most beautiful of all plants. Regrettably they are subject to wilt disease, *Botrytis paeoniae*, but this should not deter the reader from growing them. There are single, semi-double and double-flowering varieties; colours include crimson, violet, white and pink. The single flowers have a dark splash of colour at the base of each petal and are particularly beautiful. The flowers produced in May and June in some instances exceed 6 inches across. Plant in September or October on a west-facing wall to avoid early morning sun striking frosted buds. In the colder northern regions they are not so prone to frost damage because growth is much later;

apart from their susceptibility to spring frosts they are quite hardy. For them to do well, a rich soil is necessary, with plenty of rotted compost, farmyard manure or spent mushroom manure dug in before planting and a generous mulch each spring. The shrub grows about 6 feet high but is fairly slow, taking some years to reach this height. During the winter it does appear gaunt, but when covered in its most attractive leaves it is superb. A mat covering on a makeshift frame is well worth while to protect the buds from frost and early morning sunshine. First Class Certificate 1943.

Parrotia persica. *Parrotia* after the German naturalist F. W. Parrot. This is a large deciduous shrub or small tree of slow growth, introduced from Persia about 1841. Its great charms are the lovely gold and crimson coloured foliage before leaf fall in the autumn, and in early spring the red-anthered stamens and rich brown bracts on bare branches. The bark and the general shape of the wide, spreading, horizontal branches are most pleasing. This shrub is very hardy, and tolerant of difficult situations. It must, however, have plenty of sunshine to give a magnificent autumn foliage display. Height and spread 10–15 feet. It thrives on all types of soil, including chalk. First Class Certificate 1884, Award of Garden Merit 1969.

Philadelphus 'Avalanche' is a hardy, small shrub, very fragrant and floriferous. AGM 1936.

Philadelphus. No garden can afford to be without this exquisitely fragrant shrub. It was mentioned by John Gerard in the sixteenth century and John Parkinson in the seventeenth century. Often confused by beginners with *Syringa*, which is the correct generic name of lilacs, *Philadelphus* species flower in June and July. They are not fussy about soil, giving a good account in clay or chalk provided it is well drained. It is important to prune immediately after flowering. The flower forms on wood made the previous year. If the wood that has just flowered is cut to the new growth just being made, this will continue to develop and produce flowers the following summer. Top dressings of rotted compost, spent mushroom manure or decayed farmyard manure will encourage new growth. Sunshine is essential to ensure plenty of flowering wood. The hybrids I favour are single-flowered, and include:

P. 'Beauclerk' A medium-sized shrub, with white flowers about 2½ inches in diameter, Award of Merit 1947, First Class Certificate 1951, Award of Garden Merit 1955.
P. 'Belle Etoile'. A medium-sized shrub with fragrant white flowers flushed maroon at the centre, 2 inches in diameter. Award of Merit 1930, Award of Garden Merit 1936.

Pieris 'Forest Flame' is a fine hybrid between *P. formosa forestii*, 'Wakehurst' and *P. japonica*.

P. 'Burfordensis'. A medium-sized shrub with erect branches and fragrant white flowers. Award of Merit 1921, First Class Certificate 1969.

P. 'Sybille'. A small shrub with fragrant white flowers. Award of Merit 1954, Award of Garden Merit 1955.

Pieris formosa forrestii 'Wakehurst Form'. An acid soil shrub requiring the same conditions as are favoured by rhododendrons. The flowers, similar to those of lily-of-the-valley, are produced in May. The shrub's brilliant red foliage of new growth in the spring is superb, making it a prince among shrubs. This hardy evergreen should be planted in a sheltered position, protected from north and east winds. Before planting, prepare the site well by digging in plenty of decayed compost and leaf mould, the latter being very superior to peat. Although this shrub is moisture-loving, it will not tolerate waterlogging. It thrives in industrial areas provided the soil conditions are right. A shady garden is ideal. Give top dressings of peat to retain moisture, and water (with rain-water) copiously in May and June to avoid any check by drought. A handsome shrub for the small garden, height 6 feet or more. Award of Merit 1957. The type plant *P. formosa forrestii* is a native of China and Burma, introduced by that indefatigable plant collector George Forrest in 1910. Award of Merit 1924, First Class Certificate 1930, Award of Garden Merit 1944.

Poncirus trifoliata. This beautiful Chinese plant is a stout, slow-growing shrub which takes four or five years to make a reasonable plant; it reaches a height of 8 feet. It has smooth green branches which have 3-inch spines. Once it is established, these spines help to make it virtually indestructible. Lovely, snowy-white and very fragrant flowers, about 2 inches in diameter, are produced in May. Globular, miniature-orange-like fruits are striking in the autumn, when the leaves turn a rich yellow before they fall. Very hardy and not particular about soil, it thrives in polluted industrial atmospheres and is an ideal town shrub, provided it has plenty of sunshine. (See also the chapter on hedges.)

Rhododendron. From Greek *rhodon*, rose, and *dendron*, tree. This is a truly magnificent genus, and I regret that it is only possible to comment on a few species and varieties of this immense tribe here. Many books have been written on this exceptionally beautiful shrub, which in my view stands head and shoulders above all others. It is not possible to grow them

Rhododendron 'Purple Splendour', which flowers in May and June and makes a bush about 12ft high.

on limy soils unless a special raised bed about 18 inches deep is constructed, with 3 parts turf loam, 7 parts leaf mould (from trees growing on an acid soil) and 1 part sedge peat, retained in peat block walls; inevitably, tap water will be about pH8 in a limy region, which means that rain-water, collected in a butt, must be the only means of watering them. The smaller-leaved species and hybrids are easier to grow under these conditions, examples being 'Blue Tit', 'Blue Diamond', 'Augfast' and *R. praecox*. They often become chlorotic and sickly, however. Sequestrene and magnesium sulphate (Epsom salts) can be given, but I think the time and effort would be better directed into shrubs which prefer chalk. Those fortunate readers who have an acid soil (pH 4.5 to 6) would be well advised to take the opportunity of cultivating some of these lovely shrubs.

Beginners may be confused to learn that azaleas are included in the genus; they are botanically considered to be a series, and are divided into sub-series in a similar way to that of other rhododendrons. The chief difference is that rhododendrons have ten stamens, whereas azaleas have only five. The cultivation of rhododendrons in Britain dates from 1656, with the introduction of *R. hirsutum*. In 1920, 651 species were known; since then the number of hybrids cultivated has been enormous.

Cultural requirements vary according to the species and hybrids; some are very much easier to grow than others. A general guide is (1) those with silvery undersides to the leaves are easier to grow than those with a russet underside. (2) Himalayan species are more difficult generally. (3) Large-leaved types dislike wind and hot sun. The smaller the leaf the more tolerant they are. (4) Azaleas are easier to grow and more tolerant of wind and sun. (5) Rough-bark types will grow from old wood if cut back. Smooth bark types will not. (6) Always remove old flowerheads unless the seed is wanted, and give plenty of water after flowering.

Large-leaved rhododendrons grow best in an oak woodland. They will thrive next to just one oak tree; they can be planted right up to the bole of the tree without adverse effect. Partial shade, created by the canopy of leaves of an oak, is ideal. Shelter from wind is vital, and a moist soil, particularly in May, June and July, is important after flowering when maximum growth is taking place. Other forest-type trees (such as ash, elm, beech, sycamore, chestnut, poplar, lime and willow) are not suitable because they will take away nourishment and moisture. Oaks are deep-rooted and do not compete in any way. For the small garden, small-leaved maples, sorbus or flowering cherries would provide a canopy of shade and some shelter from wind, without being too competitive.

Any of the following would be suitable:

Acer nikoense, A. pensylvanicum, A. hersii, A. griseum, or *A. capillipes; Prunus* 'Accolade', *P. sargentii, P. subhirtella* 'Autumnalis', or *P.* × *yedoensis; Sorbus aucuparia* 'Aspleniifolia', *S. discolor, S. esserteauana, S. hupehensis, S. sargentiana,* or *S. vilmorinii.*

Preparation is, as always, a wise investment. The border ought to be bastard dug (see the chapter on soil), incorporating plenty of rotted bracken or leaf mould. The drainage must be good; on heavier soils a barrowload of ¼-inch lime-free grit or shingle per 8 to 10 square yards dug into the top spit will improve surface drainage and aeration. If the soil is water-logged in the winter it will be necessary to drain with land drains. That is, as long as a satisfactory outlet exists, for all drainage systems are only as good as the outlet. September-October is the best time to plant evergreens; the deciduous types can be planted between November and March, provided the weather is open and not frosty. When planting, try to keep the rootball intact, and remember that the level of planting should be at the level of the original planting. A common fault is to plant too deeply, killing the shrub in so doing. Rhododendrons are surface rooters, and even large specimens transplant well if the rootball is preserved and handled carefully. On light soils it is useful to plant and leave a slight depression to assist in watering. Heavy mulches of bracken, leaf mould or compost should be applied each year to conserve moisture and provide a cool root run.

Azaleas are generally easier to grow than rhododendrons, and will tolerate wind and sunshine. By fairly close planting, when young, the shelter obtained does help growth, but it is a mistake to allow them to become drawn and 'leggy'. Transplanting is essential if they are to have adequate space to develop into shapely and well-proportioned plants. The species and varieties I particularly favour are not the most difficult to grow, and are a suitable size for the average garden. They are as follows:

Rhododendron 'Britannia' is a hardy evergreen which flowers in May and June.

R. augustinii (Triflorum series). Hardy in south and west, not for cold regions or frost pockets. Fine blue flowers,

April-May. Evergreen, shelter from wind and sun. 10 feet high and 6 feet wide. Award of Garden Merit 1924, Award of Merit 1926.

R. lutescens (Triflorum series). Hardy evergreen. Yellow flowers, February-March. Needs shelter from wind and sun, avoid sun shining on frosted buds. 6 feet high and 4 feet wide. First Class Certificate 1938, Award of Garden Merit 1969.

R. mucronulatum (Dauricum series). January flowering, very hardy deciduous shrub. Rose-purple flowers. Avoid early morning sun on frosted flowers; put against north- or west-facing wall. 5 feet high and 4 feet wide. Award of Garden Merit 1969.

R. orbiculare (Fortunei series). Hardy, pink flowers, April. Needs shelter from wind. 3 feet high and 5 feet wide. Award of Merit 1922.

R. racemosum (Virgatum series). Very hardy evergreen. Pink flowers, April-early May. 4 feet high and 3 feet wide. Award of Garden Merit 1930.

R. scintillans (Lapponicum series). Hardy evergreen. Lavender to purple blue flowers, April – May. 2 feet high and 2 feet wide. Award of Garden Merit 1969.

R. souliei (Thomsonii series). Hardy. Pink to white flowers, May. Attractive foliage. Needs shelter from wind and sun. 6 feet high and 5 feet wide. First Class Certificate 1909.

R. yakusimanum (Ponticum series). Hardy evergreen. Pink flowers, May. Attractive foliage. 3 feet high and 5 feet wide. First Class Certificate 1947, Award of Garden Merit 1969.

R. yunnanense (Triflorum series). Very hardy, semi-deciduous. White flowers, May. 6 feet high and 4 feet wide. Award of Merit 1903, Award of Garden Merit 1934.

Hybrid rhododendrons

R. 'Augfast' (*augustinii* × *fastigiatum*). Blue flowers. 5 feet high and 3 feet wide. Very hardy and fairly easy to grow. Ideal for the smaller garden.

R. 'Blue Bird' (*intricatum* × *augustinii*). Violet-blue flowers, April-early May. A small-leaved shrub, up to 4 feet high and 3 feet wide. Award of Merit 1943, Award of Garden Merit 1969.

R. 'Bo-Peep' (*lutescens* × *moupinense*). Hardy. Creamy-yellow flowers, March. 4 feet high and 3 feet wide. Award of Merit 1937.

R. 'Dairymaid' (*campylocarpum* × ?). Hardy. Pale yellow

flowers, early May. Attractive foliage. Award of Merit after trial 1934.

R. 'Damaris' (*campylocarpum* × 'Dr Stocker'). Very hardy. Canary-yellow flowers, April–early May. A broad, dome-shaped shrub about 10 feet high and 10 feet wide.

R. 'Elizabeth' (*griersonianum* × *forrestii* var 'Repens'). Hardy. Red flowers, April–early May. 3 feet high and 5 feet wide. Award of Merit 1939, First Class Certificate 1943, Award of Garden Merit 1969.

R. 'Humming Bird' (*haematodes* × *williamsianum*). Hardy. Crimson-pink flowers, May. Very attractive foliage. 3 feet high and 5 feet wide.

R. 'Matador' (*griersonianum* × *strigillosum*). Dark red-orange flowers, April–early May. 6 feet high and 8 feet wide. Award of Merit 1945, First Class Certificate 1946.

R. 'Naomi Glow' (*aurora* × *fortunei*). Hardy. Pink flowers, May. Good foliage. 5 feet high and 6 feet wide.

R. 'Praecox' (*ciliatum* × *dauricum*). A lovely, hardy hybrid. Lilac-pink flowers, February–March. Compact growth, 5 feet high and 3 feet wide. An ideal shrub for the smaller garden. Award of Garden Merit 1926.

R. 'Temple Bell' (orbiculare × *williamsianum*). Hardy. Pink bell-shaped flowers April–May. Excellent foliage. 3 feet high and 5 feet wide.

R. 'Tessa'. Hardier than one of its parents, R. 'Praecox'. Lilac-pink flowers with a ray of crimson spots, March–early April. 3 feet high and 3 feet wide. Award of Merit 1935, Award of Garden Merit 1969.

Azaleas

All these are excellent for the average-sized garden with suitable soil:

A. *kaempferi*. Hybrids. May.
A. *mollis*. Hybrids. Early May.
A. Ghent hybrids. Late May.
A. Occidentale hybrids
A. Knaphill and Exbury hybrids
A. Kurume group (Wilson's Fifty)

***Romneya coulteri* (tree poppy).** Named after T. Romney Robinson, an Irish astronomer of Armagh, in 1844; *coulteri* after Dr Coulter, who discovered it in California in 1844. This plant is semi-shrubby, growing up to 8 feet high. It is generally cut to the ground by frost, but new growth springs up from the base each spring. It is an appealing plant with most attractive

These lovely dwarf evergreen Kurume Azaleas originated in Kurume, Japan.

grey foliage and white, poppy-like flowers, throughout July and August, up to 5 inches across, with a central mass of golden stamens. It resents root disturbance, so leave plenty of space – up to 6 square feet – when planting; once established it spreads by underground rhizomes. An ideal position is a well-drained sunny border or bank. In cold gardens and northern regions a sheltered, south-facing wall should give adequate protection. This shrub is very tolerant of industrial and town atmospheres, and thrives on all soils, including chalk. It is also an ideal coastal plant. First Class Certificate 1888, Award of Garden Merit 1929.

Rosa (rose). From the Greek *rhodos*.

'If Zeus chose us a King of the flowers in his mirth,
He would call to the Rose and would royally crown it,
For the Rose, oh the Rose! is the grace of the earth,
Is the light of the plants that are growing upon it.'

It is not possible to discuss roses in any great detail in this book. I have recommended some rambling and climbing roses in the chapter on climbing plants. For the shrub borders, selected shrub roses are most appropriate. Hybrid Tea roses, Floribunda and Polyantha varieties (the traditional groupings) abound, and increase annually. I prefer the fragrant varieties and recommend the following:

Hybrid Tea type

'Alec's Red'. Fragrant.
'Crimson Glory'. Red. Very fragrant.
'Isabel de Ortiz'. Deep pink, silver reverse. Fragrant
'Mischief'. Coral salmon. Fragrant.
'Wendy Cussons'. Cerise, flushed scarlet. Fragrant.
'Whisky Mac'. Bronze yellow-apricot. Fragrant

Floribunda type

'City of Belfast'. Scarlet.
'Elizabeth of Glamis'. Pink. Fragrant.
'Iceberg'. White. Slightly fragrant.
'Matangi'. Orange. Slightly fragrant.
'Orange Sensation'. Fragrant.
'Woburn Abbey'. Orange with yellow and red shades. Fragrant.

Shrub type

The shrub roses are not planted as much as their beauty and perfume merit. Those which I think are suitable for the average small garden, and which do not require pruning, are:

The fine polished fruits of *Rosa moyesii* 'Geranium' follow a magnificent display of red flowers.

Rosa moyesii 'Nevada'.

R. alba 'Belle Amour'. Blooms semi-double, pink, free-flowering. Very fragrant. 5 feet high and 5 feet wide. A lovely rose for any garden.

R. 'Ballerina' (hybrid musk). Apple-blossom-pink, single flowers with a white eye, small flowers but huge clusters. Glossy, light green foliage. 4 to 5 feet high.

R. bourboniana 'Boule de Neige'. Very fragrant, creamy-white flowers, June-October. Upright growth, 5 feet high and 3 feet wide, an excellent shrub rose.

R. centifolia muscosa 'Blanche Moreau'. A lovely moss rose. Pure white flowers with crimson, moss-like hairs on the calyx and flower stems, flowering June-July and again in the autumn. Attractive dark foliage. Up to 5 feet high. A fine shrub rose.

R. centifolia muscosa 'Gabrielle Noyelle'. A lovely pink flower with golden shading at the base of the petals. Up to 4 feet high.

R. centifolia 'Parfait de Flandres'. Red buds, opening to large, lilac-pink blooms, June-July. 4 feet high.

R. damascena 'Madame Hardy'. Beautiful white blooms, with good, dark foliage. Up to 5 feet high. A superb rose.

R. 'Felicia' (hybrid musk). One of the best. Silvery-pink flowers, very fragrant, foliage matt, medium green and very attractive. 5 feet high and 5 feet wide.

R. gallica 'Cardinal Richelieu'. Maroon-purple, fragrant, flowers. Very few thorns. 5 feet high and 4 feet wide. An excellent rose.

R. gallica 'Versicolor' (*R. mundi*). Lovely semi-double flowers, red striped white. 4 feet high and 4 feet wide. Named after Rosamond Clifford, mistress of Henry II.

R. moyesii 'Geranium'. Raised at Wisley Gardens and introduced in 1938. More compact than *R. moyesii*, erect habit with bright green foliage and red flowers. Grows up to 8 feet high and 6 feet wide. Award of Merit 1950, Award of Garden Merit 1969.

R. moyesii 'Marguerite Hilling'. A sport from 'Nevada'. Single deep pink flower, a fine shrub.

R. moyesii 'Nevada'. A hybrid of a *moyesii* seedling with a 'Frau Karl Druschki' seedling, 'La Giralda'. Large single white flowers and good foliage. An excellent shrub rose, growing to about 8 feet high and 6 feet wide.

R. 'Penelope' (hybrid musk). Creamy-salmon, semi-double flowers, fragrant. Semi-glossy foliage. 4 feet high and 4 feet wide. A fine shrub.

R. rugosa 'Frau Dagmar Hastrup'. Free-flowering, rose-pink single blooms. Dark foliage, very large, attractive crimson hips. Grows up to 4 feet. Award of Merit 1958, Award of Garden Merit 1969.

R. rugosa 'Roseraie de l'Hay'. Raised by Gravereaux, this is one of the finest of all shrub roses. Large, fragrant, purplish-crimson flowers. Grows about 6 feet high and 5 feet wide. Award of Garden Merit 1969.

R. spinosissima 'Frühlingsgold'. The first of the Kordes hybrids, and one of the best. Lovely, semi-double, fragrant, pale yellow flowers in May-June. Up to 6 feet high.

R. spinosissima 'Frühlingsmorgen'. Similar to 'Frühlingsgold'. Semi-double, deep pink flowers with yellow centre, in May-June. Grows up to 6 feet tall.

Rubus. Probably from Latin *ruber*, red, the colour of the fruit. There are a considerable number of species; blackberries and raspberries belong to this tribe.

R. tricolor. A fine prostrate hardy evergreen with long trailing stems, excellent for banks or cascading over retaining walls. A native of China, and introduced by Wilson in 1908. It is not fussy about soil, is shade-tolerant, and does well in a polluted atmosphere. No pruning is required, other than keeping it within bounds.

R. × tridel 'Benenden'. An excellent, vigorous, thornless shrub, quite hardy. It grows up to 8 feet high and 6 feet wide, and has attractive white flowers, 2 inches across, with a golden centre of stamens. It is suitable on all types of soil, and is a superb town shrub. Award of Merit 1958, Award of Garden Merit 1962, First Class Certificate 1963.

Rubus × tridel 'Benenden', a lovely hybrid raised by Captain Collingwood Ingram in 1950.

Sambucus racemosa 'Plumosa Aurea'. This is a most attractive shrub with golden foliage and a height and spread of 8 feet or so. It is ideal for the small garden. Award of Merit 1956.

Syringa. This is the generic name for lilac, not for the mock orange *Philadelphus*, which is often commonly called 'syringa'. This is a most showy group of small trees and shrubs, many of which have a strong perfume. They are happy in all types of soil and flourish in chalk. Most tolerant of industrial pollution, traffic fumes and salt-laden winds, they thrive in sunshine and require a moist, well-manured, well-drained soil. The flowers are borne in April and May. They are not difficult to cultivate; remove seed heads immediately after flowering, and mulch with farmyard manure, spent mushroom manure or compost each spring. No pruning is required. A superb shrub for all gardens.

Those I particularly favour are:

S. × *chinensis.* A hybrid between the Persian lilac and the common lilac *S. vulgaris*, raised in the Botanic Gardens of Rouen by M. Varin. This is an exceptionally handsome shrub which grows up to 10 feet high. The soft lavender-coloured flowers are fragrant and produced in May. Award of Garden Merit 1969.

S. × *josiflexa* 'Bellicent'. Lovely pink flowers, May-June. Height 12 feet. First Class Certificate 1946, Award of Garden Merit 1969.

S. *microphylla.* As the name implies, this is a small-leaved shrub. It is very hardy and reliable, growing up to 10 feet tall, and produces abundant, fragrant, lilac-coloured flowers. An excellent town shrub, it makes an attractive informal hedge. A native of China. Award of Merit 1937, Award of Garden Merit 1955.

S. × *prestoniae.* Vigorous, very hardy, attractive shrubs, flowering in late May, these Canadian hybrids raised by Miss Isabella Preston in 1920 are very suitable for the small garden. Height up to 10 feet.

'Audrey'. Deep pink flowers, June. Award of Merit 1939.
'Elinor'. Dark purplish-red buds opening to pale lavender-blue flowers, May-June. Award of Merit 1951.
'Isabella'. Purple flowers, May-June. Award of Merit 1941.

S. *vulgaris* varieties grow 8–12 feet high. I recommend the following:

'Charles Joly' Purplish-red, double flowers.
'Congo'. Lilac-red, single flowers.
'Hugo Koster'. Purple-crimson, single flowers. Award of Merit 1913.
'Madame Francisque Morel'. Mauve-pink, single flowers.
'Madame Lemoine'. White flowers. Award of Merit 1937.
'President Grevy'. Lilac-blue, double flowers. Award of Merit 1892.

This is *Syringa × josiflexa*, which produces fragrant rose-pink flowers in May and June.

'Souvenir de Louis Spath'. Red single flowers. Award of Garden Merit 1930.

Viburnum. This genus has many handsome flowering and fruiting species. They are most accommodating, being tolerant of industrial and town conditions and not particular about soil. They are excellent on chalk and clay.

*V. **betulifolium**.* A deciduous shrub, a native of China discovered by Potanin and introduced by Wilson in 1901, 1907 and 1910. This is one of the most beautiful of all fruiting shrubs. It has white flowers in June, but is chiefly grown for the fine autumn display of large trusses of redcurrant-like fruit. Plant two or three different clones to ensure fruiting. Award of Merit 1936, First Class Certificate 1957, Award of Garden Merit 1960.

*V. × **bodnantense*** 'Deben'. A medium-sized deciduous winter/early spring-flowering shrub. It has clusters of white, fragrant, frost-resistant flowers, pink in the bud, and is a lovely shrub for the small garden. Award of Merit 1962, First Class Certificate 1965, Award of Garden Merit 1969.

*V. **dilatatum**.* A deciduous shrub about 6 feet high, of erect growth. It flowers in June, but is grown for its large bunches of berries carried from autumn well into winter. A native of Japan and China. Award of Merit 1968. *V.d.* 'Xanthocarpum' is a yellow fruiting form. Award of Merit 1936.

*V. **plicatum*** 'Mariesii'. A magnificent flowering shrub with horizontal tiers of branches carrying dense heads of white flowers. The foliage is attractive. This is a reliable, hardy shrub. Award of Garden Merit 1929.

*V. **plicatum tomentosum**.* This deciduous hardy shrub, growing 6 feet high, is a native of China and Japan. It has white flowers, 3 inches across, in May and requires a sunny position. No pruning is required. Award of Garden Merit 1969.

Recommended hardy shrubs suitable for a heavy clay soil and exposed cold gardens

Aesculus parviflora is a miniature horse chestnut which flowers in July and August.

Abelia × grandiflora
Aesculus parviflora
Amelanchier canadensis
Aucuba japonica 'Crotonifolia'
Berberis darwinii

Berberis stenophylla
Berberis thunbergii
Buddleia alternifolia
Buddleia colvillei
Buddleia davidii varieties

Calluna vulgaris varieties
Camellia japonica
   'Donckelarii', 'Jupiter'
Chaenomeles speciosa
   'Cardinalis', 'Moerlosii'
Chaenomeles × *superba*
   'Knaphill Scarlet',
   'Rowallane'
Choisya ternata
Clethra alnifolia
Cornus alba 'Sibirica'
Cornus mas
Cornus stolonifera 'Flaviramea'
Corylus avellana 'Contorta'
Cotinus coggygria
Cotoneaster species
Daphne × *burkwoodii*
Daphne mezereum
Deutzia × *elegantissima*
   'Rosealind'
Elaeagnus × *ebbingei*
Elaeagnus pungens 'Maculata'
Enkianthus campanulatus
Erica carnea varieties
Euonymus alatus
Euonymus yedoensis
Exochorda giraldii
Forsythia × *intermedia*
   'Spectabilis'
Fuchsia 'Mrs Popple'
Fuchsia magellanica riccartonii
Genista hispanica
Hamamelis mollis
Hibiscus Syriacus 'Blue Bird'
Hydrangea bretschneideri
Hypericum patulum 'Hidcote'
Kerria japonica
Magnolia denudata
Magnolia kobus
Magnolia sieboldii
Magnolia × *soulangiana*
   'Amabilis', 'Lennei'
Mahonia bealei
Mahonia 'Charity'

Osmanthus heterophyllus
Parrotia persica
Philadelphus 'Beauclerk',
   'Belle Etoile', 'Virginal'
Pieris floribunda
Pieris taiwanensis
Potentilla fruticosa
   'Grandiflora', 'Klondyke'
Pyracantha rogersiana
Rhododendron augustinii
Rhododendron luteum
Rhododendron ponticum
   hybrids
Rhus typhina 'Laciniata'
Ribes sanguineum 'Pulborough
   Scarlet'
Ribes speciosum
Rosa spinosissima
   'Frühlingsgold'
Rosa moyesii 'Marguerite
   Hilling'
Rosa moyesii 'Nevada'
Rubus cockburnianus
Rubus tricolor
Sambucus racemosa 'Plumosa
   Aurea'
Skimmia japonica
Spiraea × *arguta*
Spiraea thunbergii
Stransvaesia davidiana
Symphoricarpos × *doorenbosii*
   'Mother of Pearl'
Syringa × *josiflexa* 'Bellicent'
Syringa microphylla 'Superba'
Syringa × *prestoniae* 'Audrey',
   'Isabella'
Viburnum × *bodnantense*
Viburnum × *burkwoodii*
Viburnum davidii
Viburnum fragrans
Viburnum opulus
Viburnum opulus
   'Xanthocarpum'

Recommended shrubs for limy soil

Abelia × *grandiflora*
Abelia triflora
Berberis darwinii
Berberis linearifolia
Berberis × *lologensis*
Berberis thunbergii
Buddleia alternifolia
Buddleia davidii 'Fascination'
Buddleia 'Lochinch'
Caryopteris × *clandonensis*
  'Ferndown', 'Heavenly
  Blue'
Ceanothus arboreus 'Trewithen
  Blue'
Ceanothus 'Burkwoodii',
  'Cascade', 'Delight'
Ceanothus divergens
Ceanothus gloriosus
Ceanothus × *lobbianus*
Ceratostigma willmottianum
Chaenomeles speciosa 'Brilliant',
  'Cardinalis'
Chimonanthus praecox
Choisya ternata
Cistus × *corbariensis*
Cistus laurifolius
Cornus alba 'Sibirica'
Cornus stolonifera 'Flaviramea'
Corylus avellana 'Contorta'
Cotinus coggygria
Cotinus coggygria 'Royal
  Purple'
Cotoneaster cornubia
Cotoneaster exburiensis
Cotoneaster rotundifolius
Cotoneaster × *watereri*
Cytisus battandieri
Cytisus × *praecox*
Daphne arbuscula
Daphne × *burkwoodii*
Daphne mezereum
Daphne odora
  'Aureomarginata'

Elaeagnus × *ebbingei*
Elaeagnus pungens 'Maculata'
Erica carnea varieties
Erica × *darleyensis*
Erica mediterranea varieties
Erica stricta (syn. *terminalis*)
Escallonia langleyensis
Escallonia macrantha
Euonymus alatus
Euonymus europaeus 'Red
  Cascade'
Forsythia × *intermedia*
  'Spectabilis'
Fuchsia 'Mrs Popple'
Garrya elliptica
Genista aethensis
Genista cinerea
Genista hispanica
Hebe 'Autumn Glory', 'Great
  Orme', 'Midsummer
  Beauty'
Hibiscus syriacus 'Blue Bird'
Hibiscus syriacus
  'Woodbridge'
Hydrangea sargentiana
Hydrangea villosa
Hypericum × *moserianum*
Hypericum patulum 'Hidcote'
Hypericum 'Rowallane'
Indigofera gerardiana
Indigofera potaninii
Kerria japonica 'Pleniflora'
Kolkwitzia amabilis
Lavandula spica 'Hidcote',
  'Munstead'
Magnolia × *highdownensis*
Magnolia kobus
Magnolia loebneri 'Leonard
  Messel', 'Neil McEacharn'
Magnolia wilsonii
Mahonia bealei
Mahonia 'Charity'
Mahonia japonica

Potentilla fruticosa 'Tangerine' has scarlet buds and orange flowers that change to a soft yellow. Ideal in partial shade.

Viburnum carlesii is a native of Korea which grows up to 4ft. Its sweetly scented flowers are produced in April and May.

Myrtus communis
Osmanthus delavayi
× *Osmarea burkwoodii*
Paeonia delavayi
Paeonia lutea ludlowii
Paeonia suffruticosa
Parrotia persica
Perovskia atriplicifolia
Perovskia atriplicifolia 'Blue Spire'
Philadelphus 'Beauclerk', 'Belle Etoile', 'Sybille', 'Virginal'
Phormium tenax
Phormium tenax 'Variegatum'
Poncirus trifoliata
Potentilla 'Elizabeth'
Potentilla fruticosa mandschurica
Potentilla 'Tangerine'
Pyracantha atalantioides 'Aurea'
Pyracantha 'Mojave'
Pyracantha rogersiana
Pyracantha rogersiana 'Flava'
Ribes speciosum
Rosa xanthina spoutanea 'Canary Bird'
Rosa spinosissima 'Frühlingsgold'
Rosa spinosissima 'moyesii' 'Frühlingsmorgen'
Rosa moyesii 'Nevada'
Rosa rubrifolia
Rosa rugosa 'Blanc Double de Coubert', 'Frau Dagmar Hastrup', 'Roseraie de l'Hay'
Rubus tricolor
Rubus × *tridel*
Sambucus racemosa 'Plumosa Aurea'
Sarcococca hookerana
Spartium junceum

Stachyurus praecox
Stephanandra tanakae
Stranvaesia davidiana
Stranvaesia davidiana 'Fructuluteo'
Symphoricarpos × *doorenbosii* 'Mother of Pearl'
Syringa × *chinensis*
Syringa × *chinensis* 'Metensis', 'Saugeana'
Syringa × *hyacinthiflora* 'Esther Staley'
Syringa × *josiflexa* 'Bellicent'
Syringa microphylla 'Superba'
Syringa × *persica* 'Laciniata'
Syringa × *prestoniae* 'Audrey', 'Elinor', 'Isabella'
Syringa reflexa
Syringa sweginzowii 'Superba'
Syringa vulgaris 'Charles X', 'Hugo Koster', 'Katherine Havemeyer', 'Maréchal Foch', 'Mrs Edward Harding', 'Primrose', 'Vestale'
Tamarix pentandra 'Rubra'
Tamarix tetrandra
Ulex europaeus 'Plenus'
Viburnum betulifolium
Viburnum × *bodnantense*
Viburnum × *bodnantense* 'Deben'
Viburnum × *burkwoodii*
Viburnum × *carlcephalum*
Viburnum carlesii
Viburnum fragans
Viburnum grandiflorum
Viburnum × *juddii*
Viburnum opulus 'Compactum', 'Sterile', 'Xanthocarpum'
Viburnum plicatum 'Grandiflorum', 'Lanarth'
Viburnum plicatum tomentosum

The carnation-pink blooms of *Rosa rugosa* 'Frau Dagmar Hastrup' set large, globular, tomato-red fruits.

Bamboos

Bamboos belong to the grass family Gramineae. Many are quite hardy and most attractive, meriting inclusion in every garden except those exposed to wind. Their cultivation is quite easy, provided that they are grown in a well-drained, moisture-retentive, fertile soil; that is, one with plenty of organic material. Chalk and clay are both suitable, but badly drained, waterlogged soils are not.

Good preparation is essential. Bastard digging, incorporating a liberal amount of decayed farmyard manure, spent mushroom manure or compost is advised to give them a good start. Subsequently, mulch each spring with similar material to sustain vigorous growth and to ensure a cool root run, which they will enjoy. Planted in shrub borders, in tubs on a patio or terrace, or in a water garden they are equally attractive they also make fine specimens, either singly or in groups on lawns. They will also make a good, labour-saving hedge.

About 30 years ago there was a fine 'Bamboo Walk' at the Royal Horticultural Society's gardens at Wisley, in Surrey. This consisted of borders of mixed bamboos, situated near the Alpine Meadow either side of a waterbound hoggin path. A delightful and interesting year-round feature of this sort is well worth including in a garden design.

Members of this remarkable tribe of plants are best planted in the spring, probably in May, just as new growth is beginning. Propagation is not as easy as some books suggest. I have found that the best method is to divide the rhizomes carefully when new leaves appear in the spring, pot them up, and place in a moist, warm propagating case in a glasshouse, until the young plants are established. They should then be hardened off gradually and grown on for a year in a sheltered nursery bed. Then they can either be planted in their permanent positions the following spring, or grown on for a further year in the nursery. Those I have suggested are all hardy and of considerable garden merit, suited to small and large gardens alike, and are not invasive types.

Arundinaria auricoma. Hardy, up to 6 feet. Golden variegated foliage.

Arundinaria fastuosa. Hardy, up to 20 feet. Upright canes, claret colour on interior surface of cane sheath.

The Chinese bamboo *Arundinaria nitida* is fast-growing and requires plenty of space.

Arundinaria fortunei. Hardy, up to 4½ feet. White variegated foliage.

Arundinaria murielae. Hardy, up to 9 feet. Slender canes, tessellated leaves.

Arundinaria nitida. Hardy, up to 15 feet. Slender purple canes, good foliage.

Chusquea couleou. Hardiest of all bamboos, a fast grower, up to 18 feet. Solid cane, not hollow. An outstanding bamboo.

Phyllostachys boryana. Hardy, up to 14 feet. Pale yellowish foliage.

Phyllostachys flexuosa. Hardy, up to 10 feet. Dark green foliage.

Phyllostachys nigra. Hardy, up to 15 feet. Canes mature to black in third year.

Phyllostachys viridiglaucescens. Hardy, up to 15 feet. Brilliant blue-green sheen on underside of leaves.

CHAPTER 4 # *Ornamental trees*

There is space for the right type of tree in all but the very smallest gardens. The experienced gardener will consider all the circumstances to ensure that all the trees in his final selection are suitable for the general environment, the type of soil, and the particular aspect. The trees will be small in stature, of proven hardiness and of special garden merit – that is, they will be noted for their beauty of flower, fruit, foliage or bark.

Trees play a very important role by giving height and breaking up the flat monotony too often found in small gardens. The sooner the decisions are made, on what trees to plant and where, the better. Permanence should be the intention – trees are not pieces of furniture to be moved at the slightest whim. Moving semi-mature trees with special equipment is expensive, and although this can work well with some species, it is fatal for others. Even the most tolerant species can take two or three years to recover. It is therefore important to plant at the outset the right type of tree, and the best of its kind, to enhance the garden layout. It is also prudent to avoid overhang and encroachment on to your neighbours' property.

Apart from adding beauty and interest to a garden, trees can perform many useful functions. Properly situated, they make windbreaks, screen objectionable views, or form effective soundbarriers. They can give privacy to a corner or shade to a terrace. Carefully sited on a lawn or towards the front of a shrub border, a tree will not only give a screening effect but will create an illusion of depth and distance.

Exploit their natural architectural qualities by using fastigiate or upright trees, which contrast well with lower shrubs; they also take up less room. Weeping trees give another kind of contrast and have a special charm of their own.

Trees can be placed either singly or in groups. Always allow plenty of room for growth – there is nothing worse than a mutilated tree. Pruning destroys its natural beauty and shape.

Opposite:
A good example of a garden in which small trees give height, colour, and shelter.

As the trees mature – which happens surprisingly quickly – it will be necessary to remove adjacent shrubs if undue competition and eventual misshapen growth is to be avoided. With maturity comes a steadily increasing beauty and you will soon be pleasantly aware 'how softly falls the foot of time'.

No attempt has been made, in compiling the following list, to include all the trees that are suitable or available. I have selected those that are especially attractive. Many have received a First Class Certificate or Award of Merit from the Royal Horticultural Society.

Acer circinatum (vine maple). *Acer*, possibly from Latin *acer*, hard or sharp, the wood having once been used for writing tablets. A small deciduous tree, suitable to all types of soil, and tolerant of industrial and coastal atmospheres. Its main feature is the superb autumn foliage.

Acer ginnala. This is a small deciduous tree with beautiful autumn foliage, suitable for all soils and industrial towns.

Acer griseum (paper-bark maple). A native of central China, this deciduous tree grows to about 14 feet high with a 10-foot spread of branches. It has a distinctive peeling orange-coloured bark throughout the year, and the leaves turn to fine shades of reds and scarlets in the autumn. This is one of the best small trees available. To produce sturdy young trees it is necessary to allow the growth of feathers, or side shoots, to increase the girth. These laterals are shortened to about eight inches long and eventually removed altogether. It is a matter of judgement to know when these should be removed: too early, and the main stem or trunk fails to develop; too late, and unsightly scars mar the bark. The tree is tolerant of all soils, including chalk, and is quite happy in an industrial or coastal area. Award of Merit 1922, Award of Garden Merit 1936.

Acer nikoense (Nikko maple). This beautiful small-to-medium-sized slow-growing deciduous tree is a native of Japan and central China. It is truly magnificent in the autumn, when its foliage turns to rich shades of red, yellow and orange. It deserves a place in every garden, being suitable for all soils, industrial and coastal areas. First Class Certificate 1971.

Acer pseudoplatanus 'Brilliantissimum'. *Pseudoplatanus* means 'false plane tree', that is, a sycamore. This is no ordinary forest sycamore, however. The variety 'Brilliantissimum' is an

Acer pseudoplatanus 'Brilliantissimum', an irresistible ornamental foliage tree.

exceptionally lovely tree, which is difficult to omit in any design. The young spring leaves are a beautiful shrimp pink which gradually turn to a soft yellow, and finally green. It is a small-to-medium-sized tree, about 14 feet to 18 feet high and with a 12-foot spread of branches. It is susceptible to black fly, but this is easily controlled by a systemic insecticide. It tolerates all soils, including chalk, and is happy in coastal and industrial areas. Award of Merit 1925.

Arbutus × andrachnoides. A hybrid between *A. andrachne* and *A. unedo*. A lovely evergreen tree of outstanding merit. Although it belongs to the family Ericaceae, which includes all the acid-loving heathers, it is remarkably lime-tolerant. It grows to about 15 feet high with a 12-foot spread of branches. It has exceptionally beautiful cinnamon-red bark, and flowers in the late autumn/early spring according to the weather conditions. Plant from a container because all *Arbutus* species (strawberry tree) transplant very badly. It is suitable for coastal and industrial areas. Award of Merit 1953, Award of Garden Merit 1969.

Ceanothus arboreus 'Trewithen Blue'. *Ceanothus*, known as Californian lilacs, are a remarkable genus of evergreen and deciduous shrubs and small trees. The magnificent 'Trewithen Blue' can grow to about 18 feet high; it is evergreen and has large panicles of deep blue flowers in June. Not for exposed cold gardens, it is ideally situated in front of a large wall or in a protected corner, provided it receives plenty of sunshine. It tolerates chalk soils and is fine for industrial and coastal locations. There is a good specimen thriving in the Rotunda Garden, London Wall, by the Museum of London. Award of Merit 1967.

Ceanothus arboreus 'Trewithen Blue'. A high south or west facing wall is ideal for this exceptionally fine tender evergreen.

Cercis siliquastrum (Judas tree). This is a small tree, about 16 feet high, which, coming from the Mediterranean region as it does, loves the sun. It is best in the south, and requires a sheltered position because the wood is brittle. It tolerates all soils, and does particularly well on chalk. Rosy pea-like flowers appear in May when the leaves are very small. The purple-tinted seed pods are a pleasing feature from July onwards. Award of Garden Merit 1927. The clone 'Bodnant' has deep purple flowers, and is better than the type plant.

Cornus mas (cornelian cherry). *Cornus*, Latin, a horn, from the hard nature of the wood. This small deciduous tree, which grows to 15 feet high, flowers profusely in February. Fortunately the flowers are very frost-resistant. They are followed by a few red berries. This tree grows well on chalk soil, is happy in coastal and industrial areas, and is particularly attractive when planted near the house adjacent to an evergreen. Award of Garden Merit 1924, Award of Merit 1929.

Cornus nuttalli. This is a native of western North America, and is one of the most beautiful of all flowering trees, though it is not easy to grow. It does not like chalk or polluted atmospheres – a country town with a good, sandy, loamy soil is the ideal place for this difficult beauty. First Class Certificate 1920.

Davidia involucrata (pocket-handkerchief tree). *Davidia* after Abbé David, who first discovered the tree in 1869 near Moupine, China. This is a medium-sized, hardy, deciduous tree, which thrives in all soils, incuding chalk. The leaves are similar to those of lime trees. The large white bracts, resembling a white handkerchief, which hang from the branches in May, are extraordinarily attractive. Award of Garden Merit 1969.

In early summer *Davidia involucrata* draws the eye upwards to its astonishing bracts of pendant white.

Drimys winteri (winter bark). *Drimys* from Greek *drimus*, acid, referring to the pungent taste of bark and foliage; *winteri* after Captain Winter, of one of Drake's ships. A handsome ever-

Drimys winteri is a fine evergreen tree.

green tree from South America, only suitable for the sheltered garden in the south. It will grow in the industrial town – the leaves are easily washed by overhead watering and rain – and is best on a loamy soil. It has fragrant ivory-white flowers in May.

Elaeagnus angustifolia. *Elaeagnus* from Greek *elaia*, an olive tree, and *agnos*, a plant like a willow. This is a fine, deciduous tree, about 15 feet high with narrow, willow-like, silver-grey leaves. It is an excellent wind-resister, and useful for providing shelter in exposed positions. It is very tolerant of chalk and is happy in maritime and industrial areas.

***Genista aetnensis* (Mount Etna broom).** *Genista* was the Latin name for flowering shrubs; *aetnensis*, of Mount Etna. It grows up to 20 feet high, and is of sparse habit, with little foliage but slender, rushlike branches. Bright yellow flowers in July make a bold splash of colour when few other hardy shrubs or trees are flowering. It tolerates industrial and coastal situations and is happy in all types of soil – a valuable addition to the small garden. Award of Garden Merit 1923, First Class Certificate 1938.

***Gleditsia triacanthos* 'Sunburst' (golden honey locust).** After Gottlieb Gleditsch, a German professor of botany in the eighteenth century and friend of Linnaeus; *triacanthos*, three-spined, i.e., in threes. This enchanting, graceful, ornamental foliage tree is a superb choice to light up a dark corner or a bleak wall. The fernlike leaves, which appear late in the spring, are tipped with gold, giving a restrained and delicate sense of light. It is quite easy to grow, doing best in the south of England. It thrives in towns, not affected by air pollution, but it does grow relatively slowly. It is one of my favourite trees, and a 'must' for every garden.

***Halesia carolina* (snowdrop tree).** *Halesia* commemorates Dr Stephen Hales, a botanical author born at Bikesbourne in Kent in 1671. This is synonymous with *H. tetraptera*. This beautiful flowering tree, native of North America, is not suitable for a chalky soil, and will do better in the south than the colder north. It blooms in May and grows to about 20 feet high. A young tree in bloom will be disappointing, but after a few years' growth it will begin to flower profusely, with clusters of snowdrop-like, silvery-white flowers on the undersides of its spreading branches. It is mystifying why it has not been planted more widely. Award of Garden Merit 1946, Award of Merit 1954.

Ilex x altaclarensis 'J. C. Van Tol'. This is an excellent holly, producing an immense crop of brilliant red berries every year. The leaves are almost spineless. Award of Garden Merit 1969.

Holly is suitable for all types of soil, tolerant of shade and very good in heavy polluted industrial or coastal areas. Other varieties which make fine trees are:

> *I. x a.* 'Camelliifolia'. Award of Garden Merit 1931.
> *I. x a.* 'Mundyi'.
> *I. aquifolium* 'Silver Queen'. Award of Garden Merit 1969; and 'Golden Queen'. Award of Garden Merit 1969.

Liquidambar styraciflua **(sweet gum).** Latin *liquidus*, liquid, and *ambar*, amber, referring to the gum (storax) yielded by some species; *styraciflua*, storax-flowing, hence the common name. A tree which has glorious autumn colour. It makes a rather large cone-shaped tree not suitable for the small garden. It should be planted at least 30 feet away from the house. It is most important to buy a good form that assumes a brilliant crimson colour just prior to leaf fall. It colours best when exposed to full sunlight. The wood is brittle, so avoid a wind-swept position. A good town tree, thriving in all soils except very shallow chalk. Award of Merit 1925, Award of Garden Merit 1969. 'Lane Roberts' is a selected clone, produced for its reliable autumn colour.

Liriodendron tulipifera. Greek *lirion*, a lily, and *dendron*, a tree; *tulipifera*, tulip-bearing. This magnificent tree is for the large garden of at least half an acre. Plant container-grown specimens, because it transplants badly. It has attractive leaves and flowers, with the bonus of leaves turning a lovely shade of yellow in the autumn. This tree will eventually grow to about 80 feet high with a corresponding spread of branches. It is quite happy in all types of soil, very successful in industrial and town atmospheres. It was introduced from North America in the seventeenth century. Award of Merit 1970.

Magnolia **(lily flower).** A genus of magnificent deciduous and evergreen trees and shrubs, named by Linnaeus in honour of Pierre Magnol, a professor of botany and medicine at Montpelier who died in 1715. Magnolias fall into two groups: those from eastern America, and the more interesting group from Asia (India, China and Japan). There is no other orna-

Magnolia × soulangiana 'Alba Superba' is a first rate small tree that flourishes in town conditions.

mental tree which surpasses a magnolia for sheer beauty. No garden can have too many. Most of them are quite hardy, and live to a great age; they are of easy cultivation provided they are given sufficient depth of good, well-drained soil in a sheltered position. They flourish in towns and industrial areas, being surprisingly most tolerant of atmospheric pollution. When preparing their planting positions, double-dig the area (see the chapter on soil), and incorporate plenty of decomposed organic material; this can be compost, well-rotted farmyard manure, spent mushroom manure, leaf mould or peat. This will provide a good rooting medium capable of retaining plenty of moisture yet still being freely drained. Magnolias, like *Liriodendron*, the tulip tree (both belong to the same family, Magnoliaceae), intensely dislike root disturbance. They are most difficult to transplant successfully, and container-grown plants are strongly recommended. If it is proposed to move an existing magnolia, think again. In the event of no alternative, take out a trench around the plant to get a really large root ball; with care this can be wrapped in sacks and placed on boards before moving. This should only be done just as the leaves are breaking, in May. Damaged roots will heal during a period of active growth. If moved in autumn or winter, it is very likely that roots will rot.

When planting in a sheltered position, avoid the morning sun, north and east winds and low-lying frost pockets, and give the plants sufficient space to develop. They resent heavy pruning. As there are a hundred or so different species and varieties, choosing is difficult. The most lime-tolerant are *M. × highdownensis*, *M. kobus* and *M. × loebneri*, including the hybrids 'Leonard Messel', 'Merrill', 'Neil McEacharn' and 'Snowdrift'. Others that are reasonably lime-tolerant, if given a good depth of loam and decayed organic material, include *grandiflora* and *soulangiana* hybrids. In my opinion the best include the following, which are easy to grow and readily available.

M. denudata (synonymous with *Magnolia conspicua*, the Yulan tree from China). This is one of the best, but unfortunately its pure white flowers are susceptible to spring frosts. It requires plenty of room, for it has a height of 30 feet and a spread of 25 feet. Plant in a good fertile soil; it is not tolerant of chalk or lime. Award of Garden Merit 1936, First Class Certificate 1968.

M. x highdownensis. A large shrub or small tree very suitable for the town garden. It has large, fragrant, pendent, pure white flowers in May-June, and does well on chalk.

M. kobus. This small Japanese tree flowers abundantly after about seven years. The flowers are small and pure white. The tree does well on chalk. Award of Garden Merit 1936, Award of Merit 1942.

M. × loebneri 'Leonard Messel'. This fine small tree, with lilac-pink flowers, does very well on all soils, including chalk. Award of Merit 1955, First Class Certificate 1969.

M. × loebneri 'Merrill'. An excellent magnolia having large, white, fragrant flowers. It is happy on all soils.

M. × loebneri 'Neil McEacharn'. This is a striking small tree with lovely pink-flushed flowers. It does well on all soils and is tolerant of town and industrial atmospheres. Award of Merit 1968.

M. sieboldii (synonymous with M. parviflora). A large, wide-spreading deciduous shrub or small tree, this Japanese magnolia grows to about 15 feet high, and has cup-shaped buds opening to fragrant, pure white flowers and later crimson fruit. It flowers over a two- to three-month period, starting about May. A few flowers bloom at a time. The leaves are attractive, being glaucous and hairy beneath. It dislikes chalk. Top dress annually with leaf mould and peat. First Class Certificate 1894, Award of Garden Merit 1935.

M. × soulangiana. This species has many forms, and is the most widely planted. Those which I consider to be the best are:

M. × s. 'Alba Superba'. White flowers. Award of Garden Merit 1969.

M. × s. 'Brozzonii'. Large white flowers, purple at base. First Class Certificate 1929, Award of Garden Merit 1969.

M. × s. 'Lennei'. Rose-purple flowers. First Class Certificate 1863, Award of Garden Merit 1969.

M. × s. 'Picture'. Flowers purple on the outside and white inside. Award of Merit 1969.

Malus. This is a genus of flowering trees and shrubs. The following species and varieties are flowering crabs, all of easy cultivation and flowering in April-May.

M. floribunda (Japanese crab). One of the most beautiful early flowering trees. The flower buds are a bright crimson, but the flowers when open are a pale rosy red. This tree grows to about 20 feet high, with a 15-foot spread. Award of Garden Merit 1923.

Malus floribunda, as its name implies, is a crab apple grown more for its flowers than its fruits.

M. 'Golden Hornet'. This very ornamental tree produces white flowers followed by a crop of bright yellow fruit, which remains on the tree until late in the year. It is one of the best fruiting crabs, and a reliable cropper. It tolerates chalk, industrial and maritime areas. Award of Merit 1949, First Class Certificate 1961, Award of Garden Merit 1969.

M. hillieri. This bears prolific large semi-double flowers, crimson in bud opening to pink. It is suitable for all types of soil and is tolerant of coastal and industrial areas.

M. 'John Downie'. An excellent fruiting crab tree with a reliable heavy crop of bright orange and red fruit. It is an outstanding tree for the small garden. Award of Merit 1895, Award of Garden Merit 1969.

M. lemoinei. A lovely tree with an abundance of large crimson flowers in April and May, and rich bronze foliage. Award of Merit 1928, Award of Garden Merit 1937.

M. 'Profusion'. An ideal tree for the small garden. It has quantities of red flowers, followed by blood-red fruits. The young leaves are coppery crimson. Award of Garden Merit 1969.

M. tschonoskii. This erect-growing tree is another good choice for the small garden. It is one of the best trees for autumn colour; the leaves turn shades of yellow, orange and scarlet. Award of Merit 1962.

***Morus nigra* (black mulberry).** This is a distinctive small tree which gives an old-world charm and tranquillity to any garden. Particularly tolerant of all soils and polluted atmospheres, it is a very successful town tree, and quite happy in coastal areas as well. It flourishes in a warm, sheltered position, and does better in the south of England than the north. It has been cultivated in Great Britain since the sixteenth century, and its rugged bark gives the impression of great age. It grows to about 20 feet high and has a 15-foot spread. Black mulberry was used in old herbal remedies for a variety of ills, making use of ripe and unripe berries, bark, roots, and the juice of both fruit and leaves. The sweet fruit, ripening in August and September, is quite pleasant as a dessert. Young trees fruit within 12 years.

Prunus is a large genus which includes many attractive flowering species. The following are some of my favourites:

P. × *hillieri* 'Spire'. A lovely conical flowering cherry suitable for a small garden. It has a profusion of soft pink flowers in the spring, with a bonus of fine autumn colours.
P. incisa **(Fuji cherry).** An exceptionally fine hardy Japanese species, with lovely pink-tinged buds opening into snowy white flowers each spring. It has attractive foliage with the bonus of beautiful autumn tints before leaf fall. The Japanese call this tree *Fuji-Zakura* on account of its abundance on the sacred mountain. It tends to remain a large spreading shrub about 10 feet high and the same wide. It is ideal for filling a corner where it has sufficient space to mature without cutting, and is a most attractive tree for the small town garden. Award of Merit 1927, Award of Garden Merit 1930.
P. sargentii. A beautiful cherry with single pink flowers in March and exceptionally fine autumn colours. Award of Merit 1921, First Class Certificate 1925, Award of Garden Merit 1928.
P. serrula tibetica. This is grown for its handsome, highly polished bronze bark, which shines and glistens in a most attractive way. It is particularly effective in the winter months when planted near the house. As it is a small tree this does not present any problems. Like *Acer criseum*, which is also grown for its bark, special care is required in removing the side shoots or feathers if large unsightly scars are to be avoided. Plant in sun; it is suitable on all soils in coastal, town and industrial areas. Award of Merit 1944.

P. subhirtella **(spring cherry).** *Subhirtella* refers to the slightly hairy leaves and young wood. Despite its common name

Prunus serrula tibetica is grown for its polished mahogany bark.

Prunus subhirtella 'Pendula Rosea' is undoubtedly one of the best spring flowering weeping trees. Excellent on top of a bank, ideal for the small garden.

there are both spring and winter flowering types, including my favourite weeping forms – which are particularly suited to the small garden to give a sharp contrast or focal point. They are most attractive when grown as a single specimen underplanted with a carpet of *Chionodoxa sardensis*. The best of these weeping forms in my opinion is *Prunus subhirtella* 'Pendula', the weeping rosebud cherry. It has a pronounced graceful weeping habit and in March-April is covered with small pink flowers. It received an Award of Merit in 1930. Another weeping form is 'Pendula Plena Rosea' which has semi-double flowers in the spring. It received an Award of Merit in 1938. 'Pendula Rosea' and 'Pendula Rubra' are the other two weeping forms suitable in sunny positions on all soils in town, coastal or industrial areas. All young weeping trees, once planted, must in their formative years be helped to form an evenly balanced head. If a tree is left to its own devices, the branches will be too close to the trunk, or the head one-sided or too low to allow sufficient space for the weeping branches to hang gracefully. Once these branches mature and thicken, it is too late to do anything about it. If top worked, i.e., grafted or budded on to an upright growing stock, make sure that any upright shoots are rubbed out immediately while they are young and soft. If they are left, and then cut out with secateurs, dormant basal buds will continually shoot out from the base of the original shoot. Although the branches fall naturally, make sure that they are spread evenly. This is best done by tying them on to a wire or light wooden frame.

Remember that:

(a)   the trunk should be at least 10 feet high to allow enough space for the weeping branches;

(b)   the wider the head the better the effect in later years; and

(c)   branches should be balanced evenly around the circumference.

P. yedoensis (Yoshino cherry). This is a small, attractive tree on which abundant bluish-white flowers appear in March-April. A lovely tree for the small garden and when underplanted with *Erica carnea* 'Vivellii' or 'Loughrigg', both of which also flower in March-April, it is truly a splendid sight. While both heathers are tolerant of chalky soils, unfortunately they dislike polluted industrial atmospheres and town air heavy with traffic fumes; in these circumstances consider underplanting with large groups of *Narcissus* 'Peeping Tom'. *P. yedoensis* was introduced from Japan in 1902. Award of Merit 1927, Award of Garden Merit 1930.

There are many Japanese hybrid cherries (some in my view overplanted), which succeed in all types of soil and are quite happy in towns and industrial areas. I do not think, however, that they are appropriate for the small garden, because after their short magnificent flowering period is over their shape and foliage do not in my opinion compare with those of other trees discussed in this book.

***Pyrus* (pear).** This generic name has in the past caused confusion because many species which used to be included in this genus have nothing in common with pears. It included apples and crabs (now *Malus*), mountain ashes and white-beams (now *Sorbus*), chokeberries (now *Aronia*) and Japanese quinces (now *Chaenomeles*). *Pyrus* now refers only to pears.

***P. salicifolia* 'Pendula' (willow-leaved pear).** This small, graceful, weeping deciduous tree has narrow, silvery leaves, and pure white flowers in April. It is excellent on chalk and very tolerant of industrial and coastal areas. Award of Garden Merit 1969.

***Robinia pseudoacacia* 'Frisia' (false acacia).** A native of the eastern United States, introduced to France about 1635 and to England in 1640. The first tree was planted by Vespasien Robin, son of Jean Robin, botanist and herbalist to Henry

Robinia pseudoacacia 'Frisia' with its striking golden-yellow foliage is prone to wind damage and a sheltered sunny position is essential.

IV of France, after whom the tree was named. 'Frisia' is an outstanding clone raised at the nursery of W. Jansen in Holland in 1935 and is without doubt one of the most decorative ornamental foliage trees available today, with its rich golden-yellow leaves making a bold splash of colour from spring to autumn. It grows well in any soil and withstands industrial and town pollution remarkably well, but does suffer badly when exposed to salt-laden air by the coast. It must be sited with care, because the wood is very brittle and vulnerable to windblow. This should be the major consideration when selecting a site for this tree. Award of Merit 1964, Award of Garden Merit 1969.

Sorbus hupehensis is a handsome small tree with attractive foliage which turns a brilliant red in the autumn, and the white fruits persist into late winter.

Sorbus. This is a huge genus, including rowans and whitebeams, of the family Rosaceae – quite easy to grow and admirably suited for the small town garden. It is particularly tolerant of atmospheric pollution. Final selection from this splendid genus is most difficult. Although in the chapter on design I stressed that restraint was necessary to avoid overplanting, some may think it difficult to plant too many rowans or whitebeams. My favourites include the following:

S. aria 'Majestica'. *Aria* is the old generic term for whitebeams, and is probably the Persian placename of origin. This is the finest of all varieties of whitebeam. It grows to 20 feet high, with a spread of up to 15 feet, and has leaves up to 7 inches long and 4 inches wide. This variety, recorded as long ago as 1858, like all whitebeams thrives on chalk, is well suited to industrial and maritime situations, and is very tolerant of wind. Award of Garden Merit 1969.

S. aria 'Lutescens'. The upper surface of the leaves is covered by white hairs in the spring, which turn to grey-green by summer. Award of Merit 1952, Award of Garden Merit 1969.

S. aucuparia (mountain ash). *Aucuparia* from Latin *aucupium*, bird-catching, from the ancient belief that the berries intoxicated birds, rendering them easily caught. The mountain ash is spread widely over Europe and Asia, and can grow 15–25 feet high, with a spread of about 10 feet. It is well suited to towns and cities and tolerant of polluted atmospheres, but is not happy in paved sunny gardens. It much prefers the moist, cooler situation associated with a north-east-facing aspect. Good varieties are:

S.a. 'Aspleniifolia'. A splendid small tree, with deeply cut leaves which give a fernlike effect. Award of Garden Merit 1969.

S.a. 'Shearwater Seedling'. A vigorous, upright, small tree. An attractive addition to any garden.

S.a. 'Xanthocarpa'. Amber-yellow fruits. Award of Merit 1895, Award of Garden Merit 1969.

S. commixta. A small, variable tree with erect branches, fine autumn colour and red fruit.

S. discolor. A superb autumn colour display, among the best, with a neat habit ideal for the small garden.

S. esserteauana (synonymous with *conradinae*). A fine tree with attractive leaves and good autumn colour. Award of Merit 1954.

S. vilmorinii. After M. Maurice de Vilmorin, who raised it. An elegant small tree with beautiful, fernlike foliage. Good autumn colour with heavy clusters of fruit, red at first turning to.white flushed rose. Award of Merit 1916, Award of Garden Merit 1953.

Malus × *atrosanguineum* is an accommodating tree which is ideal in the small garden.

Recommended ornamental trees suitable for heavy clay soil and exposed cold gardens

Acer negundo 'Variegatum'
Betula jacquemontii
Betula papyrifera
Betula pendula 'Dalecarlica'
Cercis siliquastrum
Crataegus crus-galli

Liquidambar styraciflua 'Lane Roberts'
Malus aldenhamensis
Malus floribunda
Malus tschonoskii
Prunus avium 'Plena'

Crataegus prunifolia
Laburnum anagyroides
  'Aureum'
Laburnum vossii
Liquidambar formosana
  monticola

Prunus incisa
Prunus lusitanica
Salix matsudana 'Tortuosa'
Sorbus discolor
Sorbus sargentiana

Recommended ornamental trees for limy soil

Acer griseum
Acer pseudoplatanus
  'Brilliantissimum'
Arbutus andrachnoides
Cercis siliquastrum 'Bodnant'
Laburnum anagyroides
  'Aureum'
Laburnum vossii
Malus eleyi
Malus floribunda

Malus tschonoskii
Morus nigra
Prunus subhirtella
  'Autumnalis Rosea'
Prunus × *yedoensis*
Pyrus salicifolia 'Pendula'
Robinia pseudoacacia 'Frisia'
Sorbus cashmiriana
Sorbus discolor
Sorbus vilmorinii

CHAPTER 5 *Hedges*

The boundaries form the outer frame of any design. As far as garden design is concerned, good looks, shelter from wind, and privacy are high on the requirement list. If a hedge is chosen to form the boundary, therefore, it is important to make the right choice of species. Those gardeners who have inherited a privet hedge are most unfortunate. Privet, in my view, is destitute of any beauty; it has a greedy, extensive root system (to the detriment of other plants) and it should ideally be removed forthwith and replaced with a suitable alternative from the list below. When replacing a hedge of any kind, never plant the same species.

Thorough preparation is essential if a hedge is to be grown successfully. A strip of ground 3 feet wide should be double dug, incorporating compost, spent mushroom manure or farm-yard manure into the bottom spit at a rate of one barrowload to 4 square yards. Every effort should be made to make this preparation, because once the hedge is planted the opportunity is lost. Every hedge should have a dressing in the form of a mulch every five years, again at about one barrowload to 4 square yards (that is, about one ton to 120 square yards).

Where a hedge has become bare at the base, the top can be cut down to about 12 to 18 inches above the ground. After cutting, growth will be quite vigorous from the hitherto dormant buds at the base of the hedge. This does not apply to conifers, except yew, or to smooth-barked rhododendrons.

A good hedge is kept wide at the base and narrow at the top, in the form of a triangle. This will prevent a heavy layer of snow from splitting the hedge apart, and will make clipping much easier. Clipping a hedge requires some skill; it helps considerably to use a builder's line to ensure that the top is level.

All the shrubs in the following list make good hedging

Opposite:
Taxus baccata – the aristocrat of all hedges.

plants, and have considerable garden merit. Hedges can, of course, be deciduous or evergreen.

***Acer campestre* (English maple).** *Acer,* hard or sharp, the wood having been used for writing tablets; *campestre,* growing in the fields. This maple colours superbly in the autumn, and is particularly good on chalky soils. Plant 18 inches apart in a single row.

Berberis darwinii. Named after Charles Darwin, who discovered it in 1835 when attached as naturalist to the *Beagle* on her famous voyage. This is a fine evergreen, which has orange flowers in April and May. Planted as a hedge, 18 inches apart in a single row, it is inclined to become bare at the bottom; to prevent this, restrict the top growth by regular pruning every year immediately after flowering. Suitable for all soils and polluted atmospheres including salt-laden gales. Award of Garden Merit 1930.

Berberis julianae. This is another good, dense evergreen with yellow flowers and narrow elliptical leaves. Plant 18 inches apart. Clip immediately after flowering.

Berberis stenophylla. A hybrid, its parents being *B. darwinii* and *B. empetrifolia*. This is a beautiful, graceful, evergreen shrub which has yellow flowers in April. It requires plenty of space, as it grows to 10 feet high and as wide. When grown as a hedge from 6 feet to 10 feet high, it should be clipped immediately after flowering every year. It is most suitable for industrial areas and makes a useful salt-resistant hedge at the seaside. It grows well on all soils, including chalk, but dislikes shade. Plant 18 inches apart in a single row.

Camellia japonica 'Jupiter' makes an exceptionally dense and handsome hedge.

Camellia japonica. Named after George Joseph Kemel (or Camellus), a Jesuit of Moravia who travelled in the East. Camellias are choice flowering evergreens. There are thousands of named varieties comprised of single, semi-double and double flowers ranging from white to all shades of pink and red, flowering early to late spring. All have superb polished foliage. This shrub is ideal for a town environment, provided the soil is not chalky. Camellias are relatively slow-growing, although some varieties are more vigorous than others. They live to be a great age. Their habit varies from spreading to columnar. On average they will grow about 12 inches per year for the first three years, and thereafter about six inches a year.

Obviously it is not suitable for the impatient, or where a hedge is wanted quickly. For those prepared to wait about 15 years, an 8-foot-high glorious flowering hedge is a possibility. Requirements are abundant water (but avoid a soggy root system, i.e., badly drained land), filtered sunlight, some protection from the wind and, above all, a slightly acid soil. It would be a complete waste of time to try and cultivate camellias on a chalky soil. 'Alba Plena', 'Apollo', 'Covina', 'Donckelarii' and 'Jupiter' are all good varieties for hedges, but avoid mixing the varieties in the same hedge as different habits destroy uniformity. A camellia hedge requires very little pruning. Plant in September or in May, not too deeply, 2½ feet apart. Prune if necessary, using secateurs, just after flowering in the spring. As a matter of interest, *Camellia thea*, synonymous with *Camellia sinensis*, is the tea plant.

Carpinus betula (hornbeam). *Betula* is the generic name for birch, which this hornbeam resembles. This is a native tree. It retains its foliage throughout the winter and makes a good hedge, suitable for all types of soil, including chalk. It stands clipping well and thrives in cold, wet, clay soil. Plant 18 inches apart in a single row.

Chamaecyparis lawsoniana (Lawson cypress). This is hardy and makes a good hedge. There are a great many varieties in shades of green, blue and gold, and variegated. A variety selected for a hedge must be grown from cuttings because seedlings vary too much to make a uniform hedge. The Lawson cypress is quite happy in exposed and shady positions, but not in a polluted atmosphere. Plant 2 feet apart and trim in early August.

Particularly suitable varieties are:

> *C.l.* 'Allumii'. Glaucous blue foliage.
> *C.l.* 'Erecta Viridis'. Bright green.
> *C.l.* 'Lanei.' Golden yellow.
> *C.l.* 'Lutea'. A golden form.
> *C.l.* 'Green Hedger'. A fine green form.
> *C.l.* 'Winston Churchill'. Golden yellow. A slow grower.

Chaenomeles lagenaria, or *Cydonia japonica* **(Japanese quince).** *Cydonia* is the ancient name for the common quince, which grew in abundance at Cydon, on Crete. The varieties 'Nivalis' (white) and 'Rowallane' (blood-crimson) are especially good. Plant 2 feet apart.

Chaenomeles lagenaria is a vigorous, twiggy shrub which makes a good small hedge or wall covering.

Fagus sylvatica 'Riversii' (purple beech). An unusual effective hedge, slower than *F. sylvatica* (common beech).

***Fagus sylvatica* (common beech).** The beech of the forest, when used as a hedging plant, retains its brown leaves from the autumn throughout the winter. It has lovely green leaves, particularly in the spring. It thrives on chalk and grows well on an acid soil, but is not happy on wet clay. Beech makes an excellent hedge, very tolerant of clipping. The purple-leaved form also makes a very good hedge and when well maintained is a fine sight. Plant in a single row, 18 inches apart.

***Forsythia × intermedia* 'Spectabilis' (forsythia).** Named after William Forsyth, Superintendent of the Royal Gardens, Kensington (1737–1805). Plant 2 feet apart. Prune immediately after flowering.

***Ilex aquifolium* (common holly).** *Ilex* is the Latin name for the evergreen oak (holm oak), to which holly was supposed to bear some resemblance. Holly is quite at home in industrial and seaside atmospheres. It makes a fine, substantial hedge, though is a slow grower. Nothing equals it for providing shelter, and it unquestionably makes the best evergreen hedge for industrial town gardens. However, it does not transplant well, and unless moved in either September or May, with a considerable amount of soil attached to its roots, it will probably die. Container-grown plants overcome this difficulty. It is very tolerant of clipping, but does not have the 'finish' of yew. While holly withstands all sorts of climatic conditions, it is not happy in cold, heavy clay soils. Because it grows slowly its timber has not been very much used; it is unsuitable for outdoor use, not being durable. Plant in September, 2 feet apart in a single row. Clip in April, but do not cut the leader until the required height is reached.

Podocarpus andinus, also known as *Prumnopitys elegans* **(plum-fruited yew, Chilean yew, plum fir).** This evergreen is a native of Chile, similar to yew in appearance, has brilliant green foliage and makes a fine hedge. However it is not suitable for gardens in very cold districts or in positions exposed to north and east winds. Being a conifer, it is not happy in an industrial environment. Plant in September 2 feet apart in a single row. Clip in early August.

Poncirus trifoliata, also known as *Aegle sepiaria*, *Limonia trifoliata* and *Citrus trifoliata* **(Japanese bitter orange)**. This is a slow-growing, hardy shrub. It has conspicuous, large, white, sweetly scented flowers in the spring. The branches are armed with formidable spines. The fruits are inedible, green ripening to yellow. It makes a beautiful, impenetrable hedge, very tolerant of clipping. Plant 2 feet apart in a single row.

Forsythia spectabilis makes an attractive hedge.

Prunus laurocerasus (**common** or **cherry laurel**). This shrub is tolerant of shade and polluted atmospheres; it thrives in all soils and, if left unpruned, makes an exceptionally elegant plant about 20 feet high. Pruned, it makes a substantial hedge. The leaves are of a leathery texture, suitable for towns, but the plant has a greedy root system, which rules it out for the small garden; furthermore it is not suitable for cold, exposed positions. Plant 2 feet apart in a single row. Never trim with shears but always with secateurs, annually, in March or April.

Prunus lusitanica (**Portugal laurel**). This is an excellent evergreen, hardier than the common or cherry laurel. It has dark, glossy, green leaves and is quite happy in all soils, including chalk. It is one of the most effective of all evergreens, withstanding both polluted town and salt-laden coastal atmospheres well. It makes a particularly fine hedge, but is not tolerant to shade or drip from overhanging trees. Plant 2 feet apart in a single row. Prune with secateurs in March or April.

Quercus ilex (**evergreen oak or holm oak**). This tree tolerates shade, and responds well to clipping. It is suitable for all soils except those waterlogged. It is particularly valuable in a polluted atmosphere and makes a splendid windbreak. When a large evergreen hedge is wanted, this is the best. I have seen fine specimen trees on the south coast exposed to the full brunt of salt-laden winds. It does not transplant, and only pot-grown plants are suitable. It will retain its foliage down to the ground. It will make a magnificent hedge up to 20 feet high if wanted. Plant 2 feet apart in a single row.

Rosa 'Zéphirine Drouhin'. This makes a lovely hedge up to 6 feet high. Very little pruning is necessary other than shortening back old flowering shoots. Plant 4 feet apart.

Taxus baccata (**common yew**). *Taxus* is possibly from Greek *taxon*, a bow (the wood was once used for making bows). Yew is the best plant for a permanent hedge in clean air, and it will grow in all soils, including chalk. The polluted atmosphere of cities and industrial towns, and the salt-laden air of coastal towns, however, are not suitable. The yew's dark foliage makes a superb background for other plants. Some may consider the yew too sombre and indeed it is a familiar sight in churchyards! The berries, leaves and partially dried clippings are extremely poisonous to man and beast. Yew timber possesses remarkable strength and durability, and was once used extensively for furniture; it is very resistant to decay. Plant a single row, 2 feet apart. Clip in early August. It must be well clipped, but the top or leaders must not be cut until the required height – up to 6 feet – is reached.

***Thuja plicata* (western red cedar).** This plant makes a handsome hedge. It has bright green foliage and withstands clipping well. It is tolerant of shade and grows well on most soils including chalk. An excellent choice, but not for industrial polluted areas. I prefer this to *Chamaecyparis lawsoniana* as a hedge. The clone 'Atrovirens' is a select form of *Thuja plicata*. Plant 2 feet apart. Trim in early August.

***Viburnum tinus* (laurustinus).** This makes a lovely evergreen hedge up to 6 feet high, flowering from December to April. Unfortunately it is subject to frost damage in exposed situations and is not suitable as a hedge in very cold districts. Large plants do not transplant very well. It is best to start with small plants, single row planted at 2 feet apart. When necessary trim in May, not too closely.

Other shrubs suitable for hedges are as follows:

> ***Cotoneaster lacteus***
> ***Cotoneaster simonsii***
> **✕ *Osmarea burkwoodii***
> ***Prunus*** 'Crimson Dwarf'
> ***Prunus*** 'Blaze'
> ***Pyracantha rogersiana***
> ***Rosa damascena*** 'Celsiana'. A damask rose, 5 feet high, 4 feet spread.
> ***Rosa kordessii*** 'Ballerina'. A hybrid musk rose, 4 feet height and spread.
> ***Rosa*** 'Felicia'. A hybrid musk rose, 5 feet height and spread.
> ***Rosa gallica*** 'Versicolor' (*Rosa mundi*). 4 feet height and spread.
> ***Rosa*** 'Penelope'. A hybrid musk rose, 5 feet height and spread.
> ***Rosa rugosa*** 'Roseraie de l'Hay'. 7 feet height and spread.
> ***Syringa microphylla*** 'Superba'
> ***Syringa palibiniana***

CHAPTER 6 *Climbing plants*

Many readers will undoubtedly have missed the experience of owning some of the best climbing plants because they do not know them, cannot get them, or mistakenly think that they damage walls and buildings. As for the latter, quite the opposite is true. Climbers and wall-trained shrubs protect the fabric from the weather. A wall stripped after a few years of plant growth will be found to be completely dry and in better condition than an exposed wall. I have been unable to convince archaeologists and architectural historians that to have climbers covering Roman and Wren walls is the finest way of protecting them for posterity. Needless to say, I do not have the vivid imagination so essential, in my view, in their profession, and very much prefer to see ruined remains with beautiful climbers cascading over them, and to have the air heavy with a fragrance that compels passers-by to stop and wonder what plant is the source of it. St Dunstan in the East, one of Wren's City of London churches destroyed in the last war, was purchased and landscaped by the City fathers in 1973 as a public open space, and clearly exemplifies the protective jacket provided by climbing plants to the wall remains. These are in fact the main feature of the garden, and when they are in flower the sheer beauty falling gracefully from these high walls is unforgettable. The layout received a Civic Award. Should you be in the area, do visit the garden.

I have selected a range of climbers to suit different situations, and which will in my view immeasurably enhance any house, garage, wall, fence, pergola, archway, pillar or shed. The south- and south-west-facing walls should be reserved for the tender aristocrats, others should be planted to scramble through and over trees and shrubs. If the selections are suitable, no harm at all will come to any tree or shrub supporting them. It is prudent to be quite sure, before planting, that the plant will not outgrow its position. This is particularly

Opposite:
Climbing plants provide a living drapery of flowers and foliage. This charming garden owes its character to climbers, ramblers and scramblers.

important around the house, where the wrong type of climber can block windows and grow under roof tiles. It is most annoying to have to remove a fine plant simply because it was incorrectly sited in the first place.

Preparation of the planting position is, as always, essential. The soil at the base of walls is generally quite unsuitable. It can be improved by adding decayed farmyard manure, compost or spent mushroom manure; but the likely cost of the plant will probably warrant a complete change of soil. John Innes Potting Compost No. 3 will prove to be a fine investment, if you replace an area of soil about 3 feet × 2 feet, and 2 feet deep, per climber. It will be necessary, for those plants that are not self-supporting, to fit either a trellis or a series of wires. Planting between October and March is advisable; autumn planting, while there is some warmth in the ground, is best. Evergreens should in any event be planted only in autumn or spring. Avoid the depth of winter and the height of summer – I do not agree with those who suggest that container-grown plants can be planted at any time of the year.

After-care is most essential, particularly watering, as plants at the base of walls are especially prone to drying out. Top dressing with a 3-inch layer of moist peat will provide a cool root run, conserve moisture and suppress weeds. As the plants grow away train them into position. Most climbers do not need any pruning other than where necessary around windows and doors, and the removal of old wood. Those clematis and rose species that require pruning will be discussed under each plant description.

Climbers for north- and east-facing aspects

Asteranthera ovata. This self-supporting evergreen was introduced from Chile in 1926. It must have a lime-free soil. Being tender, it is not for the cold northern areas, and even in the south-west it should have some protection during the very harsh weather that occurs every ten years or so. It supports itself by aerial roots, and must be grown in a shady position such as a north or east wall, or a sheltered, shady tree trunk. The tubular flowers, which are carmine red with a white throat, appear in June. Award of Merit 1939.

Berberidopsis corallina. *Berberidopsis* from *Berberis* and Greek *opsis*, a resemblance, i.e. 'like a berberis'; *corallina* refers to the coral-coloured flowers. This is a lovely climbing evergreen from the forests of Chile. It must have a moist, shady position and completely lime-free soil. Because it is not completely hardy it is unsuitable for colder areas, unless it can be put in an unheated conservatory that faces north, east or west. In the milder parts of the country it is excellent for a north, east or west wall. It is not self-supporting, and needs either a trellis or wires; it will grow to about 18 feet high and 16 feet wide. The crimson-scarlet flowers begin to appear in July and continue throughout the summer. Award of Merit 1901.

Hedera colchica 'Dentata Variegata'. This is the most impressive of all the ivies. It certainly has the largest leaves of the genus, up to 7 inches across and some 10 inches long. They are bright green shading to grey with a creamy yellow edge when young, and creamy-white when mature. It is much hardier than *Hedera canariensis* 'Variegata' and just as attractive, providing a most accommodating plant which grows to about 12 feet high on a north or east wall. This variegated Persian ivy is quite distinct from our native species. Award of Merit 1907, Award of Garden Merit 1969.

Hedera helix 'Goldheart'. Another magnificent ivy which has small, dark green leaves with a striking splash of yellow. It is quite hardy and most suitable for a north or east wall, being an excellent plant to brighten up a dark, ugly spot. Award of Merit 1970.

Hydrangea petiolaris. *Hydrangea* from Greek *hydor*, water, and *aggeion*, a vessel or vase, in reference to the shape of the

Hydrangea petiolaris scales house walls with the greatest of ease.

113

seed capsule. This useful, hardy, and very attractive deciduous plant was introduced from Japan in 1878. It is a vigorous climber, supporting itself by aerial roots. There are three species of climbing hydrangea, and *petiolaris* is the best one. It is very effective on a north or east wall, but wants a lot of space as it matures; 50 feet × 50 feet is not an unusual area for this plant to cover. It will also climb a very large tree. The white flowers are freely produced in June. It is quite happy on chalky soils, and town, country or coastal areas are all suitable for this lovely plant. Award of Garden Merit 1924.

Lonicera × tellmanniana. Named after Adam Lonicer, a sixteenth-century German naturalist. This is a fine hybrid honeysuckle, quite suitable for chalky soils and industrial and coastal environments. The yellow, scentless flowers are produced in June and July. This hardy plant is an excellent climber that prefers shade and is ideally positioned against east and north walls. Award of Merit 1931, Award of Garden Merit 1969.

Lonicera tragophylla. A lovely, deciduous honeysuckle that needs a moist, shady position and is very suitable for alkaline soils. It is the largest flowered and most showy of the *periclymenum* group, the rich yellow flowers appearing in June and July. They are about 3 inches long, and produced in clusters of about 20 at the tips of the shoots. Unfortunately this is also a scentless honeysuckle, nevertheless it is a splendid plant for a 30-foot north or east wall. Award of Merit 1913, Award of Garden Merit 1928.

Pileostegia viburnoides. A very hardy evergreen climber, a native of Japan, China and India. This plant is particularly useful in polluted industrial areas because its dark green, attractive, leathery leaves, which are about 6 inches long, are easily cleaned from grime by overhead watering. It is a slow-growing plant, self-supporting by aerial roots, and is happy on a north or east wall where it has space to mature. Flowers are a creamy white, produced in panicles at the end of shoots in September. It grows to about 20 feet high in a good, well-drained soil. Award of Merit 1914.

Vitis henryana. *Vitis*, Latin, a vine. Named after Dr Augustine Henry, who discovered it. Synonymous with *Parthenocissus henryana*. This lovely, self-clinging climber which has tendrils with sticky disks, is grown for its beautiful foilage. The leaves are composed of 3 or 5 leaflets, attractively variegated with white and pink along the main veins. In the autumn they colour to a brilliant red. For the best results it should be grown on a sheltered north or east wall, where the leaf markings are more pronounced, not being exposed to the sun. It is quite happy in industrial and coastal towns, and it will flourish on chalk. It grows to about 30 feet high. Award of Merit 1906, Award of Garden Merit 1936.

Climbers that require sun

The Chinese gooseberry vine *Actinidia chinensis* is a decorative climber.

Actinidia chinensis (**Chinese gooseberry** or **kiwi fruit**). *Actinidia*, from Greek *aktis*, a ray, refers to the star-like flowers or to the rayed stigmas of female blooms. This unisexual or hermaphrodite plant was first seen by Robert Fortune in 1847 when travelling in China on behalf of the Royal Horticultural Society, and was introduced in 1900. It is a hardy, handsome, deciduous, vigorous climber, ideal on a pergola, wall or fence. It has lovely red hairy shoots and large, attractive, heart-shaped leaves. The flowers are creamy white, turning to buff yellow with age. Male and female flowers are usually on separate plants, but sometimes both flowers are borne on the same plant. In New Zealand selected clones are cultivated for their fruit, now known as kiwi fruit. It does best in a deep loam but will grow on chalk, and is well worth cultivating. It is very tolerant of industrial and coastal atmospheres and the cold garden. Award of Merit 1907.

Actinidia kolomikta. This is an exceptionally lovely, very slender, deciduous climber which grows to about 10 feet high. The heart-shaped leaves, about 4 to 6 inches long and up to 3 inches wide, are purple when young. The plant is grown for its striking mature leaf colouring of green with white and pink variegation which sometimes extends to half the leaf. It should be planted on a sunny south or south-west wall, is suitable for town and coastal locations and will thrive on all but very chalky soils. Award of Merit 1931.

Campsis grandiflora (synonymous with *Tecoma grandiflora*). This plant, a native of China and Japan and introduced to Britain in 1800, is one of the most beautiful climbers available. It is vigorous and self-clinging by aerial roots, although it is wise to tie some growths in if it is grown on a wall. It grows to 30 feet and more. Because it is not so hardy as *C. radicans* (see below) it must have a sheltered position in full sun. It is the ideal plant to scramble over a summerhouse, pergola or shed but is not, unfortunately, suitable for cold northern areas. The flowers, which are produced in August, are a deep orange and rich red, funnel-shaped, about 3 inches long, in terminal pendulous panicles. A good, loamy, well-drained soil is best, but it will grow on chalk if it is well prepared. It is advisable to prune in late winter, cutting laterals back to 6 inches from the old wood to form spurs. Award of Merit 1949.

Campsis radicans. A native of south-eastern North America: a magnificent plant. It is self-supporting by aerial roots, but does need tying in if grown on a wall – again, it is just right over a pergola, summerhouse or shed. Hardier than *C. grandiflora*, but just as vigorous, growing to 30 feet or more. The brilliant orange and scarlet trumpet flowers, produced in August and September, are up to 3 inches long and 1½ inches wide. Prune in late February or early March, cutting back the growth to about six buds from the old wood, to form spurs as in *C. grandiflora*. It must have full sun and a good fertile soil, and will grow on chalk if well prepared. An ideal plant for a sunny town garden where there are plenty of walls to cover. There is a hybrid between *C. radicans* and *C. grandiflora* called 'Flava', with yellow flowers, which received an Award of Merit 1969.

Clematis. A plant of calcareous regions, the clematis rightly enjoys as much popularity as the rose. There are over 200 species and many hybrids, all of which vary in size, habit and flowering time. They all enjoy a loamy, moist soil, and thrive when the pH is 7.5 to 8 – you could provide some old mortar rubble to increase the pH for them. Place the plants on the north side of a tree or shrub, if they are to be allowed to grow naturally and scramble through the branches. If you want them against a wall, ensure that the roots are in the shade and their tops in the sun. Plant a small shrub in front of them, or a mulch of washed shingle. It is essential to have a well-drained soil for all clematis.

Most of the species should be planted to allow them to grow naturally. The space required varies from *C. macropetala* (8 feet) to *C. montana* (30 feet). The species do not want pruning, but just the occasional cutting to keep them within bounds. The hybrids are divided into groups: *florida, lanuginosa, patens, jackmanii, texensis* and *viticella*. No pruning is required on *florida, lanuginosa* and *patens* groups because their flowers, which appear in May and June, grow from the wood of the previous year. If this is pruned, there will be no flowers for a year.

However, *jackmanii, texensis* and *viticella* groups flower on the growth of the current year, and it is necessary to prune these in March or April, depending on the weather and garden aspect, to within 6 inches of the previous year's pruning cuts. The subsequent growth will flower in August-September. It is not my intention to discuss many species or hybrids here. There are many excellent books on clematis available, and those readers in chalky areas are well advised to refer to them, and plant as many as possible. The species and hybrids I favour are:

C. alpina. A deciduous climber, and native of north Europe and north Asia. It grows up to 8 feet high, various shades of solitary blue flowers appearing in April and May. One of the very best. Award of Merit 1894. Varieties of *C. alpina* are 'Frances Rivis', which has larger flowers than the type plant, 'Ruby', with rose-red flowers, and 'Sibirica', with creamy-white flowers. All are well worth growing, but they are not easy to please. Keep the tops in the sun, bottoms in the shade; no pruning required.

C. macropetala. A lovely, slender climber from Siberia and North China. It grows up to 8 feet, with beautiful, light blue flowers in May or June. It makes a superb combination with C. 'Markhamii', which is similar except that it has soft pink flowers. The pink and blue flowers are quite exceptional together. No pruning is required. *C. macropetala*, Award of Merit 1923, Award of Garden Merit 1934. C. 'Markhamii', Award of Merit 1935.

C. montana. This vigorous Himalayan climber grows to a height of at least 25 feet. The varieties are exceptionally fine and flower in great profusion in May. No pruning is required of *C. montana* or varieties, which include:

C.m. 'Alexander'. Creamy-white flowers.
C.m. 'Elizabeth'. Pink flowers. Award of Garden Merit 1969.
C.m. 'Grandiflora'. White flowers. Award of Garden Merit 1969.
C.m. 'Rubens'. Bronze-purple shoots with rose-pink flowers. Award of Merit 1905, Award of Garden Merit 1969.

C. rehderana. This deciduous climber grows up to 25 feet and has beautiful, nodding, fragrant, cowslip-like flowers in August–September. A native of western China. No pruning required. Award of Merit 1936, Award of Garden Merit 1969.

C. viticella. This species from southern Europe has small, reddish-purple flowers from July to September, and grows to about 12 feet high. Cut back to 9 inches from the base in February, as recommended for the *jackmanii* group. Varieties include:

'Abundance'. Purple flowers.
'Alba Luxurians'. White tinted mauve flowers. Award of Garden Merit 1930.
'Kermesina'. Crimson flowers. Award of Garden Merit 1969.
'Minuet'. Creamy-white flowers.
'Royal Velours'. Purple flowers. Award of Merit 1948. Award of Garden Merit 1969.

Clematis hybrids. The garden varieties are the most showy, and rival climbing and rambling roses, although when grown together they make splendid combinations. The rose makes an ideal support for them.

Clematis 'Jackmannii Superba' like all clematis, flourishes in a limy soil.

Jackmanii group. This group flowers from July to October. Prune in February/March, cutting back growth of the previous year to within 9 inches of the base (old wood). Varieties include:

'Comtesse de Bouchaud'. Pink flowers, June-August, Award of Merit 1936, Award of Garden Merit 1969.
'Gipsy Queen'. Purple flowers, July-September.
'Jackmanii Superba'. Purple flowers, July-September.
'Madame Edouard André'. Crimson flowers, June-August.
'Perle d'Azur'. Light blue flowers. June-August.

Lanuginosa group. This group flowers from May to October. Prune in February/March, cutting back growth of the previous year to within 9 inches of the base (old wood) for late flowers, or prune old flower growth immediately after flowering for early flowers. Varieties include:

'Beauty of Worcester'. Violet blue flowers, May-August.
'Blue Gem'. Pale blue flowers, June-October.
'Fairy Queen'. Pink flowers with deep pink bar, May-June. First Class Certificate 1875.
'Henryi'. Large white flowers, May-June and again August-September.
'Lady Northcliffe'. Lavender blue flowers, June-October.
'Marie Boisselot'. Pure white flowers, May-October.
'Mrs Cholmondeley'. Light blue flowers, May-August. First Class Certificate 1873.
'W. E. Gladstone'. Pale lavender flowers, June-September. First Class Certificate 1881.
'William Kenneth'. Deep blue flowers, June-August.

Clematis 'Nellymoser' which flowers on the previous year's wood, therefore, prune back immediately after flowering.

Patens group. This group flowers in May and June on shoots grown on the previous year's wood. Pruning should be done after flowering, but only to keep the plant within bounds.

'Barbara Dibley'. Violet flowers, May-June and again September.
'Lady Londesborough'. Mauve flowers, May-June. First Class Certificate 1869.
'Lasurstern'. Deep blue flowers, May-June. Award of Garden Merit 1969.
'Nelly Moser'. Pale mauve flowers with pink bar, May-June and again August-September. Award of Garden Merit 1969.
'The President'. Purple flowers, June-September. First Class Certificate 1876.

Texensis group. This group flowers from July to September. Pruning should be carried out during February/March, cutting back to live wood. This may be just above ground level because this group is tender. Plant in a sheltered position against a wall or on the south side of an evergreen shrub.

'Duchess of Albany'. Rose-pink flowers. July-September. Award of Merit 1897.
'Gravetye Beauty'. Cherry-red flowers. July-September. Award of Merit 1935.

Florida group. This group contains a number of double-flowered varieties. They bloom on short lateral growths from the previous year's wood. Prune immediately after flowering, cutting back the flowering shoots to strong first buds. Keep the main growth tied in and trained to enable the side growths to be pruned easily.

'Belle of Woking'. Double, pale mauve flowers, May-June.
'Countess of Lovelace'. Double, violet-blue flowers, May-June.
'Duchess of Edinburgh'. Double, white flowers, May-June.

Ercilla volubilis. This climber is synonymous with *Bridgesia spicata*. It is a native of Chile, introduced in 1840 by Thomas Bridges, a collector of South American plants. This useful self-clinging evergreen climber is quite hardy, and is excellent for covering walls, which it does by the aid of aerial roots. It has leathery leaves which are easily washed by overhead watering, and is thus a good plant for towns and cities. Sun and shade are both acceptable. It flowers in March and April, but it is not a showy plant, being recommended for its foliage and tolerance of shady, north-facing walls in polluted atmospheres.

Rosa. There are many splendid rose species and hybrids of climbing habit, and it is not possible here to mention more than a few. The reader's choice must be based on observation combined with reference to the many books on roses. The Royal National Rose Society publishes a selected list of varieties which is very helpful in many aspects of rose culture. I am not a rosarian, but must admit that I favour the old Shrub roses to the new Hybrid Teas and Floribundas. The climbers and ramblers which I prefer include:

Rambler roses reaching 20 feet or more

* 'Albéric Barbier'	'Excelsa'
'Alexandre Gérault'	'Jersey Beauty'
'American Pillar'	'La Perle'
'Auguste Gervais'	'Mary Wallace'
* 'Dr Van Fleet'	'New Dawn'
'Emily Gray'	

Rambler roses reaching up to 10 feet

'Breeze Hill'	* 'Princess Louise'
'Felicité et Perpetue'	'Spectabilis'
'Flora'	'Thelma'
'Gerbe Rose'	

Climbing roses reaching 20 feet or more

'Allen Chandler'	'Mermaid
'Chaplin's Pink Climber'	'Raymond Chenault'
'Clair Jacquier'	'Reine Marie Henriette'
* 'Cupid'	'Vicomtesse Pierre de Fou'

Climbing roses reaching up to 10 feet

'Blaze'	'Norwich Pink'
'Cocktail'	'Phyllis Bide'
* 'Coral Satin'	'Ruth Alexander'
* 'Dr J. Nicholas'	'Souvenir de la Malmaison'
'Lady Waterloo'	'Summer Snow'
'Maigold'	'Zéphirine Drouhin' (thornless)
'Morning Dawn'	

'Chaplin's Pink Climber' is a very hardy 20ft rambler. Raised in 1928 it is a hybrid between 'Paul's Scarlet' and 'American Pillar'.

* extremely hardy: ideal for cold exposed gardens and northern areas.

Climbing and rambling roses may be grown against walls, on pergolas, arches or pillars; some species and varieties are superb when climbing through trees, while others are effective scrambling over sheds or summerhouses. November is the best planting month, when the young plants take advantage of the summer warmth in the soil and become established before any hard winter frosts. Preparation, as always, should be thorough. It is worth giving the plants a good start, and very satisfying to see plenty of healthy new wood at the end of the first year's growth. If planting against a wall, remove soil to a 2-foot depth, 2-foot length and 2-foot width. Dig in plenty of decayed manure, well-rotted straw, leaf mould, compost or spent mushroom manure, and replace the soil with John Innes Compost No. 3 or fresh loam mixed with plenty of peat. It is impossible to rectify any shortcomings later, other than by lifting the plant – which, of course, is best avoided. After planting, cut back climbers to about 18 inches from the base, ramblers 6 inches. Apply a good mulch to conserve moisture and provide a cool root run.

Ramblers and climbers differ in habit and flowering, and must be pruned in different ways. Ramblers bloom prolifically for a short period in midsummer, and make a large amount of new wood each year. Immediately after flowering, cut out the old flowering wood and tie in the new growths, which will produce the flowers the following year. Cut the old flowering shoots as low as possible, to within 6 inches from the ground, to encourage new basal growth, most of which will be growing vigorously by this time. A large amount of wood is cut out each year. If this is not done the plants will quickly become a mass of dead wood. 'Crimson Shower', 'Dorothy Perkins' and 'Excelsa' are examples of the varieties that must be pruned in this way. However some ramblers, such as 'Albéric Barbier', 'Albertine', 'American Pillar' and 'Dr Van Fleet', do not make as many basal shoots. The new growth – anything up to 12 feet long – springs from the old wood between 2 feet and 5 feet from the ground. Cut the old flowering wood back to these new shoots immediately after flowering, and tie them in to flower the following year.

Climbers require different treatment. Having cut back the shoots to about 18 inches from the base after planting, up to five strong growths should be retained the following year for tying in to form the main framework. These shoots are cut back to half their length in March to promote further side-shoots which themselves become leaders and are tied in.

Climbing roses flower on lateral growths made the previous year, and therefore should be only moderately pruned. Cut the laterals to about five buds from the leader. The leader growths should be tied in to a fan shape, as low as possible, to restrict top growth and encourage laterals to develop. Old wood should be removed as soon as it is worn out. If the rose is growing on a pillar, it is most important to wind the leader growths around the pillar in a nearly horizontal position, to promote the lateral growths which provide the blossoms.

Rosa 'Madame Grégoire Staechelin'. Raised by Pedro Dot of miniature rose fame. Mildew free foliage and outstanding rich perfume.

Roses for east- and north-facing walls
'Danse du Feu'. Climber, 10 feet.
'Felicité et Perpetue'. Rambler, very vigorous.
'Gloire de Dijon'. Climber, 10 feet.
'Leverkusen'. Climber, 10 feet.
'Mme Alfred Carrière. Climber, 10 feet.
'Madame Grégoire Staechelin'. Climber, 20 feet.
'Parkdirektor Riggers'. Climber, vigorous, 15 feet.
'Paul's Lemon Pillar'. Climber, vigorous, 12 feet plus.

Roses for south- and west-facing walls
'Casino'. Climber, 10 feet.
'Chaplin's Pink Climber'. 20 feet.
'Handel'. Climber, 10 feet
'Mermaid'. Climber, 30 feet plus.
'Guinée'. Climber, 10 feet.
Rosa banksiae 'Alba Plena'. 20 feet plus.
Rosa banksiae lutea. 20 feet plus.
'Royal Gold'. Climber, 8 feet

Climbing roses for pillars
'Aloha'. 10 feet.
'Casino'. 10 feet.
'Golden Showers'. 8 feet.
'Meg'. 12 feet.
'Parade'. 10 feet.

Roses for climbing trees
Rosa brunonii, 40 feet.
Rosa filipes. 30 feet.
Rosa moschata. 40 feet plus.

Schizophragma integrifolium. *Schizophragma* from the Greek *schizo*, to cut, and *phragma*, wall of an enclosure, referring to the peculiar splitting of the seed capsules. This superb deciduous climber, a native of China, is similar to *Schizophragma hydran-gioides* (meaning hydrangea-like), but is better and more frequently seen. It attaches itself to its support by aerial roots, and is best on a north-facing wall, out of the sun. It needs plenty of space because, after a slow start, it will grow to 30 feet or more. Flowering in July, it has enormous white bracts surrounding the flowers. This is an excellent climber, suitable for all types of soil, and quite hardy. It will become a lovely feature. Award of Merit 1936, First Class Certificate 1963, Award of Garden Merit 1969.

Solanum crispum 'Glasnevin'. *Solanum* is a name given by the Roman naturalist Pliny to one of the nightshades, possibly from the Latin *solamen*, a solace, from its medicinal virtues. This fast-growing, showy, semi-evergreen from Chile is at its best in full sun, in a chalky soil, in a sheltered position on a south-facing wall. It must, however, have room to develop to give of its best, and will grow to 20 feet or more. Pruning should be limited to thinning out in the spring, selecting and tying in the strong growths. This beautiful plant belongs to the potato family, and is a native of Chile. The type plant was introduced about 1830. The varietal form 'Glasnevin' is much hardier and longer flowering. It has lovely blue flowers with conspicuous golden yellow stamens from July to September. Award of Merit 1955, Award of Garden Merit 1969.

Trachelospermum asiaticum. A magnificent evergreen climber with handsome, leathery foliage and fragrant, jasmine-like flowers produced in July and August. This is an ideal plant for towns where pollution is a problem. A wall with plenty of space is required if it is to develop properly – an area of 15 feet × 15 feet is not too much. This lovely climber is hardier than *Trachelospermum jasminoides*, and has smaller leaves and flowers. All types of soil are suitable, including limy. Once it is established, very little attention is needed other than keeping it within bounds.

Vitis coignetiae. Latin *vitis*, vine; *coignetiae* refers to its intro-duction from Japan to France by Madame Coignet in 1875. This deciduous climber is very vigorous, and plenty of space is essential. It will, if planted against a large tree, scramble to the top. It is magnificent in the autumn when the leaves colour to rich shades of yellow, orange and crimson. Award of Garden Merit 1969.

Vitis vinifera 'Purpurea' **(*Teinturier grape*).** This is the common vine, and its many varieties are grown mainly for their fruit. Of the several ornamental varieties, 'Purpurea' is the best. It has beautiful, claret-red foliage throughout the summer, which turns to a rich purple in the autumn. It is a vigorous climber which needs plenty of space and is happy on all types of soil. A sunny south-facing wall is ideal. Award of Merit 1958, Award of Garden Merit 1969.

Wistaria floribunda 'Macrobotrys'. Named after the American anatomist Caspar Wistar. A splendid, hardy climber, growing to 100 feet or more and producing racemes of blue flowers in May and June. When grown on the walls of a house it must be kept within bounds, and not allowed to get under roof tiles or round gutters. It is easy to grow in all types of soil, but a sunny position is necessary. Pruning should be done in August and February. In August, cut lateral growth back to about six buds from the old wood, to form spurs. In February, reduce these further to three or four buds of the older wood. Reduce all leaders by half the previous year's growth to encourage lateral growth, which will eventually form flowering spurs. Award of Garden Merit 1969.

Recommended climbers for limy soil

Actinidia chinensis
Actinidia kolomikta
Campsis grandiflora
Campsis radicans
Clematis alpina
Clematis armandii
Clematis 'Comtesse de
    Bouchaud', 'Duchess of
    Albany', 'Gravetye
    Beauty', 'Jackmanii
    Superba'
Clematis macropetala
Clematis markhamii
Clematis montana 'Elizabeth',
    'Grandiflora', 'Rubens'
Clematis orientalis
Clematis rehderana
Clematis 'Sensation'
Clematis viticella 'Alba

Luxurians', 'Kermesina'
Clematis 'William Kennet'
Hedera colchica 'Dentata
    Variegata'
Hedera helix 'Goldheart'
Hydrangea petiolaris
Lonicera americana
Lonicera sempervirens
Lonicera × *tellmanniana*
Lonicera tragophylla
Parthenocissus henryana
Passiflora caerulea
Passiflora caerulea 'Constance
    Elliott'
Rosa 'Albéric Barbier', 'Danse
    du Feu', 'Golden
    Showers', 'Handel',
    'Leverkusen', 'Mermaid',
    'Paul's Lemon Pillar',

Lonicera sempervirens, the trumpet honeysuckle, is a vigorous climber.

'Zéphirine Drouhin'
Schizophragma hydrangioides
Schizophragma integrifolium
Solanum crispum 'Glasnevin'

Trachelospermum jasminoides
Vitis coignetiae
Wistaria floribunda
  'Macrobotrys'

Climbers for north- and east-facing walls in cold, exposed gardens

Ercilla volubilis
Hedera helix 'Buttercup',
  'Cavendishii', 'Goldheart'
Hydrangea petiolaris
Lonicera × *brownii*
Lonicera × *hectrotii* 'Gold
  Flame'
Lonicera × *japonica halliana*
Lonicera × *periclymenum*
  'Belgica', 'Serotina'

Lonicera sempervirens
Lonicera tragophylla
Pileostegia viburnoides
Rosa 'Allen Chandler',
  'Chaplin's Pink Climber',
  'Coral Satin', 'Cupid', 'Don
  Juan', 'Dr J. Nicholas',
  'Paul's Scarlet Climber',
  'Zéphirine Drouhin'
Schizophragma integrifolium

Shrubs for north- and east-facing walls in cold, exposed gardens

Cotoneaster horizontalis
Garrya elliptica 'James Roof'

Jasminum nudiflorum
Pyracantha atalantioides

CHAPTER 7 *Lawns*

William Robinson wrote that 'the lawn is the heart of a true English Garden'. A fine lawn is an asset and joy to garden and gardener alike, creating a tranquil foil for trees, shrubs and flowers. Unfortunately, there are no short cuts to achieving and caring for an immaculate lawn, despite the fact that the British climate is most favourable for grass. It is very sad that some landscape architects in this country are so keen to copy the vast paved squares of Italy and Spain. They do not seem to realize that Italy and Spain are unable to grow fine lawns, and surely would if they could, because there is no finer way to complement a building. As Francis Bacon wrote, 'God Almighty first planted a garden; and, indeed it is the purest of human pleasures; it is the greatest refreshment to the spirits of men without which buildings and palaces are but gross handy-works; and a man shall ever see that, when ages grow to civility and elegance, man comes to build stately sooner than to garden finely; as if gardening were the greater perfection.'

When one of these hideous paved areas is constructed in Great Britain, it is immediately seen to be a mistake, and plant tubs and containers are quickly introduced in an attempt to soften the lines and allay public criticism. Regretfully this is not always possible, because a cubic foot of soil weighs approximately a hundredweight, and loading constraints in many instances prevent any landscaping as an afterthought. However, having expressed this opinion, I do think that there is no purpose in having a lawn in a very small garden, where a variety of plants would be more effective.

There are three ways of making a lawn: from seed, turf or tumbledown. The last is an excellent method in a large garden, because the grasses are native to the site, thriving on soil and climatic conditions which may not suit imported grasses. This particularly applies in town gardens, where in some instances

127

only *Poa annua* will survive. Tumbledown requires the same preparations as seeding and turfing. The only difference in this kind of lawn is that all kinds of native grasses will grow of their own accord, unless subsequent regular mowing prevents coarser grasses getting established. However it is not possible to make a silk purse out of a sow's ear, and the only way to make a perfect lawn is from a seed mixture which contains the right grass species. The larger the area of lawn, the more effective the general appearance will be.

The first task is to grade the site, construct paths and terrace if required and install a drainage system if necessary (as discussed in the chapter on soil). The base of the house is a useful bench mark from which to set out levels. You may want a series of different levels, undulations, a gradual slope or just a flat expanse, but in all circumstances the top spit of soil is all important, and should be set aside if any change of level is contemplated. It is essential that any alterations and new levels are made to the subsoil. The topsoil is then replaced evenly over the finished levels. A 12-inch depth of topsoil for a lawn is ideal, but there are many exceptionally fine lawns, including bowling greens, which have only 6 inches of topsoil over a 6-inch drainage layer of ash. Single digging or rotovating the topsoil is necessary. On heavy clay soil it is very beneficial to fork into the top six inches one barrowload of coarse sand, or ⅛-inch grit to 4 square yards, to assist surface drainage, and one barrowload of spent mushroom manure or compost to 6 square yards to improve the soil structure. On light sandy soil, one barrowload of spent mushroom manure, compost or wet peat per 6 square yards would improve water retention and also supply plant nutrients and food for beneficial soil bacteria.

There is a considerable advantage to fallow the site one summer, to eradicate weeds by regular hoeing or spraying with contact and/or systemic weedkillers. Where alterations to levels have taken place this gives time for consolidation and settlement, which is most helpful when preparing final levels prior to seeding or turfing. A roller is necessary only for the preparation of the surface for games such as tennis, cricket or bowls and then, once the game is over, aeration equipment must be used to rectify the damage caused by the roller. If you wish to construct a bowling green or tennis court, reference to R. B. Dawson's *Practical Lawn Craft* will prove to be extremely helpful. If you do not, sell your roller! Some amateur gardeners are convinced that a heavy roller will level a site, and have difficulty in accepting that it is actually harmful to an estab-lished lawn. Levelling can be achieved only by pegging out the site in approximately 10-foot squares and, with the aid of a tight line (a builder's line is ideal), by levelling each square to a running or flat level using a spade and fork.

Seeding

After cleaning the site during the summer months, the final seed bed preparation should be undertaken in the middle of August. This is best done by treading the ground both ways: any soft areas are quickly discovered by the soles of the feet. The site is then raked, firmed again by treading in both directions and cross-raked to produce a fine tilth. By keeping the rake fairly upright a good level is easily obtained; stones are raked into lines and barrowed off. Do not sieve the top few inches to remove stones, because this adversely alters the soil structure, encourages panning and subsequently inhibits aeration and germination of grass seed. Treading and raking should be done when there are good drying conditions. Once you have made a good, firm, friable, level seed bed, your next job is to put on an even application of fertilizer ten days before sowing, raking it lightly into the prepared seed bed. Use ½ ounce sulphate of ammonia, 1 ounce superphosphate and ¼ ounce sulphate of potash per square yard. Mix the fertilizers with dry sand to act as a carrier.

Sow the seed at the end of August. The seedlings will then be well established to survive the winter, and will grow away strongly in the spring to form a good sward. For a fine ornamental lawn the seed mixture should be 70% by weight *Festuca rubra* (Chewing's fescue) and 30% by weight *Agrostis tenuis* (New Zealand brown top). In hot dry situations sow *Poa pratensis* (meadow grass) and/or *Cynosurus cristatus* (crested dogstail). These can be sown either singly or as a mixture in equal parts. In a shady area, provided it is not under the drip of trees or under conifers, sow *Poa nemoralis* (wood meadow grass) or *Poa annua* (annual meadow grass), or a mixture of the two. An April sowing can be badly affected by a summer drought, but a spring sowing is preferable to a late September or October sowing. The best results are undoubtedly achieved by an end-of-August sowing, when there is plenty of warmth in the ground to promote and establish good sturdy growth before the winter. Always choose a windless day.

The seed should be divided into lots, that is, halves, quarters, or eighths depending on the area to be sown, and the area divided into equal sections accordingly. This will ensure uniform sowing (1 ounce per square yard). It is helpful to mix the seed with a quantity of dry sand or dry sieved soil to act as a carrier, which assists even sowing. Sowing one way and then cross-sowing is also recommended. When the soil surface is dry, after sowing, the seed should be very gently raked in. Some experts recommend, after sowing and raking in, a light roll. I prefer to leave the surface loose. Rolling, in my view, only seals the surface, and indeed it cakes a heavier clay soil to the detriment of the germination process.

Germination will be about 14 days. Heavy dews will encourage rapid growth, and it will be necessary to cut the grass before winter. This should be done when the grass is about 2 inches high. Set the blades of the mowing machine to cut at 1 inch or just over. The object is just to tip the leaf top to encourage basal growth (tillering). In the spring the established grass will grow quite strongly, but on no account be tempted to shave it by cutting too low. Cutting at 1 inch high is advised twice a week. In town gardens it is advisable to protect the seed from birds by threading black cotton on pegs over the seeded area. Only in the event of an Indian summer, when the dry weather will delay germination, will it be necessary to water artificially with a sprinkler. Avoid this if possible, because of the panning effect to the soil surface. If it is unavoidable, irrigate with a good sprinkler only during the evenings – watering in the sun tends to cake the soil surface even more.

Turfing

Turfing has various advantages. It produces immediate results; it is usually done between September and March, when general gardening work is minimal; and above all the amateur finds it much easier to produce a lawn by turfing than by seeding. The grass species in the turf, however, will not be as good as those bought in seed form. When buying turf, ensure that it is weed-free and that coarse grasses do not predominate, or the results will be very disappointing. Preparation of the soil bed for turfing is exactly the same as for seeding, with the exception of substituting the recommended fertilizers with an application of bonemeal at 2 ounces per square yard. This should be applied before the turf is laid. Because turf should not be laid in frosty conditions and badly discolours if left stacked for a relatively short period of time, it is wise to complete all turfing by December. If left until March or April it will be necessary to irrigate the turf after laying and before it is affected by dry weather, otherwise it will crack and shrink badly. Turves supplied commercially are machine-cut 3 foot by 1 foot to a uniform thickness of 1 inch, and on a properly prepared soil bed laying them is as easy as rolling out a carpet.

The best method is to lay from boards, without walking or barrowing turf on the prepared soil. Lay the first row adjoining a path or terrace and place the scaffold boards on top of the turf. Then, facing the soil bed and working from the boards, work forward, laying the turves by bonding them like bricks in a wall. As each line is completed the boards are moved forward in order to lay the next row. This method adequately compresses the turf without the use of a roller or the need to beat it with a large wooden mallet. Once the turf has been laid, top dress with a mixture of equal parts peat and sand. This should be brushed well into the cracks and base of the grasses. It is important to cut the grass when it is established and is about 1½ inches high. Pick a dry day when no frost is forecast, cut to about ¾ inch high and keep it topped to this height throughout the winter.

Mowing

Once a lawn is established by turfing or seeding, the type of maintenance will eventually determine its quality. A first-class sward will not be achieved by a weekly cut. Mowing has a very significant effect on density, weed infestation and the type of grass species in a lawn. The cardinal points with regard to mowing are:

1. Mowing should be done regularly at frequent intervals. Shaving the grass in an endeavour to mow less frequently does permanent damage and opens up the sward to weed invasion. Mowing three times a week at the same height results in a good, high-density sward. Mowing every day at the same height produces an even better sward. Controlled experiments have shown that mowing once a week produces more clippings than the total clippings removed when cutting three times a week. Mowing every day produces less in a week than a thrice-weekly cut. This means that fewer plant foods are removed by regular, frequent cuttings at the same height.

2. Mowing has a very positive effect on the type of species in the turf and, again, should be done daily to encourage a finer lawn. Most people purchase pasture turf, in which the leafy coarser meadow grasses and rye grass predominate; however, when this type of turf is mown regularly three times a week at the same height (start at ⅜ inch high and reduce to

⅛ inch high), these coarser grasses gradually die out and in their place the finer bent grasses begin to flourish, producing a uniform, high-density sward.

3.   It is important to have a good-quality cylinder mower in proper repair with the blades set correctly. Place a piece of a cigarette packet between the bottom blade and cylinder, turn the cylinder by hand and adjust until the blades are cleanly cutting the packet along the entire length of the bottom blade. Avoid having the cylinder adjusted too tightly on to the bottom blade. Ribbing of the grass by the mower indicates one of three things: the cutting has been too long delayed, the cylinder is set too tightly on to the bottom blade, or the mower is not good enough. A mower with eight blades or more, to give 100 cuts per yard, is necessary; the more expensive machines are geared to turn the cylinder at a higher number of revolutions per yard. Rotary mowers are not suitable for fine ornamental lawns. It is important to avoid a severe check to grass in the spring by not allowing it to grow too long during the winter.

Mowing should always be undertaken during dry weather. Keep the grass topped to about ½ inch high and avoid periods of frost. Mowing in different directions helps to control creeping weeds and grasses. It is a good idea to fit a scarifying comb to the mower to lift grasses up to the cutting cylinder. During drought conditions it is wise to let clippings fly, that is, remove the box from the mower. These clippings act as a mulch and prevent the lawn from drying out so quickly.

Autumn maintenance

Autumn maintenance is especially important. It consists of scarifying, aerating and top dressing to improve soil structure, texture, water retention and the turf surface. Top dressings are not high in manurial value, and are not intended to be; a high-density turf with a good surface is the result of uniform close mowing, which promotes the growth of desirable finer grass species. Prior to top dressing, the lawn should be scarified with a wire rake or a mechanical scarifier (now available from some small tool hire companies). Scarifying must be done vigorously to remove matted growths of dead herbage and the runners of creeping plants. This is followed by mowing to box off the debris and to prepare the surface for solid or hollow tine forking (see below). This can then be done either by hand or by machine, and the holes should be made 6 inches deep and 4 inches apart. This relieves compaction, improves surface water drainage and assists aeration. Forking also enables top dressings to be worked in by lute or brush. Regular top dressing significantly improves the turf surface, but it is most important to work the material into the base of the grasses. Leaving the dressing on top weakens the grass and encourages fungus diseases. Make a top dressing by mixing 1 part (by volume) loam (sieved $^3/_{16}$-inch mesh), 2 parts sand, and 1 part peat. Apply one hundredweight to 50 square yards. This can be broadcast by hand or by a fertilizer distributor.

Two light top dressings, about four weeks apart and well worked in, are much better than one heavy dressing not worked in.

On heavy soils a top dressing of sand is very helpful. This should be applied at one hundredweight to 30 square yards and well worked in. Dressings of sand should not be overdone; a heavier soil should have more sand dressings than a lighter one, to improve surface drainage and also to encourage the grass to tiller, that is, to promote basal growth. For the golfer or bowler who would like to use his ornamental lawn for practising, sand dressings make the surface fast and true. Charcoal, applied at one pound weight per square yard, sweetens the soil, and this can be included in the top dressing.

Hollow tining is usually done every fourth year. The plugs left on the surface by machine or hand fork should be swept up and put on to the compost heap. Solid tining should be done every autumn. The removal of grass clippings depletes the soil of nitrogen, phosphorus and potassium, and even though more frequent mowing reduces the loss, it is necessary to replace these lost plant foods regularly. An effective and simple method is to apply a compound fertilizer in the spring at 3 ounces per square yard. Make this of 3 parts (by weight) sulphate of ammonia, 3 parts dried blood, 8 parts bonemeal, 5 parts superphosphate, and 1 part sulphate of potash. By adding dry sand or soil as a carrier to this mixture it will be much easier to apply evenly. Because grass is grown so intensively, it is necessary to supplement the compound fertilizer with further nitrogenous fertilizers between May and August to replace the nitrogen removed by mowing throughout the season.

The old gardening adage 'what is taken out must be put back' is most appropriate in lawn care. The main fertilizers are as follows: sulphate of ammonia and dried blood (both supply nitrogen, an essential major element for plant growth), bonemeal and superphosphate (phosphatic fertilizers to promote a good healthy root system, which enables the turf to withstand periods of drought and also produces a vigorous dense turf); and sulphate of potash (potassium, which has the same effect as sunlight. It hardens growth and increases resistance to disease.)

From the middle of May, apply sulphate of ammonia at four-weekly intervals up to August at the rate of 2 ounces per square yard. In a wet summer, when the grass is too lush, reduce the nitrogen by omitting one feed, or apply only 1 ounce per square yard. Do not apply any nitrogenous fertilizers after August, or the grass will be susceptible to disease in the autumn/winter. Calcined sulphate of iron has a marked inhibitory effect on fungus diseases and also, when used with certain fertilizers, acts as a weed and moss killer. A mixture for general weed control for use between April and June is: 3 parts (by weight) sulphate of ammonia, 1 part calcined sulphate of iron, and 20 parts sand (lime-free), applied at 4 ounces per square yard. This will scorch and blacken the grass quite seriously, but within a few weeks the grass will be growing strongly.

Tap-rooted weeds will require spot treatment with a stronger mixture made up of: 35 parts (by weight) sulphate of ammonia, 15 parts calcined sulphate of iron, and 50 parts dry sand (lime-free). For very weedy turf this mixture can be used at the rate of 4 ounces per square yard, but there will be considerable scorching of the grass and recovery will take longer.

If a lawn is well maintained there should not be any difficulty with weeds or moss, but if there has been neglect and weeds have flourished, an application of a selective hormone weed-killer such as MCPA or 24D, available under several trade names, is very effective. Always follow the manufacturer's instructions and do not be deceived by these powerful, slow-acting weedkillers. Overdosing at worst will kill the grass, but in any event the serious check to the grasses certainly will not do them any good. Treatment in the spring is most effective when the grass is growing vigorously. Choose a dry, windless day and leave the grass uncut for 24 hours after application, to enable the weeds to absorb the chemical. It is very helpful not to cut the grass for seven days before applying the weed-killer; this will expose the maximum leaf surface. Once the hormone is absorbed it is translocated throughout the plant, stimulating rapid growth, causing the cells to collapse and the plant to die. The presence of moss is clear evidence of neglected turf; it is most common during the autumn/winter. Bad aeration, insufficient drainage and low fertility are certainly the main causes, but moss can still be a problem on well-drained, chalky soils. Nitrogenous fertilizers with an alkaline reaction such as nitro chalk, nitrate of soda and nitrate of lime favour growth of moss. Sulphate of ammonia discourages it and superphosphate applied at 2 ounces per square yard will scorch and check it. Lawn sand is also very effective. The only solution to the problem is an adequate maintenance programme of feeding, aeration and mowing – and when you have regularly carried this out you will relish the joy of having a first-class lawn.

CHAPTER 8

Herbaceous border plants (hardy perennials)

There is an immense range of hardy perennials available, and they are not planted as widely as their versatility and beauty merit. The great garden reformers Miss Gertrude Jekyll and William Robinson admired and recommended the planting of hardy perennials at the turn of the century. It was Gertrude Jekyll who advised that they should be carefully selected and planted in narrow drifts, whereby the group just coming into flower should screen the group just passing out of flower.

Gardening fashions change, and the demise of the 'herbaceous border' during the last twenty-five years has, in my view, been regrettable. The reason for it is obscure. It may be that these plants die down in the autumn and are not attractive during the winter – which in a small garden is a situation best avoided – or it may be they are generally time-consuming, needing staking, lifting, dividing and replanting. Hybrid Tea and Floribunda roses are equally unprepossessing between November and April, and they require quite a lot of attention too, yet they have not fallen from favour; indeed the reverse is true.

The ideal and, I think, what most people want, is variety and beauty from as many different types of plants as possible in the garden space available to them. This will not give a spotty effect; on the contrary, the skill of a good plantsman will capture subtle combinations and contrasts in foliage, fruit, bark and flowers. Be ever mindful of year-round interest, and aware of the added bonuses of fragrance and autumn colour. Very large drifts of just one plant do not look lavish; they simply have a disastrously boring effect. The best herbaceous borders were usually double borders, each about 15 feet wide on each side of a 15-foot-wide grass path, with a fine clipped yew hedge in the background. There was a splendid example at the Royal Horticultural Society Gardens, Wisley, thirty years ago, and fine borders do still exist, maintained by those skilful

Opposite:
Moist, humus-rich soil, shelter and partial shade make a haven for iris, meconopsis, hosta and candelabra primulas.

gardeners who have recognized, without making the garden too much of a chore, that reward is related to effort. Many municipal authorities have led the way, by demonstrating the suitability of certain plants in a particular district. This is the way to encourage wider planting – by example.

Borders of hardy perennials may be of any size or shape, and may be single or double-sided. The larger they are the more effective they become – but of course they must be in scale with the garden overall. The majority of hardy perennials are not difficult to grow, and there is a large selection suitable for the smaller garden, including those which are happy in shady positions. The mixed border of shrubs, roses, sub-shrubby plants, hardy perennials and bulbs has gained in popularity in recent years. There is a good example at the Royal Horticultural Society Gardens, Wisley (Broad Walk), which I hope has played a part in stemming the decline of the hardy perennial. This type of border provides plenty of colour and interest throughout the year, the shrubs giving a fine background and shelter for the hardy perennials and bulbs. While it is always difficult to decide on what to plant, extra care is necessary here to avoid those shrubs which are greedy feeders, otherwise there will be serious root encroachment to the detriment of the border as a whole. The best position for hardy perennials is where they will get the maximum amount of sunshine, and shelter fom north and east winds. The other requirements for a successful border are that it should have a well-drained soil, and definitely not be in a frost pocket. The width of the border or island bed devoted solely to hardy perennials should govern the height of the planting, if it is to be in scale. The simple rule is that the maximum height should be half the width.

Planning a border is a great pleasure. There are many delightful decisions to be made in arranging leaf or colour associations, choosing those plants that you think will give a good account of themselves, planning a display from spring to autumn, or restricting the flowering period to June, July and August. You may decide to confine the border to a specific colour or association of colours; for example, white and grey, red and yellow, yellow and gold, yellow and blue, blue and pink, blue and silver, and so on. Colours of the same hue grouped together avoid colour clashes; this of course includes foliage as well as flowers. The planting can be designed for foliage effect or fragrance only.

For all types of borders, it is important that the site should be thoroughly prepared by bastard digging (see the chapter on soil) and incorporating plenty of compost, spent mushroom manure or rotted farmyard manure at a rate of one 4-cubic-foot-sized barrowload per 10 square yards. This should be completed before Christmas in order to take advantage of the hard weather, which has such a beneficial effect on soil.

Plan the border on paper, to scale. (Graph-paper is ideal.) This will avoid over-purchase of plants, and will help enormously when you are actually planting the border in the spring, after it has been firmed by treading and raked down to a fine tilth. The border itself should be marked out in one-yard squares, corresponding to the prepared plan. Put a few key markers throughout the border, which should enable you to plant out the whole bed in accordance with the drawing.

Plants should be planted in groups of, say 3, 5, 7 or 9. The smaller the plant the more will be required to make an effective group. There should be no single plants, as these would be lost in the overall display. Some plants, such as peonies, hellebores, *Romneya coulteri*, alstroemerias and *Eremurus*, resent root disturbance, and take a little longer to become established, so do not be disappointed if they appear to be slow in the first year. Never stake plants unless it is absolutely necessary. If required, this should be done in the spring, before growth gets too advanced. Brushwood is very suitable for staking; place it around and inside the group and, just below the top of the estimated height, turn over the twiggy branches. The plants will subsequently grow up through and hide the brushwood. While looking quite natural, they will be firmly supported and protected from strong winds and summer storms.

Endeavour to arrange groups which flower at the same time to be sited throughout the border or bed. Avoid having all the flowers in one section at any one time, or having specific colours in one area. Remember to limit the height of the tallest plants to half the width of the border. Use whites and yellows to break strong colours that would otherwise clash.

The majority of hardy perennials need lifting, dividing and replanting every four or five years. This is best done in September or October. Take the opportunity to dig in a generous amount of compost or spent mushroom manure. Before lifting, it is a good idea to label everything, especially varieties, to avoid mixing them up. The identification of different genera, for example *Sidalcea* or *Solidago*, is one thing, but it is quite another matter to identify *Sidalcea* 'Sussex Beauty', a clear pink, 4 foot high, from *Sidalcea* 'Croftway Red', a rose-red, 3 foot high. When clumps are divided, select the strongest outside shoots for replanting. These should be planted about 12 inches apart within the group, leaving 24 inches between groups. Try to avoid planting rank growers near weak ones or those that resent disturbance. For outer groups, use low-growing plants in every other space. Vary the heights and habits throughout the border or bed. A spiky group, for example, should be next to a bushy type to give an interesting contrast.

A border skirted by grass is easy on the eye; a strip of stone about 12 inches wide along the edge allows plants to tumble over without being damaged by the mowing machine, and also prevents grass from being spoiled. Single-facing or double-sided borders are both appropriate for herbaceous plants. However, the single-facing borders, if backed by a hedge or shrubs, will suffer some root encroachment; plant the perennials at least 3 feet away from hedges or shrubs so that they have a chance to give a good account of themselves.

Frequent hoeing will keep the weeds down, but a 3-inch mulch of pulverised bark, peat, compost or spent mushroom manure will not only keep weeds suppressed but will also reduce the need to water. If watering is necessary – and this should be avoided if possible – water thoroughly. Do not do what most amateurs do, just lay the dust. Leave a sprinkler in one position for an hour to give a good watering that will last three to four weeks or more.

It is not possible to discuss at length more than a few species and varieties in this book. A few of the plants I particularly favour are as follows:

***Achillea* (yarrow, milfoil).** Named after the Greek hero Achilles, who first used the plant in medicine. It is also mentioned in that most interesting book, Culpeper's *Complete Herbal* (1616–54) as a treatment to induce sleep, ease pain and lessen bleeding. There are a number of species from this large genus which are worthy of cultivation in the rock garden and herbaceous border. All are stout, durable, hardy plants which thrive in all types of soil and all conditions. They are excellent for the cold, exposed garden and northern regions.

A. decolorans. 'W. B. Child' is undoubtably the best form. It is of Swiss origin, and is not an invasive plant. Growing to a height of 2 feet, it has finely cut leaves and produces clusters of pure white flowers throughout the summer, the individual flowers being about ⅜ inch in diameter. The attractive flowerheads make a fine display in the border, and are all useful for flower arrangers.

A. eupatorium (synonymous with *A. filipendulina*). This 4-foot-high plant from the Caucasus has large, flat heads of yellow flowers from July to September. If these are picked when fresh, and dried, the colour is retained for quite some time. It is a good cut flower and a superb border plant. 'Parker's', 'Spark's and 'Gold Plate' are all first-class varieties.

A. millefolium. This is one of the weeds so difficult to eradicate from fine lawns. Its varieties, however, make a very appealing display from June to August. They grow 2 feet tall, have fine cut foliage and flat heads of red or carmine flowers. 'Lilac Beauty', 'Cerise Queen', 'Rose Queen,' 'Fire King' and 'Crimson King' are all good varieties.

A. taygetea. This is a very fine border plant, thriving in full sunshine. It has grey foliage and flattish heads of lemon-yellow flowers from July onwards. It grows to about 2 feet high, is a good cut flower for the house, and dries well.

Aconitum. All the aconites dislike root disturbance and, once planted, should be left for many years. Best planted in the spring, they take a couple of years to settle down. All prefer a moist, retentive soil, and are equally at home in sun or partial shade. *A. napellus* (monkshood) is the plant which provides

Achillea 'Moonshine' is a hybrid between *A. taygetea* and *A. clypeolata.*

A lovely association of pink and blue cranesbill (*Geranium*) with yellow achillea.

the drug aconite. All of them, however, are poisonous, particularly the root; but this should not deter the reader from growing these handsome plants, which are not unlike small delphiniums. Mulching with compost each spring works wonders, ensuring the cool, moist root run which these plants enjoy so much.

A. arendsii. This hybrid between *A. wilsonii* and *A. fischeri* displays all the fine characteristics of both parents. It is well worth growing.

A. fischeri. Flowering in September-October, this 3-foot-high plant has most attractive foliage and violet-blue flowers on strong, stiff spikes, which do not need staking.

A. henryi 'Sparks Variety'. This is another fine variety, which grows up to 4 feet high. It has deep Oxford-blue flowers, June-August.

A. napellus 'Bicolor'. An attractive plant flowering in July-August, it has light blue and white flowers on stout stems, up to 3 feet high, and good foliage.

A. wilsonii. 'Barker's' and 'Kelmscott' are both excellent varieties, growing up to 6 feet high. The strong stems produce lovely blue flowers, September-October.

Agapanthus. The blue African lily is a truly magnificent plant for tubs, cut flower arrangers and borders alike. All species are quite easy to grow, provided they have full sun and rich feeding. Not particular about soil, they flourish in limy and well-drained clay soils. In cold, exposed gardens and northern regions, however, it is prudent to put a heavy mulch of straw or bracken over the crowns to give the tough, deep-rooting, fleshy roots some winter protection.

A. africanus (synonymous with *A. umbellatus*). This rewarding plant has strap-like leaves developing into large clumps, and produces umbels of dark blue flowers in August. It grows to about 18 inches high.

A. campanulatus. This has large heads of paler blue flowers, 2 to 3 feet high.

A. 'Headbourne Hybrids'. This is a fine plant, with smaller blue umbels of flowers, August-September, 18 to 24 inches high.

Anaphalis yedoensis. A useful silver-grey plant, about 2 feet tall, producing off-white everlasting flowers, August-September. It flourishes in full sunshine and is not invasive.

Artemisia lactiflora. This is a fine plant, growing up to 4 feet high in a moist soil, which it prefers. It has attractive, deeply cut foliage and spiraea-like plumes of creamy-white flowers. It will not be happy in dry, light soils unless plenty of moisture-retaining organic material is dug in, and more subsequently applied as a mulch.

Artemisia ludoviciana. This is a good white-grey foliage plant which grows up to 4 feet high. It is invasive, and should not be sited near plants that resent disturbance.

Astrantia major (masterwort). An umbelliferous plant, easy to grow, with distinct star-like flowers, greenish white tinged with pink. It is not showy, but is pleasing and useful as a cut flower. It prefers a moist soil and partial shade, and is an excellent plant for a shady town garden.

Baptisia australis (false indigo). Some species of *Baptisia* provide tinctures for dyers. *B. australis* is an attractive, hardy plant producing spikes of blue flowers in June. The average height is 2 feet, but in rich, fertile soils it will grow to 4 feet. It resents root disturbance, and takes a couple of years to get established.

Brunnera macrophylla (synonymous with *Anchusa myosotidiflora*). This pleasing plant from the Caucasus is not particular about soil, and excels in partial shade. It has deep green, heart-shaped leaves, about 18 inches high, and in May-June produces sprays of delicate forget-me-not-like flowers. It is a good plant for the shady town garden.

Campanula lactiflora. This is a plant which will grow in a dry, shady position, although it prefers a sunny site. It will grow up to 5 feet high in good, fertile soil, but about 3½ feet is usual. Bell-shaped flowers are produced from June onwards. Varieties worth growing are 'Pritchard's Variety' (lavender blue) and 'Loddon Anna' (pale pink).

Campanula latifolia. A strong-growing, 4 foot-high plant, which does not require staking. It thrives in shade, and is excellent for the shady town garden. Flowers appear June-July. The best form is 'Macrantha' (violet-blue).

Cimicifuga japonica (bugbane). This plant was once used to ward off fleas! It flowers in late September, growing to about

Campanula latifolia 'Brantwood'—a splendid variety.

3 feet high, with graceful spikes of white flowers. 'White Pearl' is a good variety for the border. It is not fussy about soil, provided that it retains moisture; it enjoys partial shade.

Clematis integrifolia. An excellent, non-climbing, upright, hardy perennial, this clematis produces small blue flowers from July onwards. Growing about 2 feet high, it is best planted in a sunny position. As with all clematis, it loves a limy soil.

Clematis recta. Another non-climbing hardy perennial, similar to *C. integrifolia*, but with small white flowers, July-September. It is a fine border plant which merits a place in the garden.

Coreopsis verticillata (tickseed). This is a graceful plant which grows up to 2 feet high. It is very free-flowering, producing rich yellow, star-like flowers from June onwards. The elegant feathery foliage is also most attractive. It is not fussy about soil, but this rewarding plant loves a sunny position.

Crambe cordifolia. From the Caucasus, this superb plant grows up to 4 feet high. Somewhat similar to a large gypsophila, it has wide, branching sprays of small white flowers in June, and striking large round leaves. It is not fussy about soil, and is easy to grow except in a windy, exposed garden.

Crinum powellii. This South African plant could well have been included in the chapter on bulbs, corms and tubers, because it is a bulbous plant; but because it is commonly planted in herbaceous borders I prefer to include it here. It has broad, strap-like leaves, about 18 inches long, forming stout clumps. From these are produced stems up to 3 feet high, carrying large, pink, trumpet-like flowers, July-August. The large bulbs should be planted during the spring, the base of the bulb being set about 8 inches deep in well-drained soil. They will take a couple of years to settle down. This plant is hardy in all but the coldest districts. A sunny sheltered border is ideal, however, and the base of a south-facing wall is best in northern regions.

Dianthus plumarius (common pink). This is a parent of many hardy garden pinks. All varieties thrive in full sun in a limy, well-drained soil, and are excellent for the front of a border or a dry wall. Cut back to ground level immediately after

Coreopsis verticillata is a ferny-leafed plant producing yellow starry flowers throughout the summer.

Dianthus 'Cherry Ripe' is a hybrid derived from *D. plumarius*.

144

flowering to encourage strong basal growth. The charm of these hardy pinks lies in their scent, their range of colours, and their particular usefulness as cut flowers.

Dracocephalum hemsleyanum. A spiky, showy plant growing to 18 inches high. It is not particular about soil, being equally at home on clay, chalk, or a light, sandy soil. It prefers a sunny spot, but is shade tolerant, and should be left undisturbed for many years. The rich blue tubular flowers appear in August. It is easily propagated from spring cutting or seed.

***Echinops ritro* (globe thistle).** An architectural plant with large, globular blue flowers and coarse, grey-green foliage, growing up to 4 feet high. Enjoying full sun and withstanding drought conditions extremely well, this easily grown plant is especially useful for light, sandy soils. *E. humilis* 'Taplow Blue' is a similar plant with lighter blue flowers.

Eremurus bungei. This is a noble, tuberous rooted plant, with immense, 5-foot-high, broad spikes of yellow flowers which are superb for large floral arrangements in a church. They are, of course, very decorative in the garden, flowering late June-early July. These plants are not easy to grow. They take two years to settle down, for the surface fleshy roots radiating from the crown resent disturbance. Cultivation is best restricted to a heavy annual mulching of decayed farmyard manure or compost each spring. Slugs can be a problem in spring, and soot or slug bait should be frequently applied around the crowns. A well-drained soil and plenty of sunshine are required. Plant the crowns 4 to 6 inches deep in September, about 3 feet apart. In colder regions, apply a protective layer of straw or bracken over the crowns in winter.

***Eryngium* 'Violetta' (sea holly).** Eryngiums are most attractive border plants, with lovely steel-blue, teasel-like flowers surrounded by spiky bracts (specialized leaves on the flower stem). *E.* 'Violetta' has extra-large, dark blue flowers with bracts coloured like the flower petals. Provided the soil is well drained, this hardy plant is equally happy on clay, chalk or sandy loam, but does best in a sunny position. It grows to a height of 30 inches and flowers July-September.

***Euphorbia* (spurge, milkweed).** Named after Euphorbus, physician to Juba, King of Mauritania. A few species of this immense genus are well worth growing. They need a sunny

White and yellow are attention-getters from a distance. A charming colour arrangement for a sunny border.

Euphorbia characias 'John Tomlinson'.

position, but very little attention, and are happy in any type of soil. They flower from March to June.

E. characias. This species has huge heads of green and gold flowers, 4 feet high.

E. griffithii. The flowers of this species are yellow and the variety 'Fireglow' has flaming orange bracts.

E. wulfenii. From the eastern Mediterranean region, this species has lime-green flowers, 4 feet high.

Galega officinalis **(goat's rue).** This is a good, hardy, common border plant, with pea-like flowers and attractive foliage. It is easy to grow, and not particular about soil, indeed it is ideal for difficult, drought-prone soils. 'Duchess of Bedford' (mauve and white flowers), 'Her Majesty' (lilac blue) and 'Lady Wilson (mauve pink/pale lilac) all grow up to 4 feet high.

Geranium **(cranesbill).** This is not to be confused with the summer bedding geraniums, which are actually pelargoniums. True geraniums are quite hardy plants, excellent as ground cover, and easy to grow in well-drained soils in full sunshine.

G. armenum. A tough, hardy, vigorous plant which in a moist soil grows up to 3 feet high and on poor, light soil, 2 feet high. The magenta flowers, about 1½ inches in diameter, with a black centre, are produced in abundance, from mid-June to August. The foliage is excellent for suppressing weeds.

G. grandiflorum. This is a bushy plant growing up to a foot high. It has lovely blue flowers and is easy to grow on any type of soil but needs a sunny position.

G. ibericum. Another fine border plant, 18 inches high, from the Caucasus. It has large violet-blue flowers, good foliage, and thrives in any soil but needs full sun.

G. wallichianum. A prostrate-growing plant which produces large purple flowers from July onwards. The variety 'Buxton's Blue' has blue flowers shading to white towards the centre.

Geranium ibericum – a hardy and long-lived plant.

Gypsophila. All gypsophilas have a preference for limy soils. *G. paniculata* 'Bristol Fairy' is a double white form, flowering in June. It grows up to 3 feet high and 3 feet wide, but is not a very long-lived plant. A well-drained soil in full sun is required. 'Flamingo' is a double pale pink form. Not as vigorous as 'Bristol Fairy', it is, however, more attractive. 'Rosy Veil' ('Rosenschleier') is an excellent plant either for the front of a border or grown cascading over a retaining wall. It has pale pink double flowers and grows up to 12 inches high and 24 inches wide.

Helianthus multiflorus. A good, sturdy, common, vigorous border plant which grows up to 5 feet high. The best double variety, in my view, is 'Loddon Gold', which has bright golden flowers 3 inches across. 'Capenoch Supreme' is a fine single variety. The flowers appear from July to September. Full sun is required and a heavy loam or clay soil is preferable.

Helleborus (Christmas rose or **Lenten rose).** There are a number of species, all of which thrive on a fertile, moisture-retentive soil. They all resent root disturbance and drought conditions. Ideally, they should be planted in partial shade, and are excellent for shady town gardens. Cultivation should consist of an annual top dressing of leaf mould, compost or spent mushroom compost to provide the cool root run which the hellebores enjoy.

H. corsicus. This species makes a dome of stout stems, 2 feet high and 3 feet wide. The glaucous-green, leathery leaves are a handsome foil to other plants. In March-April big heads of lovely pale apple-green flowers are produced. This is a first-class plant for the small garden.

H. foetidus. A British native, it makes an attractive display of purplish-green flowers and has dark green, elegant, shiny leaves. Another fine plant for the small town garden.

H. orientalis. A dome-like evergreen plant with leaves up to 18 inches long. The flowers are creamy-white, greenish-white, pink and purple.

Hosta (synonymous with *Funkia*; **plantain lily**). Named after N. T. J. Host (1761–1834), an Austrian botanist. Hostas are Japanese foliage plants which thrive in well-cultivated, fertile soils in partial shade. A woodland garden or shady town garden is the ideal location. If plenty of decayed organic material is dug in prior to planting, and if subsequently mulched with compost each spring, hostas will thrive in a more sunny position.

Hosta fortunei 'Albopicta' is a beautiful choice foliage plant for garden and flower arrangements.

H. fortunei. This species has large, bold, handsome, bluish leaves, 18 inches high, and lilac-mauve flowers, July-September.

H.f. 'Albopicta' has large, heart-shaped leaves, 24 inches high, with bright yellow centres and an edge of green. The central yellow area fades to pale green with age.

H. glauca (synonymous with *H. sieboldii* and *H. sieboldiana*). The blue-green leaves grow up to 9 inches wide and 12 inches long. The flowers are a pale lilac.

Iris innominata is a delightful plant producing golden flowers, 9 inches high, May-June. It dislikes a limy soil, but is otherwise not difficult to grow.

Kniphofia (red hot poker). Named after Johann Hieronymus Kniphof, a German professor of medicine. Its common name describes it well. There are many hybrids varying from 18 inches to 5 feet, and in colours from fiery red through yellow to cream. All require sun, a well-drained, light soil and a sheltered position. They are not for exposed, cold gardens. *K. galpinii* is a species from the Transvaal. It has grass-like foliage, from which 24-inch-high stems carrying lovely orange flowers are produced. Other good varieties are 'Bee's Sunset' (3 feet high, orange flowers), 'Bee's Lemon' (3½ feet high, light yellow flowers) and 'Samuel's Sensation' (6 feet high, red flowers).

Lavatera olbia. *Lavatera* after J. K. Lavater, a seventeenth-century Swiss naturalist. Most species are very free-flowering, colourful annuals. *L. olbia* is a fine flowering sub-shrub, growing up 5 feet high. It revels in hot, dry, sunny positions. It is not fussy about soil, but does prefer a lighter one. It resents root disturbance and is not long lived; the large, pink, showy flowers so freely produced prompt those familiar with the plant to propagate some every few years from seed or cuttings in spring or late summer in order to keep it. It is a common sight in the south of France where it flourishes.

Liatris (snakeroot, blazing star or gay feather). A North American hardy perennial which flowers from the top of the flower spike downwards. It grows from a fleshy tuber. A well-drained, light soil in full sun is essential; winter wet is very much resented.

> **L. callilepis.** This species produces purple-rose flower spikes, up to 3 feet high, from July to September. It is a useful cut flower for the house.
> **L. spicata.** This has purple, feathery spikes, about 18 inches high, from June onwards. Plant in the spring.

Malva alcea. This is a vigorous plant, 4 feet high by 2 feet wide. It is very similar to *Lavatera* and *Sidalcea*, requiring similar growing conditions: full sun and a well-drained soil. Easily raised from seed and cuttings, this plant has large, saucer-shaped, rose-pink flowers from July to September. *M.a.* 'Fastigiata' is more compact, growing up to 3 feet high.

Mertensia. Named after F. C. Mertens, a professor of botany at Bremen. *M. virginica* (Virginian cowslip) grows from a tuber, and has lovely 18-inch sprays of blue flowers from April to early June. A cool shady position and a moisture-retaining soil are essential. It is resentful of root disturbance and drought conditions. Annual top dressings of leaf mould or peat are very beneficial.

Monarda (bee balm, bergamot). Named after N. Monardez, a physician and botanist of Seville. This is a North American plant of easy culture, growing up to 3 feet high in full sun or partial shade. It is not fussy about soil. The tubular flowers are produced from June onwards. The best varieties include 'Cambridge Scarlet', 'Croftway Pink' and 'Mrs Perry' (crimson).

Oenothera (evening primrose). This is an immense genus from North America containing several good border plants. Full sun and a well-drained soil are needed to grow them.

Monarda didyma 'Croftway Pink' produces its honeysuckle-like flowers from June to September.

Oenothera missouriensis is an excellent, reliable dwarf border plant.

Paeonia officinalis 'Rubra Plena' is a long-lived, very hardy, double-red, old cottage garden type.

O. fyrverkeri (synonymous with *O. tetragona*). A splendid plant, 18 inches high, with yellow flowers on reddish stems from June onwards.

O. missouriensis. A prostrate plant, ideal for the front of a border, or for a retaining or dry wall. It produces large, yellow flowers, 3 inches across, from June onwards.

O. speciosa. This species grows up to 12 inches high. It has large, white flowers from July to September.

Paeonia. Peonies are divided into two groups: the tree peony, discussed in the chapter on shrubs, and the herbaceous kind. The latter type come mainly from *P. officinalis*, the European, and *P. albiflora*, the Chinese species. These magnificent hardy plants are easy to grow provided that they have full sun and a well-manured, deep, fertile, limy soil. All peonies love chalk. Because they resent root disturbance, give them sufficient space to develop. Plant preferably in September-October – the earlier the better – and no later than February, and ensure that the top of the crown is 2 inches below the soil surface. They take two or three years to settle down. Because they flourish in the richest of soils, top dress with well-decayed farmyard manure or compost every spring. Flowering in May and June, they range in colour from red and crimson to pink and white, with single, semi-double and double flowers on 2-to-4-foot-high stems. The considerable number of varieties of *P. officinalis* and *P. albiflora* are now classed under *Paeonia lactiflora*. The late Sir Frederick Stern was a great specialist in peonies as well as in other plants, and his publications are well worth reading.

P. cambessedesii. A native of the Balearic Islands, this species has deep green leaves, purple on the underside; 18-inch-high stems produce lovely, single, rose-pink flowers, 3 inches across with red and yellow centres, in late April-early May. It is not hardy in cold, exposed gardens. Avoid north and east aspects; a sheltered border or the base of a south-facing wall is ideal.

P. mlokosewitchii. Discovered in the Caucasus by a Mr Mlokosewitsch, this species first came to the attention of British botanists in 1908. It has fine foliage and many cup-shaped yellow flowers with red stamens, flowering April-May. It grows up to 2 feet high and 3 feet wide. It is at home in either a shrub or a herbaceous border. A truly lovely plant. Award of Merit 1929.

***Perovskia atriplicifolia* (Russian sage).** Named after M. Perowsky, one-time governor of the Russian province of Ouenberg. This is a lovely sub-shrub with grey foliage, native to an area from Afghanistan to Tibet. It is cut to the ground every winter, but from the old stool each spring grow up stems 3 feet high, which produce striking, lavender-blue flowers in August and September. It thrives in a light, dry soil in a sunny position, and is also quite happy in clay if it is well drained.

Phygelius capensis (Cape figwort). A handsome South African plant, suitable for a sunny, sheltered position in a well-drained soil. It grows up to 3 feet tall and produces many tubular scarlet flowers with yellow throats from August to October.

Polygonum (knotweed). This is a large genus, of which some species are valuable for the garden. They are easy to grow, but prefer a moisture-retentive soil, and are equally good in sun or shade.

> ***P. amplexicaule.*** A fine bushy plant for the border, growing about 3 feet high and 3 feet wide, and producing 6-inch spikes of red flowers from August to October.
> *P.a. atrosanguineum* has deeper red flowers, and the variety 'Firetail' has scarlet flowers.
> ***P. campanulatum.*** This species has spiky pink flowers, on a plant 4 feet high and 3 feet wide, in August and September. It is not particular about soil.

Rhazya orientalis. This is an easily grown plant which has dainty blue flowers, similar to those of a periwinkle, from August. It grows up to 18 inches high, and has elegant foliage. It does best in sunshine and is not fussy about soil except that it should be well drained.

Rudbeckia deami (coneflower). This is an easily cultivated plant, which makes a colourful display from August onwards. It is very free flowering, having yellow flowers with a black centre. It has greyish-green foliage up to 30 inches high, is not fussy about soil, but does best in a sunny position.

Rudbeckia speciosa (synonymous with *R. newmanii*). This species is taller and bushier than *R. deami*, and flowers a little later. Full sun and any well-drained soil are all that is needed.

Salvia (sage). A drought-resistant group of plants, providing a few excellent species for the garden.

> ***S. haematoides.*** Grey-green foliage produces stout flowering spikes of pale lilac-blue flowers from June to September. A native of Greece, it prefers the sun and a well-

151

Salvia superba lives up to its name!

drained soil. It grows up to 4 feet high. Although it is not a long-lived plant it is so easily grown from seed that replacements are not a problem.

S. superba. Aptly named, this is a superb border plant. It grows up to 3 feet high and bears masses of Oxford-blue flowers, set off by purple bracts on stiff flower spikes, from June to September. It is a great favourite with bees. Best grown in full sun, it is not particular about soil. Varieties of *superba*, for example 'Lubeca' – synonymous with 'Compacta' (30 inches high), 'East Friesland' (18 inches) and 'May Night' (30 inches) are all easy to cultivate, flowering at their best in July-August.

Sidalcea (Greek mallow). There are several hybrids, all fine border plants and also excellent for cutting. They are sun lovers, will grow in any soil, and flower prolifically in July-August. All are very effective when planted in association with *Salvia superba*.

The varieties which are particularly worth growing include the following:

S. 'Croftway Red'. Rose-red flowers, 3 feet.
S. 'Elsie Heugh'. Rose-pink flowers, 4 feet high.
S. 'Loveliness'. Pink flowers, 30 inches high.
S. 'Oberon'. Pink flowers, 24 inches high.
S. 'Rev. Page Roberts'. Light-pink flowers, 4 feet high.
S. 'Sussex Beauty'. Rose-pink flowers. 4 feet high.

Solidago (golden rod). This genus has been significantly improved by plant breeders during the last 30 years. They have fine plumes of yellow flowers, are not fussy about soil and are very easy to grow. 'Golden Falls', 'Golden Gates' and 'Golden Shower', all up to 3 feet high, are worth growing.

Veronica gentianoides. This is a showy, spiky plant with pale Cambridge-blue flowers in May-June. It will grow in any soil, but is best in a sunny position.

Recommended perennials and bulbs suitable for well-cultivated, average soil

Achillea decolorans	*Achillea taygetea*
Achillea eupatorium hybrids	*Aconitum fischeri*
Achillea millefolium hybrids	*Aconitum henryi*

An interesting combination of purple tradescantia, feathery astilbes and the pale yellow flowers of *Roscoea cautleoides*.

Crinum powellii.

Aconitum napellus hybrids
Aconitum wilsonii hybrids
Agapanthus africanus
Agapanthus umbellatus
Agapanthus 'Headbourne Hybrids'
Alstroemeria aurantiaca
Alstroemeria 'Ligtu Hybrids'
Anaphalis yedoensis
Anemone japonica hybrids
Artemisia lactiflora
Artemisia ludoviciana
Aruncus sylvester
Astrantia major
Baptisia australis
Brunnera macrophylla
Campanula lactiflora
Campanula latifolia
Campanula persicifolia
Cimicifuga japonica
Cimicifuga racemosa
Clematis integrifolia
Clematis recta
Coreopsis verticillata

Crambe cordifolia
Crinum powellii
Dianthus plumarius
Dierama pulcherrimum
Dracocephalum hemsleyanum
Dracocephalum ruyschianum
Echinops humilis 'Taplow Blue'
Echinops ritro
Eremurus bungei hybrids
Eryngium tripartitum
Eryngium 'Violetta'
Euphorbia characias
Euphorbia griffithii
Euphorbia wulfenii
Galega officinalis 'Duchess of Bedford', 'Her Majesty', 'Lady Wilson'
Geranium armenum
Geranium grandiflorum
Geranium ibericum
Geranium wallichianum 'Buxton's Blue'
Gypsophila paniculata 'Bristol Fairy'

153

Veronica gentianoides,
which grows to 20 inches
high.

Gypsophila 'Flamingo'
Helenium 'Butter Pat',
  'Kupfersprudel', 'Wyndley'
Helianthus multiflorus 'Loddon
  Gold'
Heliopsis magnifica 'Light of
  Loddon'
Helleborus corsicus
Helleborus foetidus
Helleborus orientalis
Hemerocallis 'Black Prince',
  'Conspicua', 'Hyperion',
  'Margaret Perry', 'Pink
  Charm', 'Saladin'
Hosta fortunei
Hosta glauca
Iris innominata
Iris sibirica varieties
Kniphofia galpinii
Lavatera olbia
Liatris callilepsis
Liatris spicata
Malva alcea
Malva alcea 'Fastigiata'
Mertensia virginica
Monarda 'Cambridge Scarlet',
  'Croftway Pink', 'Mrs
  Perry'

Nepeta × 'Six Hills Giant'
Oenothera fyrverkeri
Paeonia cambessedesii
Paeonia lactiflora varieties
Paeonia mlokosewitschii
Paeonia suffruticosa varieties
Papaver orientale varieties
Perovskia atriplicifolia
Phygelius capensis
Physostegia virginiana 'Vivid'
Polygonum amplexicaule
Polygonum campanulatum
Rhazya orientalis
Rudbeckia deami
Rudbeckia speciosa
Salvia haematoides
Salvia superba
Sidalcea 'Croftway Red', 'Elsie
  Heugh', 'Rev. Page
  Roberts', 'Sussex Beauty'
Solidago 'Golden Falls',
  'Golden Gates', 'Golden
  Showers', 'Leda', 'Lemore'
Verbascum olympicum
Veronica gentianoides
Veronica spicata varieties

Recommended perennials and bulbs suitable for moist soil

Artemisia lactiflora
Aruncus sylvester
Caltha palustris
Caltha polypetala
Cimicifuga americana
Cimicifuga japonica
Cimicifuga racemosa
Eupatorium purpureum
Filipendula camtschatica
Filipendula hexapetala 'Flore
  Plena'
Filipendula magnifica
Gentiana asclepiadea

Helleborus corsicus
Helleborus foetidus
Helleborus orientalis
Helonias bullata
Hemerocallis varieties
Hosta fortunei
Hosta fortunei gigantea
Hosta glauca
Hosta lancifolia
Kirengeshoma palmata
Ligularia clivorum
Ligularia hessei
Ligularia veitchiana

Ligularia wilsoniana
Lysichitum americanum
Lysichitum camtschatcense
Lythrum salicaria 'Brightness',
    Lady Sackville', 'Morden's
    Pink', 'Robert', 'The
    Beacon',
Lythrum virgatum 'Rose
    Queen', 'The Rocket'
Mimulus cardinalis
Mimulus cupreus varieties
Mimulus langsdorffi
Mimulus luteus
Monarda didyma varieties
Oenothera fruticosa
Oenothera fyrverkeri
Oenothera glabra
Oenothera riparia
Peltiphyllum peltatum
Phlox paniculata 'Brigadier',
    'Prince George', 'Professor
    Went'
Primula aurantiaca
Primula beesiana
Primula bulleyana
Primula burmanica
Primula chronantha
Primula florindae
Primula heladoxa
Primula japonica

Primula pulverulenta 'Bartley
    Strain'
Primula rosea
Primula secundiflora
Primula sikkimensis
Rheum nobile
Rheum palmatum
Rheum palmatum tanguticum
Rodgersia aesculifolia
Rodgersia pinnata 'Superba'
Rodgersia podophylla
Sidalcea 'Croftway Red',
    'Sussex Beauty', 'Rose
    Queen' and many other
    varieties
Silphium asperrimum
Smilacina racemosa
Smilacina stellata
Solidago 'Golden Falls',
    'Golden Gates', 'Mimosa'
Thalictrum dipterocarpum
Thalictrum flavum
Thalictrum glaucum
Tiarella cordifolia
Tiarella wherryi
Trillium grandiflorum
Trollius 'Canary Bird',
    'Golden Monarch',
    'Orange Glow', 'Pritchard's
    Giant'

Primula bulleyana, a
candelabra primula
which belongs to the bog
section of primulas.

Recommended hardy herbaceous perennials and bulbs suitable for a heavy clay soil and exposed gardens

Acanthus mollis
Achillea filipendulina 'Gold
    Plate'
Achillea millefolium 'Cerise
    Queen'
Aconitum henryi 'Sparks
    Variety'
Aconitum napellus bicolor
Aconitum napellus 'Newry
    Blue'

Agapanthus 'Headbourne
    Hybrids'
Artemisia lactiflora
Aruncus sylvester
Bergenia cordifolia
Campanula lactiflora 'Loddon
    Anna', 'Pritchard's variety
Campanula latifolia
    'Macrantha'
Caltha palustris

Chrysanthemum maximum
'Everest', 'Phyllis Smith',
'Wirral Supreme'
Cimicifuga racemosa
Digitalis 'Excelsior Strain'
Echinops humilis 'Taplow Blue'
Echinops ritro
Eryngium planum
Eryngium planum 'Blue
Dwarf'
Euphorbia epithmoides
Euphorbia griffithii
Euphorbia wulfenii
Galega officinalis 'Duchess of
Bedford', 'Her Majesty',
'Lady Wilson'
Geranium ibericum
Geranium × 'Johnson's Blue'
Geranium sanguineum
'Lancastriense'
Helenium 'Butter Pat',
'Crimson Beauty',
'Kupfersprudel'
Helianthus multiflorus
'Capenoch Supreme',
'Loddon Gold'
Heliopsis scabra
'Goldgreenheart',
'Incomparabilis'
Helleborus corsicus
Helleborus foetidus
Helleborus orientalis
Hemerocallis 'Hyperion',
'Margaret Perry', 'Marie
Ballard', 'Pink Charm'
Heuchera 'Coral Cloud', 'Mary
Rose', 'Red Spangles'

Hosta fortunei
Hosta glauca
Hosta plantaginea
Hosta undulata
Iris sibirica varieties
Liatris spicata
Ligularia clivorum 'Orange
Queen'
Lysimachia clethroides
Lysimachia leschenaultii
Lythrum salicaria 'Robert',
'The Beacon'
Monarda didyma 'Cambridge
Scarlet', 'Mrs Perry',
'Croftway Pink'
Paeonia delavayi
Paeonia lutea
Paeonia lactiflora hybrids
Paeonia suffruticosa
Physalis gigantea
Polemonium caeruleum 'Blue
Pearl'
*Polygonum amplexicaule
atrosanguineum*
Rhazya orientalis
Rudbeckia speciosa
Rudbeckia sullivantii
'Goldsturm'
Salvia superba
Sidalcea 'Loveliness', 'Rev.
Page Roberts'
Solidago 'Golden Mosa',
'Golden Shower'
Thalictrum flavum
Veronica spicata 'Blue Spire',
'Minuet'

Euphorbia wulfenii, which
grows up to 4 feet high
and 4 feet wide.

Some hardy perennials suitable for cut flowers

Achillea eupatorium 'Gold
Plate'
Achillea serrata
Achillea taygetea
Aconitum napellus bicolor

Aconitum henryi 'Spark's
Variety'
Agapanthus 'Headbourne
Hybrids'
Chrysanthemum maximum

Dianthus 'Pike's Pink'.

'Esther Read', 'Wirral
Supreme'
Dianthus varieties
Echinops ritro
Eremurus varieties
Eryngium 'Violetta'
Euphorbia characias
Euphorbia griffithii
Euphorbia wulfenii
Gypsophila 'Bristol Fairy'

Heuchera 'Coral Cloud',
'Sparkler'
Paeonia double varieties,
'Felix Crousse', 'Karl
Rosenfeld', 'Lady
Alexandra Duff',
'Madame Calot'
Solidago 'Lemore', 'Lesden',
'Mimosa'

Ornamental grasses, rushes and sedges

Ornamental grasses, rushes and sedges have, surprisingly, been very neglected, yet they are particularly suitable for both town and city gardens. While being especially tolerant of atmospheric pollution, they have a grace, beauty and elegance which makes them comparable to any other plant. Their diversity is worthy of consideration. They extend from low-growing varieties to 12-foot-high plants – and this does not include the bamboos. Many flourish in full sun; others prefer partial or complete shade; a few, such as the genus *Luzula*, are superb in the shade of trees. Most suppress weeds effectively and are in all respects labour saving.

Apart from the various habits and forms, the subtle colours of leaf and flower are quite distinctive, ranging from different shades of green, blue and purple, and variegations. Many are at home in the bog garden. Some are excellent rock garden subjects, and others are useful for screening. Herbaceous and shrub borders are also good locations for several species. Having established a selection of these lovely plants, readers interested in floral art will have a good supply of invaluable fresh and dry material for their arrangements.

The preparation of planting sites for the majority should be similar to that for other plants, as discussed in the chapters on shrubs and herbaceous plants; that is, bastard digging, preferably in the autumn and certainly before Christmas, incorporating plenty of organic material, such as decayed farmyard manure, compost or spent mushroom manure. Planting is best carried out in the spring. Plant at ground level in a container, pot, or open ground, and subsequently mulch every spring to sustain vigorous growth.

Notwithstanding their beauty or appeal, if you are planting invasive types, I strongly advise that these be confined to

These elegant ornamental grasses successfully soften hard landscaped surfaces.

containers and tubs, and kept above ground level. If they are planted in open ground they will rapidly over-run the whole garden. Most perennial grasses should be cut back to ground level in late autumn. Propagation is best carried out by careful division in spring, just as new growth is emerging from the base. There is a considerable range of ornamental grasses, rushes and sedges, and I am able to mention in this book only a few – those which I think are the best of their kind, and are most suitable for the town garden.

Alopecurus pratensis 'Aureo-Variegatus' (**meadow foxtail**). This is a fine, hardy, golden-striped grass, up to 3 feet high. It will grow in sun or partial shade, and is not particular about soil provided that it is well drained.

Arundo donax 'Macrophylla' (**giant reed**). A vigorous evergreen grass, up to 12 feet high, 'Macrophylla' has broader leaves than the type plant. A sheltered position in full sun, in a moisture-retentive soil, is ideal; it is not suitable for cold gardens or northern regions. This is an excellent plant for isolated groups or a small lawn. It is advisable to cover the crowns with a layer of straw, bracken or leaf mould for the winter.

Festuca gigantea (**giant brome**). This grass is extremely tolerant of shade, and is ideally grown under trees provided that the soil is fertile and fairly moist. It grows up to 3 feet high.

Miscanthus sacchariflorus (**Eulalia grass**). A moist soil in full sun is essential for this 8-foot-high grass from China and Japan. The form 'Aureus' has striped golden leaves, 5 feet tall, and the 7-foot 'Variegatus' has pure white stripes. Cover in winter with a protective layer of bracken or straw.

Molinia caerulea 'Aureo-Variegata'. A hardy, very attractive, variegated (cream and yellow) grass which is only successful on an acid soil. It grows up to 18 inches high.

Pennisetum orientale. A fine grass, about 2 feet high, with lovely pink flowers on graceful, slender foliage. It is very useful for cutting and drying. A sheltered, well-drained, sunny position is vital. Protect in winter with a layer of bracken or straw.

Scirpus tabernaemontani zebrinus. A beautiful, hardy sedge, which could equally well fit into the chapter on water and bog plants. Its leaves, up to 5 feet high, are banded in green and white. It is best grown at the margin of ponds or in a bog garden in full sun.

Spartina pectinata. A fertile, moisture-retaining soil in full sun is needed to grow this vigorous, hardy grass. It has elegant leaves, about 4 feet high, which turn a lovely yellow in autumn. 'Aureo-marginata' is a golden variegated form of considerable merit.

Stipa gigantea. A striking grass from Spain, growing to 3 feet high, and quite hardy in all but the very coldest gardens. It is best planted as a specimen in a lawn, in full sun, and a well-drained, fertile soil. Its flowers are as fine as the the best pampas grass.

Stipa pennata. A fine, graceful grass, 2 feet high. It needs full sun and a well-drained soil.

The following grasses, rushes and sedges are also recommended:

Arundo donax
Briza media
Calamagrostis canescens
Carex × acutifolia 'Aureo-Variegata'
Carex morrowii
Cortaderia selloana
Festuca gigantea
Festuca glauca
Miscanthus sacchariflorus
Oryzopsis miliacea
Pennisetum orientale
Spartina pectinata
Stipa gigantea
Stipa pennata
Stipa splendens

CHAPTER 9

Bulbs, corms and tubers

A garden without bulbs, corms and tubers, which give so much grace and beauty during the cooler months, is unthinkable. Regrettably, there are many genera, species and varieties which are not grown as extensively as their merit deserves. With a wider understanding of their individual requirements, you may be encouraged to rectify any omissions.

The distinctions between bulbs, corms and tubers are simple. *Bulbs* are composed of a number of scales (onions and daffodils are good examples). *Corms* consist of a solid mass of thickened stems which are covered with membraneous sheaths (such as begonias, crocuses and gladioli). *Tubers* have solid flesh similar to corms but do not have sheaths (such as anemones, potatoes and dahlias).

Bulbs, corms and tubers can all be planted in herbaceous borders or rock gardens, or under deciduous trees and shrubs; also, a number will naturalize in grass. Because the flowers are generally formed within the bulb when you buy them, the first year gives a fine show, only moisture being needed to produce the flower. The second and subsequent years, however, are another matter. If the soil, aspect and climate are suitable they will thrive and increase until obvious over-crowding, with fewer flowers and abundant foliage, makes it necessary to lift, divide and replant. If they are unhappy there will be very few or no flowers, and probably no bulbs in the following year. The majority of bulbs, corms and tubers flourish in soils extending from chalky to slightly acid. Very few indeed will grow in the very acid soils that are suitable for rhododendrons and heathers. Heavy clay to light sandy soils are acceptable, provided they are well drained. On no account plant them in waterlogged sites. The only solution in wet situations or on very heavy clay soils, other than providing a drainage system (as discussed in the chapter on soil), is to

Opposite:
This is *Lilium* 'Rosenfinger', a lover of light shade and well-drained, fertile soil.

plant them in prepared raised beds with sharp drainage. Some, like tulips and alliums, prefer full sun, while others, such as snowdrops, like partial shade. Erythroniums, cyclamens and trilliums want complete shade. Individual treatment varies, although they all have storage organs which allow for long periods of dormancy without food or water. During this period some are best lifted and kept dry until replanted. Others are best left in the soil to get a good baking in a well-drained, sunny position. For the majority of spring-flowering types, September is the best month for planting, although tulips can be planted as late as December. Summer and autumn-flowering types should be planted in March. Only experience with particular genera, species and varieties can be the true guide as to their suitability to your garden. You will find that some will flourish and others fail; indeed, some will thrive in specific areas of the garden and will prove to be difficult in other parts.

The main pests are without doubt *slugs and snails*, which are commonest on calcareous soils. Fortunately these can be controlled with the slug killer Metaldehyde or Methiocarb as a bait, or trapped on pieces of old sacking laid on the soil surface or in jars of sweetened beer sunk up to their necks in the soil, which remains effective for three or four nights.

Narcissus, galanthus, leucojum and scilla can be attacked by the *large and small narcissus flies*. The large fly is on the wing during May and June, laying eggs on the surface near the daffodil leaves or neck of the bulb. On hatching, a solitary larva eats a tunnel through the middle of the bulb via the bottom root plate. Fortunately there is only one generation per year. The small narcissus fly also lays eggs on the surface near the bulb foliage, but a second generation appears at bulb-lifting time, and will lay eggs on the bulbs if they are left on the surface for any length of time. Several larvae of the small narcissus fly eat their way from the top of the bulb inwards, turning it into a wet, brown, rotten mass. Control is achieved by surface cultivation, drawing the soil over the holes left by dying foliage to discourage the flies from laying eggs near the bulbs. Inspect the bulbs at lifting time, and if any are soft or spongy burn them immediately. Chemical control, which is difficult, may be attempted by an application of HCH dust over plants in June and July. This may be partially effective, but once the larvae are in the bulb it is generally too late.

Eelworm is a serious pest, but commercial growers on lifting give the bulbs a hot-water treatment, that is, the bulbs are immersed in water and kept at a temperature of 100°F for five hours or 112°F for three hours. It is very unlikely that you will buy infected bulbs from reputable suppliers. The hot-water treatment also kills the fly larvae. Buying cheap bulbs is a false economy, because a few bulbs infested with eelworm will contaminate the whole garden. The symptoms of eelworm attack are soft spongy bulbs with no evidence of fly attack, and brown rings of decay among the white scales when the bulb is cut open. Burn infected bulbs immediately, and avoid growing on contaminated land for at least five years. If foliage is weak and discoloured, it is a sign that something is wrong; dig it up and examine for pests.

Mice are particularly fond of crocus corms. Trapping is the only sure method of control.

Sparrows can be most destructive, creating havoc with crocus flowers; the use of black thread is as good a control as any.

Diseases are fortunately few, and the most common is *tulip fire*. The first symptoms are distorted leaves and shoots which appear soon after emergence from the soil; greyish patches then appear on the foliage until it withers, and many small yellow spots with dark green surrounding areas develop, destroying the whole plant. This is a particularly troublesome disease on wet clay soils in a wet season. To prevent the disease from spreading, avoid planting tulips on the same site year after year. Alternatively change the soil or sterilize the site to 12 inches deep, if badly affected. Spraying with benomyl as a precaution, and soaking the bulbs in benomyl for 12–30 minutes before planting on wet clay soils or where previous outbreaks have occurred, is advisable.

I have selected bulbs, corms and tubers that are widely available, reasonably priced and in my opinion are of sufficient merit to secure a place in any garden and above all are not difficult to grow if their individual requirements are provided.

Allium. Latin name for garlic, and now the name for the onion family. This is a very attractive genus, but much neglected because most species have an onion smell when bruised. Alliums, which all have showy globular heads of flowers, are all sun-lovers and will grow in most well-drained soils. They can be grown from seed, which germinates very well, and most form plenty of offsets on established bulbs. Plant in late summer or early autumn in a sunny position, the smaller bulbs about 2 inches deep and 3 inches apart, and the taller species 4 inches deep and 18 inches apart. Leave the bulbs undisturbed for three or four years until overcrowding is obvious, then lift, divide and replant immediately in August-September.

Recommended species and varieties are:

A. albopilosum. Lilac, 18 inches high, summer-flowering.
A. beesianum. Blue, 12 inches high, summer-flowering.
A. caeruleum. Lilac, 12 inches high, summer-flowering.
A. giganteum. Violet, 5 feet high, summer-flowering. Very useful in the herbaceous border.
A. moly. Yellow, 12 inches high, flowers in May.
A. narcissiflorum. Violet-pink, 6 inches high, flowers, in June-July. Narcissus-like flowers.
A. ostrowskianum. Red, 6 inches high, named after the Russian botanist Ostrowsky.
A. pulchellum. Violet-pink, 12 inches high, flowers in June-July.
A. sphaerocephalum. Purple, 18 inches high, summer-flowering.

Alstroemeria. Named in honour of Baron Alstroemer, a Swedish botanist. This is a most attractive tribe; regretfully they are difficult to establish, but it is well worth trying. The tuber is joined to the crown by a brittle thread; if this is broken it will never grow. Only plant pot-grown specimens, in the spring, and make sure that the crowns are planted about 6 inches below the surface. Mark the spot, and be careful with subsequent cultivation for the first two difficult years. Hand weeding, only as and when necessary, is really all that is required. Hailing from South America, alstroemerias must have a sunny position in a well-drained, sandy loam. Once they are established, leave them for many years, and allow them to spread where they will. They are useful cut flowers for the house.

Alstroemeria ligtu hybrids. These strongly resent disturbance.

The following are recommended:

A. aurantiaca. Golden or orange, 3 feet high.
A. 'Dr Salter's Hybrids'. Carmine, flame-yellow and pink, 3 feet high.
A. Ligtu Hybrids. Pink and flame colours, 2 feet high.
A. ligtu pulchra. From Chile, white to pink, overlaid yellow, 3 feet high.
A. 'Orange King'. Orange flowers, 3 feet high.
A. pulchella. Scarlet blooms, 3 feet high.

Anemone (windflower). From Greek *anemos*, wind, and *mone*, habitation. Some species enjoy windy places, hence the English name. There are many types of anemone, some of which are tuberous or have thickened rhizomes, and it is these

Anemone blanda.

that are discussed in this chapter. *A. coronaria* has parsley-like leaves. The semi-double 'St Brigid' strain and the single-flowered 'De Caen' strain are hybrids from this species, both 6–12 inches high. They require a fertile, well-drained soil with plenty of leaf mould or peat. Plant the tubers 2 inches deep and about 4 inches apart in October and, provided they have an application of bone meal at 4 ounces per square yard and hoof and horn at 2 ounces per square yard each winter, with a 3-inch top dressing of sieved leaf mould or peat, they can be left to give a good display for some years. *A. fulgens* has vivid scarlet flowers on 12-inch stems in May; with good cultivation they should flower quite well for two or three years if they are in full sun. Plant in October, 2 inches deep and 8 inches apart. The two most outstanding species which are quite happy on chalky soil are *A. apennina*, which has attractive, bright blue flowers, about 6 inches high, and will flourish in considerable shade and *A. blanda*, which grows about 3 inches high but requires full sun. The varieties of *A. blanda* ('Atrocaerulea', 'Blue Star', 'Charmer', 'White Splendour' and 'Radar') are particularly charming and well worth growing. Plant *A. apennina* and *A. blanda* in September or October, 2 inches deep and 4 inches apart. If the conditions suit them they will rapidly increase. *A. nemorosa*, the wood anemone, has good varieties, such as 'Allenii', 'Blue Bonnet', 'Vestal' and 'Robinsoniana'.

All flower in April, as does *A. ranunculoides*, a lovely native of northern European deciduous woodlands. These should be planted in the shade about 2 inches deep in a leafy soil. They are quite happy on alkaline soils.

Camassia. This genus is easy to cultivate, thriving as it does in full sun or shade in any type of soil provided it is well drained. Plant the bulbs 3 inches deep and about 3 inches apart in October. The flowers appear from May to July. They will seed quite readily *in situ* if left alone.

> **C. cusickii.** Pale blue, 3 feet high.
> **C. esculenta.** Deep blue to white, 3 feet high.
> **C. leichtlinii.** Named after Leitchlin, an Austrian botanist. White to blue, 3 feet high.

Chionodoxa. From Greek *chion*, snow, and *doxa*, glory. This is a splendid, easy-to-grow genus, which is especially appealing when established in large drifts. The small sprays of starry flowers appearing in the spring vary, and include blue, white and pink. They are happy in all types of soil, and seed profusely if left alone. Plant 3 inches deep and about 2 inches apart in September in a sunny position.

> **C. gigantea**. Violet blue with white eye, 10 inches high.
> > *C.g.* 'Alba'. White, 3 inches high.
> **C. luciliae**. Violet blue with white eyes, 6 inches high.
> > *C.l.* 'Alba'. White, 5 inches high.
> > *C.l.* 'Rosea'. Pink with white eye, 5 inches high.
> **C. sardensis**. Deep blue, 6 inches high.

Colchicum. From Colchis, a province of Asia Minor, where the bulbs are to be found. An exquisite genus of elegant autumn flowers, ideally planted under deciduous trees and among shrubs. The flowers on long tubes appear before the leaves in the autumn. Care is needed to ensure that the foliage, which appears in the spring and grows very large, does not smother adjacent plants. Autumn winds and heavy rain can damage the flowers although when planted among shrubs these afford some protection. Foliage, flowers and bulbs are very poisonous to cattle and man. Plant in July, 5 inches deep and 6 inches apart. There are a considerable number of hybrids available, all worth growing.

The species recommended are:

> **C. autumnale.** Lilac flowers in August, 4 inches high.
> > *C.a.* 'Album'. White flowers in August, 4 inches high.
> **C. byzantinum.** Rose-lilac flowers in August, 4 inches high.

Camassia cusickii is a beautiful summer flowering bulb.

C. cilicicum. Rose-lilac flowers in October, 4 inches high.

C. speciosum. Deep rose-lilac flowers in September-October, 6 inches high.

C.s. 'Album' White flowers in September-October, 6 inches high.

Crocosmia includes montbretias. This native of South Africa bears 3-foot arching sprays of flower in July and August. They should soon develop into strong clumps, and should be lifted every third or fourth year, divided and replanted during March or April. Plant 3 inches deep, about 3 inches apart, in a well-drained, sunny position. There are number of hybrids, all well worth growing.

Crocus chrysanthus 'Goldilocks' is one of many crocus hybrids.

Crocus. Greek *krokos*, saffron, probably from *kroke*, a thread, the filaments of the styles being the source of the dye. The familiar large Dutch garden crocuses are much easier to grow than the species, needing nothing other than a well-drained soil. The many Dutch varieties range in colour from white, lilac and mauve, to deep purple and yellow, and some are striped. They are from 2½ to 5 inches high. All are a welcome addition to the spring display, particularly when grown in large drifts. If they are grown in grass, do not mow until the foliage has died down.

The species can be divided into autumn-, winter- and spring-flowering. All prefer a sheltered, well-drained, sunny position in a light soil. The winter- and spring-flowering species should be planted in September or October and the autumn-flowering species in July or early August. Plant all of them 3 inches deep, and about 3 inches apart. Unfortunately, mice are especially fond of the corms. If the plants are successful they will rapidly multiply. When overcrowding becomes obvious, lift only when the foliage has died down naturally, and replant immediately. The species which are quite easy and particularly beautiful are as follows:

Autumn-flowering species

C. longiflorus. Pale lilac and purple striped.

C. medius. Bright purple.

C. pulchellus. Blue.

C. sativus. Lilac.

C. speciosus and varieties. Pale to deep violet.

Winter-flowering species (December to February)

C. ancyrensis. Orange.

C. asturiensis 'Atropurpureus'. Violet.

Crocus tomasinianus 'Ruby Giant' will rapidly increase more than most in suitable conditions.

Spring-flowering species
C. biflorus and varieties. White striped and shaded.
C. chrysanthus and varieties. White, cream, orange, blue and yellow.
C. susianus. Gold with mahogany stripes.
C. tomasinianus and varieties. Pale blue to purple.

Cyclamen. The name is a contraction of Greek *kyklaminos*, from *kyklos*, a circle, alluding to the coiled stem of the seed vessel (after the flower has been fertilized, the stem coils like a spring). Cyclamen are not the easiest plants to grow; this may be because the soil is too acid, or is poorly drained, or there is too much sun or dense shade, or the corms are too old. *C. neapolitanum* and *coum* are the easiest species to grow.

Plant young plants of the autumn-flowering *C. neapolitanum* in August, 1½ inches deep and about 3 inches apart, in a chalky, loamy soil with good drainage under deciduous trees. *C. neapolitanum* roots from the top of the corm. Top dress with sieved leaf mould when established and if happy they will readily increase. *C. coum* flowers in February-March but requires similar treatment. All resent root disturbance, therefore hand weeding, top dressing with sieved leaf mould about 2 inches thick and bone meal at about 4 ounces per square yard is all the cultivation necessary. They will not suffer from overcrowding for many years. *C. neapolitanum's* foliage is ivy-shaped and heavily mottled with silver markings. The flowers vary from pale to deep pink, and are about 4 inches high. *C. neapolitanum* 'Album' is a fine white form. *C. coum* has crimson flowers and deep green kidney-shaped leaves, 3 inches high.

Eranthis hyemalis **(winter aconite).** From Greek *er*, spring, *anthos*, a flower. The early-flowering hyemalis flowers in the winter, starting in January with yellow flowers on 2-inch-high stems. They are ideally placed in the shrub border, particularly near the house, where they can be enjoyed on a cold winter's day. Plant 2 inches deep and 2 inches apart in August, preferably in a moist, loamy soil. They resent disturbance and take two or three years to get established. *Eranthis cilicica* and the hybrid *Eranthis tubergenii* also merit places in any garden.

Erythronium. From Greek *erythros*, red, being the colour of the flowers of the earlier introduced species. This genus belongs to the lily family and is restricted with the exception of the European species *Erythronium dens-canis* to the continent of America. All are easy to grow if planted in partial or complete shade in a leafy or peaty soil. The corms should never be

The nodding six-petalled flowers of *Erythronium tuolumnense*.

allowed to dry out, or they will quickly shrivel and die. *E. dens canis*, the dog's-tooth violet, is so called because of the shape of the corm. It was at one time used as a powerful remedy for worms in children. Plant all species and varieties in September, 2 inches apart and 4 inches deep, and leave them for many years without disturbance if they like the position.

E. dens-canis. Very variable in colour from lavender to rose, flowers in March and April, 2 inches high.
E. revolutum. Deep pink flowers in April, revolute, or rolled-back leaves, 8 inches high.
E. tuolumnense. Yellow flowers in April-May, with green foliage, 8 inches high.

Good hybrids include 'White Beauty' and 'Pagoda'.

Fritillaria imperialis (crown imperial). From the Latin *fritillus*, a dice-box. This is a large, upright plant with attractive bell-shaped flowers, either yellow or reddish-orange, appearing in May. It needs full sun and a well-drained, chalky soil. Plant in September or October, 6 inches deep and 18 inches apart, and leave for many years – these plants resent disturbance.

Fritillaria meleagris. The markings on the flowers resemble those on a chess board. There are many forms of these very appealing, dainty, bell-shaped flowers which appear during April and May, ranging in colour from white to violet and rose. Plant 3 inches deep and 2 inches apart during September-October, in partial shade and in moist soils. These are ideal under shrubs and may also be naturalized in grass.

The flowers of the snake's head fritillary, *Fritillaria meleagris*.

Galanthus (snowdrop). Greek *gala*, milk, and *anthos*, flower, alluding to its whiteness. This lovely plant is a 'must' in every garden. It likes full or partial shade and a good, well-drained soil. Plant 1 inch apart and 3 inches deep in August-September. The base of a deciduous hedge, under deciduous trees and among shrub borders are ideal situations. A dressing of sieved leaf mould about 1 inch thick and an application of bone meal at 4 ounces per square yard and hoof and horn at 2 ounces per square yard each year is all they require. They are best left undisturbed until overcrowded. Then lift, divide and replant immediately in July.

G. byzantinus. Flowers January to February.
G. elwesii. Flowers February-March.
G. ikariae. Flowers March-April.
G. nivalis and varieties. Flowers January to March.

169

Galtonia. Commemorating Francis Galton, anthropologist. The only species worth growing is *G. candicans,* the spire lily. A native of southern Africa, it is hardy in southern England, enjoying full sun in a well-drained position. The scented white bell-shaped flowers, up to a dozen on 3-foot-high stems, are most welcome in the months of July and August. Sometimes known as *Hyacinthus candicans,* it is like a hyacinth but much larger in all its parts. Plant bulbs 6 inches deep, 12 inches apart in October and leave until they get overcrowded. It can also be grown from seed. Slugs appear to be fond of them; put 1 ounce Metaldehyde mixed with 3 pounds moist bran around the plants in warm, damp weather. Soot is a good deterrent.

Iris reticulata is a natural inhabitant of rock gardens and dry walls.

Iris. Greek *iris,* a rainbow, presumably in reference to the many colours of the flowers. This is a genus of bulbous, rhizomatous and herbaceous perennials producing striking flowers from January well into the summer. Although the herbaceous perennials (dealt with in Chapter 8) are easy to cultivate, most of the bulbous and rhizomatous types are somewhat difficult in the open garden and are best grown in a bulb frame. However, *Iris reticulata* (*reticulata,* a net, refers to the netted bulbs) and its many varieties are easy, and will rapidly increase if planted in a very sunny position where they will get a good baking during the summer, and where the drainage is very sharp. A native of Turkey, Iran and Iraq, it grows there on scree and bare stony places, which indicates the ideal conditions. Plant in September 2 inches deep, about 1 inch apart, leave for a number of years until they become overcrowded. They flower in February-March about 6 inches high with four-sided, grass-like foliage. 'Cantab', 'J. S. Dijt', 'Clarette', 'Joyce' and 'Violet Beauty' are among the many varieties well worth growing.

Leucojum (**snowflake**). Greek *leukos,* white, *ion,* a violet, referring to the colour and possibly the fragrance of the flowers. This charming genus is not grown enough. The three species recommended provide spring, early summer and autumn flowers. Sometimes they do not flower for a couple of years following planting; avoid disturbance.

L. aestivum (*aestivum,* summer, season of flowering). The summer snowflake has smaller flowers than the *vernum,* but is just as delightful. The cultivar 'Gravetye', named after the garden of William Robinson in Sussex, is by far the best form. It flowers in May, grows to between 12 and 24 inches high, is best in a damp rich soil and quite happy in water-logged conditions. Plant 3 inches deep and 3 inches apart in September.

L. autumnale is a superb plant, flowering in October, about 4 inches high. Plant in a sunny position about 1 inch deep and 1 inch apart in July.

L. vernum (*vernum*, spring, season of flowering). The spring snowflake is easy to grow in any moist soil in shade or partial shade. It flowers in March, and is about 6 inches high. Plant 3 inches deep and 3 inches apart in September.

Leucojum vernum is an exquisite flower but it does resent disturbance.

Lilium. There are many good and interesting books available on lilies and their cultivation, and I do not intend here to attempt to cover the subject. It is true that many lilies are very difficult to grow, and the bulbs are expensive to buy, but the way to start is to understand the cardinal points, and to plant for the time being only those lilies that are relatively easy. Once you have embarked on their cultivation – which will undoubtedly give immeasurable pleasure, because they are so lovely and so full of grace – progression to the more demanding types will, I am sure, be inevitable.

The first point to understand is that the lily bulb does not have any dormancy period; furthermore the scales of the bulb are unprotected, unlike a daffodil bulb. In fact the bulb is very easily bruised and damaged. Some shops and garden centres are oblivious of this, judging by the sorry state of many bulbs offered for sale. Also bulbs quickly dry out and shrivel when lifted. Buy only those bulbs that are not damaged or shrivelled, and that are carefully packed in moist peat and moss by a specialist grower. Plant them immediately. Obviously, the planting positions should have been properly prepared well before you buy the bulbs. A hurried job will give disappointing results; indeed it would be a complete waste of money.

The ideal soil for lilies is one that has been well cultivated, for many years, with generous, regular dressings of well-decayed organic material. It will have the right moisture-holding properties, nutrients, drainage and aeration, as discussed in the chapter on soils. *Avoid* (a) a heavy, wet, uncultivated clay; this will be too wet in the winter and hard baked in the summer; (b) a light sandy soil, which will be too dry in the summer, when water is wanted in the growing season; and (c) chalky soils; these are not the best because of the intolerance of some species and varieties, and they also tend to be too dry during the summer months.

171

Where soil conditions are not suitable, construct a raised bed about 12–15 inches high to achieve good drainage, and use a mixture of equal parts of loam, leaf mould and grit or washed ⅛-inch pea shingle. This is an ideal growing medium for most lilies. Where you have double-dug and added plenty of organic material to establish a reasonably fertile soil, it is prudent to dig holes about 12 inches deep and fill them with the above mixture for each lily bulb – after all, they will be there for some years. Never use fresh manure or artificial fertilizers. 4 ounces per square yard of bonemeal and 2 ounces per square yard of hoof and horn are adequate if applied annually with a top dressing of leaf mould about 3 inches thick in May.

Some lilies dislike full sun, and none will thrive in complete shade: most prefer their bulbs in shade and tops in sun. Partial shade is very good. All dislike wind and draughts. Planting among shrub or herbaceous borders is ideal, giving the required amount of protection, shelter and shade, provided they do not have to compete with tree and shrub roots. Rhododendrons and pieris are splendid plants to associate with lilies, having the right type of foliage, and hardy ferns give the right amount of shade over the bulb without being too competitive.

Recommended species, most of which grow to about 5 feet high, are:

L. hansonii. Lime-tolerant, stem-rooting. Plant 8 inches deep.

L. henryi. Lime-tolerant, dislikes acid soil. Among the latest to flower. Up to 8 feet high. Stem-rooting. Plant 8 inches deep.

L. martagon. Likes chalky soils. Makes little growth the first year. Plant 6 inches deep.

L. pardalinum. Prefers lime-free soil, likes moisture. Will increase rapidly if happy. Plant 5 inches deep.

L. superbum. Lime-free soil, in position that is well drained but does not dry out. Plant 5 inches deep.

Apart from the basal roots, some species and hybrids have stem roots which help to nourish the plant. A bulb planted up to 8 inches deep is not too deep, and thereby encourages the development of stem roots on those which have this characteristic. Many hybrids are quite outstanding, in many instances being much better than the parent species and often much easier to grow. Mid-Century and Olympic hybrids, Backhouse and Paisley strains excel on chalky soils – a bonus for those

Lilium × 'Golden Clarion' has pleasantly scented flowers.

gardening in these conditions. The hybrids which I suggest you start with are:

Aurelian hybrids: 'Golden Clarion' (5–7 feet) and 'Limelight' (6–8 feet) are especially lovely.

Backhouse hybrids: the result of crossing *Lilium martagon* and *L. hansonii*; the hybrids are all free-flowering and strong growers. Once planted, they will last many years in one position. Height up to 6 feet, each spire carrying up to 30 flowers.

Bellingham hybrids: very attractive, easily grown, vigorous plants which grow up to 7 feet high and carry up to 40 lovely flowers.

Fiesta hybrids: particularly valuable in July, making a wonderful contribution to the sheer beauty of the summer-flowering lilies. 4 feet high.

Mid-Century hybrids. These are possibly the easiest to grow. Some of the named varieties are exceptionally fine lilies. Up to 4 feet high.

There are many other hybrids and strains – far too many to mention here – and all are well worth growing. Visiting fine gardens during the summer months and actually seeing them flowering, noting their growing conditions, and above all growing some of the easier hybrids to begin with yourself, can be the only path to success – and remember to take great care to buy good, virus-free, undamaged bulbs, preferably from a specialist grower. Do not expect too much the first year after planting, as lilies take time to get established. But after that your enthusiasm will blossom; you will become an avid reader of lily books, and will raise lily bulbs from seeds and bulb scales in a small frame. When you have established flowering groups of 4- to 8-foot-high lilies with strong stems carrying dozens of lovely flowers in your garden during the summer months, the delight, excitement and astonishment will be beyond description.

Muscari. From Greek *moschos*, musk, the flowers of some species having a musky smell. This hardy genus is easy to grow in any good, well-drained soil in sun, and is particularly useful for carpeting the front of a shrub border. Plant in September or October about 3 inches deep and 4 inches apart; lift when they get overcrowded in July and replant immediately. Recommended varieties are:

M. armeniacum. Purplish blue flowers in April, 6 inches high.

The grape hyacinth *Muscari armeniacum* is ideal for a border edge.

M. azureum. There is a good white form flowering in April, 6 inches high.

M. comosum 'Monstrosum'. Blue/violet flowers in May, 12 inches high.

M. tubergenianum. Pure blue flowers in April, 8 inches high.

Narcissus. This is the botanical name for the genus; daffodil is the common English name. A daffodil is a narcissus, and any narcissus is a daffodil. There is a limited number of species, but a considerable number of varieties; indeed, new varieties are produced each year, but as they can only be increased vegetatively it takes many years to build up a stock to commercial levels. This genus is, rightly, appreciated widely. The Royal Horticultural Society's Narcissus Committee classification falls into eleven divisions. Narcissus species grow wild in the Northern Hemisphere, extending from Switzerland, southern France, Spain, Portugal and North Africa. The northern limit is the British Isles, and the southern limit is the Canary Islands and Mediterranean region through Asia to Japan. With the exception of a few species, all narcissi will flourish in a well-drained soil in the sun. The bulbs of different varieties and species vary in size and shape. Daffodils prefer a slightly acid soil, but are tolerant of chalk. All except *Narcissus cyclamineus* dislike shade. The best planting time is August and early September; depth depends on the size of the bulb: 3 inches for the smaller bulbs, up to 6 inches for the largest.

Plant in sheltered positions, such as the front of shrub borders, or under deciduous trees; many varieties will naturalize in grass. Avoid the use of fresh manure or fresh compost. Spent mushroom manure is ideal. Confine fertilizers to 4 ounces bonemeal per square yard and 1 ounce sulphate of potash per square yard, applied in February. The leaves are the main food supply, that is, the plant food factory. After flowering their task is to build up sufficient food to produce next year's flowers. On no account should any leaves be either cut off or tied into bundles; these practices weaken the bulbs and if they are continued the bulbs will eventually fade away. Remove the foliage only when it has turned yellow and withered.

The choice of species and varieties is a matter of personal taste. Some of my favourite varieties are 'Golden Ducat', 'Beersheba', 'Broughshane', 'Mount Hood', 'Edward Buxton', 'Riante', 'Verger', 'Kilworth', 'Grand Prospect', 'Irish Minstrel', 'Farnsfield', 'Jewel Song', 'Brunswick' and 'Knowehead.'

The miniature species and hybrids are exceptionally lovely,

and most are quite easy to grow. They are particularly suited to a rock garden in a sunny, well-drained, sheltered position. Those I like include the following:

N. bulbocodium. *Bulbocodium* probably from Greek *bolbos*, a bulb, and *kodion*, a little fleece, that is, the covering of the bulb. This is the hoop-petticoat daffodil. It forms long, rush-like, dark green foliage from which are borne small, single, bright yellow flowers in March, on 6-inch stems. This species will naturalize in grass on sandy soils. The Alpine Meadow at the Royal Horticultural Society's Gardens, Wisley, and Windsor Great Park include delightful examples.

N. triandrus. *Triandrus*, having three stamens. The common name for this group is Angel's Tears, which refers to the Portuguese boy who burst into tears when reprimanded by his father for bringing back the wrong plants when collecting. All have small cups and bear several flowers in April, and the petals turn back like those of a cyclamen. They will grow well in a sunny place with good drainage; a sandy soil suits them best. All except the first have an 8-inch stem.

N.t. albus. White, 6 inches high.
N.t. 'Liberty Bells'. Lemon-yellow.
N.t. 'Rippling Waters'. White.
N.t. 'Silver Chimes'. Creamy white with lemon cups.
N.t. 'Thalia'. Cream with white cups.
N.t. 'Tresamble'. Creamy white.

N. cyclamineus. *Cyclamineus* means 'like a cyclamen flower'. This fine miniature plant has grass-like foliage from which grow 4-inch high stems bearing lovely single yellow flowers with a long narrow cup and reflexed petals. It prefers a damp situation, and has naturalized in the Wild Garden at Wisley. It flowers in March. All the *cyclamineus* hybrids are very endearing; those that have a special appeal to me are:

N. 'Charity May'. Clear yellow.
N. 'Dove Wings'. White petals, yellow cup.
N. 'February Gold'. Lemon yellow; will grow to about 12 inches high. Flowers in March.
N. 'February Silver'. Pale, creamy petals, darker cup. Flowers in March.
N. 'Jenny'. White petals, pale to white cup.
N. 'Peeping Tom'. Yellow, very attractive long cup.
N. 'Tête à Tête'. A lovely, small, clear yellow flower.

Narcissus 'February Gold' is a sturdy hybrid of *N. cyclamineus*. Appropriate for rock garden or shrub border.

N. jonquilla. *Jonquilla* refers to the rush-like leaves. The little jonquilla, about 12 inches high, has bright yellow scented flowers in May, two to six on each stem. Varieties which I strongly recommend are:

N.j. 'Juncifolius'. Two yellow, scented flowers on each stem; ideal in a rock garden. Half-shade and good drainage required. Flowers in April, 4 inches high.
N.j. 'Rupicola'. Single, scented, yellow flowers; again, would suit a rock garden. Half-shade with good drainage is necessary. Flowers in April, 4 inches high.
N.j. 'Trevithian'. Several flowers on each stem, pale yellow and sweetly scented.

Nerine. Named after a princess of Greek mythology. *Nerine bowdenii* flowers in the autumn. It is fairly hardy, although a native of South Africa. It increases quite readily, and it does best at the base of a sunny south wall. The lovely umbels of pink flowers on 18-inch stems appear before the leaves; they are good cut flowers for the house. Plant in July or August in a well-drained soil. They are best left undisturbed until overcrowding necessitates lifting and replanting.

Ornithogalum nutans is a useful bulb for naturalizing under shrubs.

Ornithogalum (star of Bethlehem). From Greek *ornis*, a bird, *gala*, milk; 'bird's milk' was said to be an expression among ancient Greeks to describe some wonderful thing. This plant is surprisingly little known. *O. umbellatum* and *O. nutans* are both about 10 inches high, flowering in early summer. They can easily become weeds, but they have attractive white and green flowers, and are worth a place among shrub borders, provided they are not mixed with choicer bulbs.

Puschkinia. Named after M. Puschkin, a Russian botanist. *Puschkinia scilloides*, synonymous with *P. libanotica*, is a native of the Caucasus, Turkey, Iraq and Iran, and is easy to grow. In March, it bears up to six flowers per stem. The flowers are whitish, with a blue strip down each petal, and 4 inches high. The pure white form is particularly lovely. A well-drained soil with full sun or partial shade is all that is required. Plant in September or October 3 inches deep and about 2 inches apart; they are very attractive when grown in a large group. Leave undisturbed until they become overcrowded, then lift in July and replant immediately.

Scilla. Also known as *Endymion*. Everyone knows *Scilla nonscripta*, the English bluebell, although the Scots think of the bluebell as *Campanula rotundifolia*, which the English call the harebell. The more robust Spanish bluebell *Scilla hispanica* has many hybrids. These vary in colour from pale to deep blue, pale rose to deep pink, and pure white. They are all very easy to grow. 'Excelsior', 'Queen of the Pinks' and 'Triumphator' are impressive when grown as groups in shady or partially shady positions. The spring-flowering scillas are most attractive with their bright blue flowers carried on 4-inch stems. They all want a rich, sandy soil, and are best in a sunny position but will survive in partial shade.

S. bifolia. A native of central and southern Europe. Many starry blue flowers in March on 4-inch stems.

S. sibirica. A native of Russia to Syria. The variety 'Spring Beauty' is a most striking blue. Ideal in shrub borders.

S. tubergeniana. Synonymous with *Scilla miczenkoana*. A native of north-west Iran, it is similar to a large-flowered puschkinia. Pale blue with dark stripes down each petal. Easily grown in a well-drained sunny or half-shady position.

Sternbergia lutea. Named after a German botanist, Count Sternberg. The English name, lily of the field, is a reference to the New Testament. This plant could be mistaken for a yellow crocus, although they belong to different families. *Sternbergia lutea* is a lovely, 4-inch-high, yellow, autumn-flowering bulb. It has wide, strap-like leaves and loves a warm, sunny spot and a really good summer baking. Plant in a light, well-drained soil, 4 inches deep, in July or August and leave quite undisturbed for many years.

Tulipa. A corruption of the Persian word *thoulyban* or *tulipant*, a turban, which the flower of the tulip was supposed to resemble. Most tulips in cultivation are hybrids bred from species which now bear hardly any resemblance to them. The tulip genus is divided into sections according to their flowering times. These consist of early single and early double tulips; Mendel, Triumph and Lily-flowered; the Darwin and Cottage types; late doubles; and Parrot tulips. Hybrids of *greigii*, *kaufmanniana* and *fosteriana* are particularly outstanding and merit wider planting. Varieties within these several divisions are considerable and are adequately described in bulb catalogues; however, it is worth noting that large stocks of a particular variety mean cheaper prices, and old or new varieties in short supply are expensive. Hybrid tulips are generally planted in

Scilla tubergeniana.

177

Tulipa tarda is a sun lover which thrives in a well-drained soil.

beds allocated to seasonal bedding, window boxes and tubs. Tulips should be planted in November, 4 inches deep and 6 to 9 inches apart. Bulbs should not be lifted until the foliage has died down naturally, but in practice this is difficult when, as is usual, summer bedding plants are to be planted. Lifting bulbs too early inhibits the food supply necessary for the formation of the following year's flower; but they can be temporarily replanted elsewhere until the foliage has died down. On lifting, retain the largest and store them in a dry shed until the autumn. They should then be planted in prepared beds. A vegetable garden is ideal for growing on; pinch out the flower buds, which will enable the foliage to build a good-sized flowering bulb for the following year. In town gardens where space is at a premium, the bulbs are not worth retaining after flowering. Buy new bulbs every year, and be sure of a first-class spring display.

The species should be planted in well-drained, sunny positions, sheltered from cold winds. They should be left for some years until overcrowding warrants lifting, dividing and replanting.

Those I particularly favour are:

T. eichleri. A native of north-west Iran. Rich red flowers in April, 6–9 inches high.

Tulipa kaufmanniana
'Peacock mixture'.

T. fosteriana hybrids. Easily grown. Colours vary, height 8–24 inches. Flowers in March-April.

T. greigii hybrids. All easy and well worth growing, with attractively marked leaves. 8–10 inches high. Flowers in April.

T. kaufmanniana hybrids. White, flushed red and yellow flowers in March-April, 8 inches high.

T. praestans. A native of Central Asia. Keep dry in the summer; white-orange, 8-inch high flowers in February.

T. tarda. An attractive tulip from Central Asia. White and yellow flowers in May, 4 inches high.

T. turkestanica. A native of Central Asia. Keep dry in the summer; white-orange 8-inch high flowers in February.

CHAPTER 10

Conifers

Conifers form a large and important group of plants which bestow a majestic elegance and tranquil grace on gardens large and small. They contribute a richness of colour ranging from gold, yellow, blue, bronze, purple and many different shades of green and, furthermore, they provide wonderful winter shelter for birds and make effective windbreaks. The name 'conifer' was used by the Frenchman Pierre Belon in the sixteenth century; it means literally, 'cone-bearing'. This description is not always applicable, however, for cypresses and junipers do not bear cones.

Conifers must have clean air to flourish. Those gardens with the misfortune to be sited in polluted atmospheres caused by industry or heavy traffic are not suitable for any conifers except the deciduous types: larch, swamp cypress, dawn redwood and maidenhair. These have a fresh start with new leaves every spring, and can cope in such atmospheres, whereas the evergreens may survive a few years but are always sickly and stunted. The chief point to be borne in mind, in the selection of all evergreens where there is a pollution problem, is that only those which have smooth or glossy leaves should be chosen. Dirt, diesel oil and sulphur deposits clog up the leaf pores which are essential to the proper functioning of any plant. Smooth or glossy leaves do not catch so much dirt, and in any event are easily washed clean by heavy rain or overhead irrigation. Conifers are not easily cleaned, and consequently suffer.

Conifers generally flourish best in a deep, rich, well-drained soil. It is always helpful to know where a particular plant comes from, as this gives an indication of the different soil requirements. Few conifers like a hot, sandy or gravelly soil, but pines flourish on them. Moisture-loving species are *Picea sitchensis* (Sitka spruce), *Abies balsamea* (balsam fir), *Taxodium distichum* (swamp cypress), *Sciadopitys verticillata* (umbrella

Opposite:
As a group, the conifers have great architectural appeal and provide winter interest. Note, however, the forest type tree which is outgrowing its station in the adjoining garden.

pine) and *Metasequoia glyptostroboides* (dawn redwood). Land with a clay or chalk subsoil suits *Pinus nigra* (Austrian pine), *Abies cephalonica* (Grecian fir), *Abies pinsapo* (Spanish fir) and *Cedrus libani* (cedar of Lebanon). If the soil contains more than 10 per cent lime, suitable conifers include *Thuja occidentalis* varieties, *Thuja orientalis* varieties, *Taxus baccata* varieties and *Cephalotaxus* species, some *Abies*, such as *bracteata*, *magnifica*, *nobilis* and *nordmanniana*, *Juniperus communis*, *sabina* and *virginiana*, *Pinus nigra*, *pinaster* and *sylvestris*, *Libocedrus decurrens* and *Ginkgo biloba*. For dry land there are numerous junipers and pines, which will cope well with droughts.

Thorough preparation of the planting site is, as always, a wise investment to ensure good vigorous growth the first year after planting. Conifers should be planted either in the autumn or in the spring. Autumn is the best time to plant, when there is some summer warmth still in the ground. Never plant in the depth of winter or in the height of summer, whether the plants are container-grown or not. Correct planting distances are of paramount importance. Conifers dislike root disturbance and after a certain age – very young in the case of pines – it is impossible to move them successfully.

As a general rule, pruning is not recommended because the wounds do not heal easily. Some species lend themselves to clipping and make fine hedges, but none except yew will break out again from old wood. It is not possible to discuss more than a few conifers, and it is of little use to mention the large forest or timber trees. I have therefore confined my remarks to those which are suitable for the average garden, which in my view are the best of their kind. Mindful that to see is to understand, a visit to Bedgebury Pinetum, Goudhurst, Kent, with camera and notebook is more instructive than the brief descriptions given here.

Abies amabilis 'Procumbens'. *Abies* is possibly from Latin *abeo*, depart, that is, from the ground, making reference to the great height of some species (*A. amabilis* reaches a height of 250 feet in Oregon and Washington, *A. concolor* grows up to 270 feet in the Rocky Mountains and Arizona, and *A. grandis* to 300 feet from California to Vancouver Island. *A. amabilis* 'Procumbens' is a low-growing variety, up to 3 feet high with wide, horizontal, spreading branches. It likes a fertile, moist soil, and is not suitable for limy or light sandy soils which suffer from drought.

Abies cephalonica 'Nana'. *Cephalonica* from Cephalonia, the

Dwarf conifers (genus *Thuja*) and anemones (*Anemone blanda*) growing together.

Balkan Peninsula. The young growth of this tree is tender and subject to frost damage in the spring. *A. cephalonica* 'Nana' is a fine prostrate form with wide spreading branches. It thrives on limy soils but, like all evergreen conifers, is not suitable for towns with a polluted atmosphere, for frost pockets, or for exposed cold gardens.

Abies nordmanniana 'Aurea Nana'. *A. nordmanniana* is known as the Caucasian Fir, Nordmann's Fir, or Crimean Fir. A tree from the Pontine Mountains, Asia Minor. *A.n.* 'Aurea Nana' is a most decorative, slow-growing dwarf form, which has wide, spreading branches. The leaves are light yellow. This is a very attractive conifer for the rock garden.

***Cephalotaxus fortunei* (Chinese plum yew).** A native of China, this conifer was introduced by Robert Fortune in 1849. It is a yew-like plant, very shade-tolerant, and not particular about soil, including chalk. It is quite an attractive, dark, evergreen shrub.

Cephalotaxus fortunei 'Prostrata'. This is a fine prostrate shrub with good foliage, useful on banks and over retaining walls. It must have space to develop. It does excellently on limy and clay soils.

183

Chamaecyparis lawsoniana
'Ellwoodii'.

***Chamaecyparis lawsoniana* (Lawson cypress).** This cypress was first introduced in 1854 by a Mr Lawson, an Edinburgh nurseryman. It is a native of Western North America, known there as the Port Orford cedar, because it thrives on the Oregon coast. It is possibly the commonest planted conifer. It is very hardy and has produced under cultivation a considerable number of forms, varying enormously in foliage, colour, size and habit. It will grow in excess of 80 feet in poor soil, and frequently grows 200 feet high in its wild state. There are a number of cultivars suitable for the small garden, provided the air is clean. They will grow in any soil but do best in a good, deep, fertile, loamy soil; they also favour a heavy rainful. There are so many attractive forms that it is tempting to overplant; but do not fall into this trap. The varieties which in my opinion merit planting are listed below:

C.l. 'Allumii'. This is a fine blue-grey form, slow-growing, of pyramidal habit, not as big as another good blue-grey variety, 'Triomf Van Boskoop'. 'Allumii', which eventually grows to a maximum of 40 feet or so, is more suitable for the smaller garden. It is quite hardy and tolerant of all soils.

C.l. 'Columnaris'. Growing up to 35 feet high or thereabouts, this is a very narrow, fastigiate (upright) tree with glaucous foliage, ideal for the small garden. Award of Garden Merit 1961.

C.l. 'Ellwoodii'. This is a slow-growing conifer with an attractive, tight, columnar habit. It has grey-green feathery foliage, grows to about 10 feet high in 18 years, and is useful in the heather or rock garden. Award of Merit 1934, Award of Garden Merit 1969.

C.l. 'Fletcheri'. Another fine conifer for the small garden or heather and rock garden. It is fairly slow growing, reaching a height of about 18 feet in 18 years, and 25 feet in 35 years. It has lovely, soft, grey-green feathery foliage, and is ideal for all types of soil. First Class Certificate 1913, Award of Garden Merit 1969.

C.l. 'Pottenii'. This is a fine conifer for any garden. It has green feathery foliage, and a very upright habit. It is fairly slow in growth – about 18 feet in 18 years. Award of Merit 1916.

C.l. 'Winston Churchill'. In my view this is the best golden Lawson. It has a fine, pyramidal habit of growth, though fairly slow. It will reach a height of 5 feet in 12 years. With bright yellow foliage, it makes an attractive feature when grown as a single specimen, ideal for the smaller garden, very hardy and indifferent to type of soil.

For larger gardens I recommend *Chamaecyparis lawsoniana* 'Green Hedger', 'Kilmacurragh', 'Lanei', 'Lutea', 'Stewartii' and 'Triomf Van Boskoop'.

Chamaecyparis obtusa 'Nana Gracilis'. This is a small tree of dense growth with very attractive dark green foliage. It is very slow growing, reaching about 4 feet to 6 feet high after 30 years' growth. It is ideal for the rock garden or terrace area. It is not for limy soils, but clay and sandy soils are suitable.

Cryptomeria japonica 'Elegans'. *Cryptomeria* from Greek *kryptos*, hidden, and *meros*, a part, that is, parts of the tree not being fully understood. *Japonica* is the only species in this genus; the variety 'Elegans' grows 12 feet tall. This is a striking tree, particularly during the winter months when its dense feathery foliage takes on a lovely red-coppery hue. Not particular about soil, it thrives on chalk. It is ideal for the small garden, and very effective when planted in association with a golden conifer. First Class Certificate 1862.

Juniperis communis 'Depressa'.

Juniperus communis 'Depressa'. This is a useful, hardy, dwarf, carpeting shrub, excellent for rock gardens, banks, tops of retaining walls and in the heather garden. It has yellowish-green leaves which turn to an attractive bronze in the winter, excels on chalk and is quite happy on clay and sandy soils.

Juniperus communis 'Hibernica' **(Irish juniper).** A very attractive, slender, upright tree which grows to about 12 feet high in about 25 years, less where the soil is poor. The columnar habit is most useful to achieve contrast among heathers or in a mixed border in a small garden. The dense foliage gives an elegant appearance. Indifferent to the type of soil; it is an excellent choice for limy soils.

Juniperus communis 'Hornibrookii'. Named after Murray Hornibrook, who collected a seedling in County Galway, Ireland. This very hardy, fine, ornamental shrub forms a dense carpet, taking on the shape it covers. It is excellent in rock gardens or cascading over retaining walls. It flourishes on chalk; clay and sandy soils are also quite suitable.

Juniperus conferta. A fine prostrate shrub from Japan. The foliage is bright green and quite prickly to the touch. This is an excellent carpeter which needs plenty of space to develop. It is indifferent to the soil, but excels on chalk.

185

Juniperis communis 'Compressa'.

***Juniperus horizontalis* (creeping juniper).** This is an attractive, creeping, mat-forming shrub – another good ground-cover plant, suitable for all types of soil. Award of Merit 1969. There are many excellent forms of *Juniperus horizontalis* which are similar in habit and just as hardy; these include 'Bar Harbor', 'Douglasii' and 'Wiltonii', which are well worth growing. All should be planted in the sun to bring out the glaucous blue colouring of their foliage.

Juniperus sabina 'Tamariscifolia'. This low-growing, hardy shrub is ideal for the rock garden, banks, the front of borders, the tops of retaining walls or in terraces to punctuate the paving. A very popular shrub, ideal on chalk and suitable on clay and sandy soils. Award of Merit 1969.

Juniperus viginiana 'Chamberlaynii'. Under cultivation, *Juniperus viginiana* (pencil cedar) has produced many varieties, and *J.v.* 'Chamberlaynii' is one of them. It is a spreading, prostrate shrub with attractive glaucous foliage, ideal for rock and heather gardens, terraces and walls. It is extremely hardy, and suitable on all types of soils.

Picea albertiana 'Conica'. This tree from Alberta is very compact, forming a perfect pyramid up to 7 feet high in 30 years' growth. Notwithstanding that it is very slow growing, it acquires a most effective and pleasing shape after about 10 years' growth. Award of Merit 1933, Award of Garden Merit 1969.

Picea orientalis 'Gracilis'. This is a slow-growing tree, conical in shape, with dark green leaves. It grows up to 7 feet tall in about 25–30 years. Its pyramidal shape is useful in a formal garden layout.

Picea pungens 'Koster'. This fine tree grows up to 18 feet high and is a very ornamental conifer with striking blue leaves. It prefers a good fertile soil, but will grow on dry, sandy soils.

Picea pungens 'Moerheimii'. A tree up to 18 feet high, very elegant, with lovely, glaucous blue leaves. An exceptionally fine tree.

Picea pungens 'Procumbens'. This is a prostrate, wide-spreading conifer, ideal for rock garden, bank or terraced area. It has intensely blue leaves.

Pinus mugo (mountain pine). An attractive small pine up to 7 feet high. Ideal in a rock garden, it has a dense, bushy habit and attractive dark green foliage. It is not particular about soil and is excellent on clay and chalk. A fine plant for the small garden.

Taxus baccata 'Repandans'. This shrub forms a wide-spreading, slow-growing mat with dark green foliage. It is an excellent plant for the front of a border, rock or heather garden, for a terrace, bank or on top of a retaining wall. Quite hardy, it flourishes on chalk and is suitable for clay and sandy soils. Like all members of the yew family, it grows reasonably well in shade.

Taxus baccata 'Semperaurea'. This is an exceptionally fine shrub of medium size, fairly slow-growing. The foliage is a lovely gold, turning to yellow. It should be grown in the sun. It contrasts well with a dark green foliage plant, such as a camellia or *Ilex camellifolia*. Award of Garden Merit 1969.

Taxus baccata 'Standishii'. This is the best upright golden yew; but it is slow-growing. It is ideally used as a contrast plant in a formal rose garden. Award of Garden Merit 1969.

Thuja occidentalis 'Filiformis'. A slow-growing bush with 'whipcord' branches. It grows up to 6 feet high, and is suitable for clay and limy soils.

Thuja occidentalis 'Globosa'. An attractively shaped bush, slow-growing. It reaches up to 3 feet high by 6 feet wide, and is suitable on chalk and clay soils. An interesting bush.

Thuja occidentalis 'Rheingold'. This is a slow-growing, golden bush, ideal for the small garden. It grows up to 5 feet tall and 4 feet wide, and is ideal on chalk and clay soils. Award of Garden Merit 1969.

Thujopsis dolabrata. A native of Japan. Seen at its best, this is a handsome tree or shrub with very attractive foliage. I have a plant growing in the shelter of an *Arundinaria nitida* (bamboo) which is about 5 feet high after 15 years' growth. It thrives on well-drained soils, including clay and limy ones.

Tsuga canadensis 'Albospica'. This is a very attractive variety, especially in spring and summer, when the growing tips of the shoots turn a creamy white. It is a slow grower, reaching a height of up to about 10 feet.

Tsuga canadensis 'Pendula'. This is a very attractive shrub or small tree of cascading branches. It thrives in a fertile, moist soil, is reasonably tolerant of chalk, and grows up to 6 feet high.

Recommended ornamental conifers for clay soil

Chamaecyparis lawsoniana
   'Allumii'
Chamaecyparis lawsoniana
   'Elegantissima'
Chamaecyparis lawsoniana
   'Fletcheri'
Chamaecyparis lawsoniana
   'Lanei'

Chamaecyparis lawsoniana
   'Lutea'
Chamaecyparis lawsoniana
   'Pottenii'
Chamaecyparis lawsoniana
   'Winston Churchill'
Cryptomeria japonica 'Elegans'

Conifers for clay soil (recommended for small gardens under ½ acre)

Chamaecyparis lawsoniana 'Lutea'.

Abies nobilis 'Prostrata'

Abies nordmanniana 'Aurea
   Nana'

Abies nordmanniana 'Pendula'
Chamaecyparis lawsoniana
    'Allumii'
Chamaecyparis lawsoniana
    'Fletcheri'
Chamaecyparis lawsoniana
    'Pottenii'
Chamaecyparis lawsoniana
    'Winston Churchill'
Chamaecyparis obtusa
    'Ericoides'
Juniperus communis
    'Hibernica'
Juniperus recurva
Juniperus sabina 'Blue
    Danube', 'Tamariscifolia'

Picea orientalis 'Nana Gracilis'
Pinus mugo
Taxus baccata 'Adpressa'
Taxus baccata 'Dovastoniana'
Taxus baccata 'Semperaurea'
Taxus baccata 'Washingtonii'
Thuja occidentalis 'Filiformis'
Thuja occidentalis 'Globosa'
Thuja occidentalis 'Rheingold'
Thuja plicata 'Hillieri'
Thuja plicata 'Stoneham Gold"
Thujopsis dolabrata
Tsuga canadensis 'Pendula'
Tsuga canadensis 'Albospica'

Conifers recommended for calcareous soil

Juniperus × *media*
'Pfitzeriana Aurea'.

Abies cephalonica 'Nana'
Chamaecyparis lawsoniana
    'Allumii'
Chamaecyparis lawsoniana
    'Fletcheri'
Chamaecyparis lawsoniana
    'Pottenii'
Chamaecyparis lawsoniana
    'Winston Churchill'
Cryptomeria japonica 'Elegans'
Juniperus chinensis 'Sargentii'
Juniperus communis
    'Hibernica', 'Hornibrookii'
Juniperus conferta
Juniperus horizontalis 'Bar
    Harbor'
Juniperus × *media* 'Pfitzerana
    Aurea'

Juniperus sabina
    'Tamariscifolia'
Juniperus virginiana
Picea abies 'Clanbrassilliana'
Picea abies 'Nidiformis'
Picea abies 'Procumbens'
Pinus mugo
Taxus baccata 'Adpressa'
Taxus baccata 'Dovastoniana'
Taxus baccata 'Semperaurea'
Taxus baccata 'Washingtonii'
Thuja occidentalis 'Filiformis'
Thuja occidentalis 'Globosa'
Thuja occidentalis 'Rheingold'
Thuja plicata 'Hillieri'
Thuja plicata 'Stoneham Gold'
Thujopsis dolabrata
Tsuga canadensis 'Albospica'

CHAPTER 11

Window-boxes, tubs and hanging baskets

Window-boxes, tubs and hanging baskets, well planted and maintained, will effectively transform a town house or flat. What is more, just one inspiration of this nature will inevitably set a trend, for neighbours will quickly follow suit, and within a relatively short time there will be a marked improvement throughout the street or estate. Neglected boxes and tubs do not have this effect, of course, and stick out like sore thumbs. It is therefore not prudent to embark on this type of venture unless you can be sure that the maintenance will be consistently good; but if you are able to invest just a little time on a fairly regular basis, you can achieve excellent results at relatively little cost, even if you are not overly blessed with 'do-it-yourself' talents.

Window-boxes

I prefer small window-boxes, about 30 inches long, 10 inches wide and 9 inches deep. This is a quite manageable size, which is an advantage when you are placing them in position from the top of a ladder or through a bedroom window. The width of the window will determine how many boxes are placed on the sill (where windows do not open outwards), and all boxes, including those on balconies, should be fixed firmly in position with brackets, to ensure that no accidents occur.

Boxes, tubs, urns and window-boxes on a terrace are enjoyed by those using the terrace. Plants in boxes on window-sills and balconies, however, turn outwards toward the light, and it must be accepted that passers-by will have the most pleasure from the display.

Opposite:
Cheerful displays of summer seasonal bedding plants.

Old ammunition-boxes, well painted, with a few ½-inch-diameter drainage holes drilled in the bottom, are excellent for this purpose, especially when simple clip-on or screw-on front panels are fitted. These can make the boxes look quite distinctive if they are painted in ivory, white, black or grey, or given a wood finish. Ammunition-boxes can be bought from some surplus stores and are also advertised in *Exchange and Mart* and elsewhere.

Other types of window-box available are made from plastic, fibreglass, or a mixture of asbestos and cement. All these are maintenance-free, and come in a variety of sizes. The handyman will no doubt make his boxes himself, from wood. A box made from a softwood, primed, with two undercoats and one finishing coat of the good old-fashioned lead paints still obtainable from a builders' merchant, will last many years; it is unnecessary to buy expensive hardwood.

There is considerable merit in planting the boxes and growing them on in a glasshouse or conservatory, if you have one, to get them established before putting them out in their final positions. In a 9-inch-deep box, place large pieces of broken crock over the drainage holes, and add a layer, about 1½ inches deep, of washed single or small stones. Over this drainage material place a layer of moss or coarse peat to prevent soil from being washed down into the drainage material, causing a blockage and subsequent waterlogging. Fill the box with John Innes Potting Compost No. 3. This is made up of a mixture of 7 parts (by volume) loam, 3 parts sphagnum moss peat and 2 parts coarse sand. To every bushel (see below) of this mixture, add 12 ounces John Innes Base Fertilizer and 2¼ ounces chalk. This should be mixed with the sand when mixing the compost. The fertilizer is made up by mixing 2 parts (by weight) hoof and horn ⅛-inch grist, 2 parts super-phosphate and 1 part sulphate of potash; all these are available from any good horticultural sundries store. A bushel is 2218.2 cubic inches. More simply, a box with internal dimensions of 25 inches long, 6¾ inches deep and 13 inches wide, filled level, holds exactly one bushel. There are 21 bushels to a cubic yard; 1 bushel will fill 40 five-inch pots.)

Sterilization of the loam in John Innes compost is necessary for plant production in a glasshouse, but for window-boxes, tubs and urns it is not necessary. There are a number of loamless composts based on a mixture of sphagnum moss peat, sand and fertilizers, but I have not found anything as good as the old-fashioned John Innes composts for plant production or subsequent growing on. A good loam is vital, however, and unfortunately the soil in town gardens is generally very impoverished and would not be suitable for making up a compost for tubs and window-boxes. The cheapest way to do this is to share a bulk purchase with members of your local

Horticultural Society, or Gardening Club, or with a group of neighbours. In this way up to 16-cubic-yard lorry-loads of good topsoil, grower's-sized bales of sphagnum moss peat and 10 cubic yards of coarse sand can be purchased from a landscape contractor or nurseryman. If bulk deliveries are somewhat daunting, smaller loads of John Innes composts are supplied by many nurserymen who have all the necessary mixing equipment. Good fibrous loam for a small project can be acquired by buying a few hundred turves which should be stacked for six months to rot down.

If the boxes are filled with John Innes Potting Compost No. 3, it will be some years before a change is required. When ordering it is necessary to have a reasonable load, and it is worth noting the high transport costs – half loads cost nearly as much as full loads. Furthermore, these materials will not deteriorate in storage, provided they are covered with plastic sheeting to prevent cats from fouling them. Boxes on balconies, rooftops and garage walls, and along the top of porches, all tend to dry out quickly, particularly during sunny periods, and also when the plants are mature and the boxes are full of roots. Some staining of the building or walls below the box is inevitable, but this can be reduced by careful watering or by fitting a galvanized strip projecting between the box and the window-sill to form a drip groove for the drainage water to run clear.

On occasions, I have overheard judges of town garden and window-box competitions comment on the need to have a wide range of plants, including herbs and alpines. In my opinion, the bolder the splash of colour the better, and the longer the display from the same plant the better; this means in practice that the range of suitable plants is reduced to seasonal bedding plants, bulbs and evergreens.

About six weeks after planting, when the plants are happily growing, feeding at two-weekly intervals should begin. A liquid fertilizer is best, and this should be applied according to the manufacturer's instructions. Any fertilizer should be applied only when the soil is wet. Overdosing can be fatal. Regular watering, removal of weeds and fading flowers are essential jobs if the boxes are to flourish and continue to thrive. If summer watering is too demanding, capillary water systems fitted to window-boxes and tubs are available, but these are not suitable for winter use, and they are expensive. Seasonal bedding plants such as geraniums should be planted 9 inches apart, petunias, verbena, African marigolds 6 inches apart; lobelia, alyssum, French marigolds 4 inches apart. Ivy (*Hedera helix*) is ideal as a permanent plant, winter and summer, cascading down the front of the box and softening the appearance of the building.

Planting out summer bedding plants too early gives the plants an immense check and they will take weeks to recover, if they do so at all. Foliage turns a dull mauve-blue and roots rot. Do not be influenced by the appearance of the plants on a market stall or in a garden centre; they may have just been taken from a greenhouse and, although looking lush and green, not been hardened off. In any event most are half-hardy plants and will not survive cold weather.

Summer bedding plants should not be planted out until the beginning of June in the south of Britain and the middle of June in the north. Without any check they will grow away rapidly and make fine plants.

Bulbs and spring-flowering plants should be planted in October. During the winter a variety of evergreens planted in window-boxes and tubs is an appealing way of continuing an attractive display. If they are kept in their pots when they are planted in the tubs or window-boxes in the autumn, the check of transplanting is avoided. In the spring, about March or April, pots of bulbs, polyanthus, wallflowers, daisies, winter-flowering pansies and myosotis can be planted to replace the evergreens. The latter should then be plunged in a spare sunny section of the garden up to their rims in a bed of peat, leaf mould or spent mushroom manure. Regular watering and feeding during the summer will keep them growing in preparation for replacing in tubs and window-boxes the following autumn. Evergreens suitable for this purpose include:

Buxus sempervirens and varieties
Daphne laureola
Elaeagnus pungens 'Maculata'
Euonymus fortunei and varieties
Euonymus japonicus and varieties
Fatsia japonica
Hebe in variety
Hedera – all green and variegated forms
Juniperus × *media* 'Pfitzerana'
Juniperus sabina
Osmanthus heterophyllus
Phillyrea angustifolia
Phillyrea latifolia
Prunus laurocerasus and varieties
Prunus lusitanica

Sarcococca humilis
Skimmia japonica
Taxus baccata and varieties
Thujopsis dolabrata
Viburnum tinus

Cuttings of the evergreens listed above can easily be rooted in June-July to keep the required stock of young plants available for use when older plants get too big and have to be either planted permanently or discarded. Where there is a wind problem it may be possible to achieve some shelter by erecting a screen or windbreak, with wooden trellis, plastic chain link or galvanized wire to support plants that are wind-tolerant. These include the following:

Elaeagnus angustifolia
Elaeagnus × *ebbingei*
Elaeagnus glabra
Elaeagnus macrophylla
Escallonia macrantha
Garrya elliptica
Hedera all green and variegated forms
Hippophae rhamnoides
Pyracantha atalantioides

These can be planted in a tub of 30 inches diameter, in John Innes Potting Compost No. 3; by careful pruning and tying in over a three-year period a good windbreak can be established.

Bulbs are particularly useful for window-box and tub planting, and those recommended are:

Hyacinthus 'Ostara'
Narcissus 'February Gold'
Narcissus 'Gold Harvest'
Narcissus 'Peeping Tom'
Narcissus 'Unsurpassable'
Tulipa 'Double Early' varieties
Tulipa 'Double Late' varieties
Tulipa fosteriana varieties
Tulipa greigii varieties
Tulipa kaufmanniana varieties

Plants recommended for window-boxes

Spring display

Bellis perennis (daisies)
Cheiranthus (wall flowers)

Iberis sempervirens (candytuft)
Myosotis (forget-me-not)
Primula vulgaris hybrids **(polyanthus)**
Primula 'Juliana' hybrids

Summer display (in full sun)

Ageratum 'Blue Mink'
Alyssum "Carpet of Snow'
Antirrhinum 'Little Darling'
Begonia semperflorens varieties
Dahlia dwarf forms
Geranium 'Sprinter'
Lobelia **'Cascade'** mixed
Petunia 'White Cascade', 'Pink Cascade'
Salvia 'Blaze of Fire'
Tagetes erecta **(African marigold)** 'Inca Gold'
Tagetes patula **(French marigold)** 'Naughty Marietta'
Tagetes 'Starfire'
Verbena **'Topic'**

Summer display (in the shade)

Begonia 'Danica Scarlet'
Calceolaria 'Golden Bunch'
Calendula 'Mandarin'
Coleus mixed
Impatiens 'Imp' or 'Futura' or 'Elfin' hybrids
Nicotiana 'Nicki'F$_1$ hybrids, mixed
Tagetes 'Starfire'
Tagetes erecta **(African marigold)** 'Inca Gold'
Tagetes patula **(French marigold)** 'Royal Canary'

Tubs and urns

A tub or an urn can be a striking focal point on a terrace or lawn. It can highlight the head, foot or landing on a flight of garden stairs, or be very effective at or above eye level on pillars or copings. Subject to cost, all types and sizes of tub or urn are available. These include English and Italian clay, concrete, a mixture of concrete and asbestos, fibreglass, plastic, metal or timber, all in classical or modern designs. Old wine-barrels are still available from coopers, of which there are a

A paved corner is an ideal spot for a tub or two and makes an excellent focal point.

number in London and elsewhere in the country. Cut in half, these barrels make excellent tubs. They are generally made of oak or chestnut, and provided they have two or three coats of a bituminous paint on the inside, holes drilled in the bases for drainage and the bands regularly painted to prevent rust, they will last for several years. Square tubs are available in iroko, teak and cedar. These should also be painted with a bituminous paint on the inside and regularly treated with teak oil or linseed oil on the outside. While secondhand bargains in the form of lovely old urns may occasionally be on offer, it is essential that they have a good drainage hole, otherwise waterlogging will occur, with fatal results for any plant. I favour large containers because summer watering is not so critical; futhermore small ones are generally quite out of scale.

Tubs give the opportunity of growing plants which otherwise would not be possible, for the soil can be varied to suit the plant. Also, a tub can be moved on rollers to a sheltered position or into a glasshouse or conservatory during the winter months. It can be watered with lime-free rain-water from a rain-butt to maintain the correct pH value. Rain-water in a barrel should have some charcoal kept in it to keep it sweet, and a lid on the barrel to prevent its use as a breeding-ground by mosquitoes.

A single urn or tub is a focal point, but a group of different sizes may be even more effective. It is important to select the right type of planting to fit the situation. Seasonal bedding plants with bold colours may be appropriate. Height in these circumstances can be achieved by standard fuchsias or *Ricinus communis gibsonii*, the castor oil plant, which grows to an imposing 4-foot-high plant in a few weeks. Cannas and *Zea mays* (Indian Corn) are excellent in the sun. In shade, in addition to those seasonal bedding plants recommended, height can be acquired by planting *Abutilon thompsonii, Eucalyptus globusus* or *Grevillea robusta*.

Where gardens are shaded by adjacent buildings, or where trees create a shady environment, woodland plants are best. As long as there is acid soil and shelter from winds, rhododendrons, camellias, Japanese maples, vacciniums, fothergillas and many similar plants are ideal. If the soil is alkaline, however – and town gardens in a hard-water district generally are – these shrubs can only be grown successfully in tubs or containers with a prepared compost.

Shrubs planted in tubs or urns eventually become too large and need repotting into something bigger. To get them out of containers without damaging either shrubs or tubs can be accomplished by inserting a liner at potting time. Man-made fibre straps or plastic-covered wire mesh would be suitable. An ideal compost for the shrubs listed, which with increasing age will produce fine exhibition specimens, giving immeasurable pleasure, is equal parts (by volume) of sphagnum moss peat, leaf mould and loam with a pH6 to 6.5. Mix with each bushel either 12 ounces John Innes Base Fertilizer, or equal parts (by volume) of well-rotted manure, well-rotted compost and loam with a pH6 to 6.5. Once the plants are established, regular feeding with a liquid fertilizer, from late spring to late summer, every two weeks, is all that is required, except for watering when necessary with lime-free water.

Camellia 'Adolphe Audusson' with its compact growth is a fine choice for a tub.

Acer japonicum 'Aureum'. A lovely Japanese maple, whose leaves are a pale golden yellow throughout the entire summer and edged red in early spring. In the autumn the yellow becomes more pronounced. This bush is a gem for a shady, sheltered garden, but it will get badly scorched in sun or cold winds. It needs acid soil and is very slow-growing. Award of Garden Merit 1969.

Acer palmatum 'Dissectum'. When mature, this is a beautiful, graceful shrub with fine, soft green leaves and a good autumn colour. It must have an acid soil and a sheltered, shaded position, because it will scorch in strong winds and full sun. Award of Garden Merit 1956. *A.p.* 'Dissectum Atropurpureum' is a similar shrub, but the leaves are a rich bronze purple throughout the summer. It is very slow-growing, taking years to develop into a large, spreading specimen. As above, an acid soil and sheltered, shaded position are essential. Award of Garden Merit 1969.

Camellia japonica 'Apollo'. A valuable and fine-quality shrub, increasing with age into a most beautiful evergreen. It has red, semi-double flowers, with occasional white smudges, in spring. It must have a lime-free soil, and be sheltered from wind and early morning sun. A moist, sheltered, woodland environment is ideal. Camellias thrive in towns, provided the soil is acid and water lime-free. Award of Merit 1956, Award of Garden Merit 1969.

Camellia Williamsii 'Donation'. Another beautiful camellia, which is free-flowering from November to May, with exquisite, large, semi-double pink flowers. Award of Merit 1941, Award of Garden Merit 1958.

Camellia williamsii 'J. C. Williams'. A fine shrub, gaining in beauty with age. The flowers are pink and single. Award of Garden Merit 1949.

Rhododendron 'Bow Bells'. A lovely, dome-shaped rhododendron with small, pretty leaves, coppery young growths and pink, bell-shaped flowers opening from rose-red buds. It grows to about 4 feet high and 4 feet wide, and needs the same conditions as Japanese maples. Award of Merit 1935.

Rhododendron 'Humming Bird'. Another attractive dome-shaped shrub with dark green foliage and crimson pink flowers, 3 feet high, 5 feet wide.

Tubs and urns planted with *Agapanthus* look exceptionally fine; the splendid foliage and lovely umbels of blue flowers are set off to good advantage in this way. *Agapanthus campanulatus*, *A.c.* 'Albus', *A. patens* 'Profusion' and *A.* 'Headbourne Hybrids' are all hardy. They like rich feeding and a warm position in full sun. The strap-like leaves are particularly suited to tubs and urns. Round heads of trumpet-shaped blue flowers on 2–2½-foot-tall stems appear in August. Pot in John Innes Potting Compost No. 3, and feed every two weeks during spring and summer months. *Phormium tenax* and varieties also look distinctive in tubs and urns. John Innes Potting Compost No. 3, feeding every other week and watering as and when necessary is all that is required, other than an open, warm, sunny position.

Hanging baskets

Hanging baskets can be most attractive in a small garden, hanging from balconies and porches and in conservatories. Preparing and planting are quite easy. Place a 1-inch layer of moss on the inside of the basket and add John Innes Potting Compost No. 3 to within 2 inches of the rim. Put in a variety of plants, placing the cascading types to fall over the edge. Ensure that all plants are watered both before and after planting. For watering, planting and weeding, place the basket

A splendid example of a well planted hanging basket.

in the top of a bucket. This provides support and keeps the basket upright.

Avoid hanging baskets in windy or draughty positions. Plants should be carefully chosen to suit the shade or sun, as recommended for window-boxes and tubs.

A much better display is possible if the baskets are made up in early April and kept in a glasshouse or conservatory to become well established before they are hung in their display positions at the end of May.

CHAPTER 12 # Dry walls and rock gardens

The heap of soil with a few assorted stones placed at random, generally called 'the rockery', should, in my view, be avoided. If a factor such as cost, or difficult access, prevents the purchase of the required number of large pieces of sandstone or limestone to construct a natural-looking rock outcrop, my advice is to forget about a rock garden and have a dry wall instead. A dry wall, free-standing or built as a retaining wall, is an ideal situation for a wide range of alpines and is admirably suited to a small garden where space is at a premium or where there are different levels. It is also an effective and attractive method of establishing external boundaries or making any internal divisions that may be wanted.

Dry walls

Considerable skill is required in building a dry wall, but this should not discourage the beginner. Predictably, there will be many attempts to get it right, but it is really worth the effort to acquire not only a perfect home for many exquisite alpines, but also an extremely attractive feature which effortlessly harmonizes with the rest of the garden.

A dry wall is made without cement or mortar. The stone is laid with a standard compost of 3 parts (by volume) loam (sieved ⅛ inch), 1 part peat, and 1 part grit (⅛ inch in diameter) or washed shingle, firmly packed into the crevices (see diagram). This can, in special instances, be made more peaty or sandy to suit the requirements of a particular plant.

Mark the position of the proposed wall with a builder's line and excavate a level trench (or running level) 6 inches deep to accommodate the foundation layer of stones. The stones should ideally be two or three times larger than a brick, and squared or dressed. Select the largest stones for the foundation layer, and ensure that these are very firmly bedded in by ramming the prepared compost round them.

Opposite:
The blue flowers and purple bracts of *Ajuga pyramidalis* and the succulent leaves of *Sempervivum tectorum* 'Mahogany' are perfect foils for two alpine phloxes in this corner of a rock garden in June.

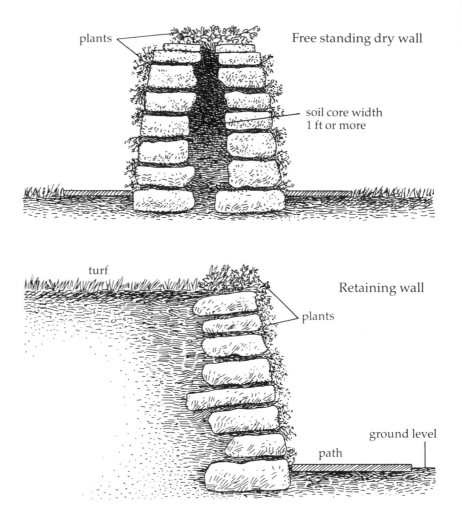

plants

Free standing dry wall

soil core width
1 ft or more

turf

Retaining wall

plants

ground level

path

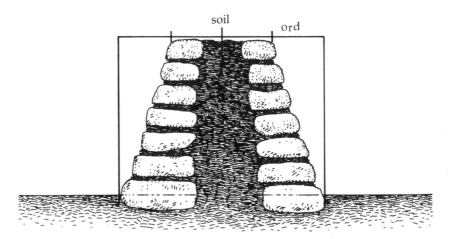

soil

ord

Having laid the first course, drive a stake in at both ends, vertically, to the required height of the wall; allow at least a 2-inch batter for every 12 inches of height. (A 'batter' is a slight inward slope, which gives the wall stability and allows rain-water to run down the face of the stone between the crevices.) A free-standing dry wall should have the same batter on both sides. A 4-foot-high wall, whether free-standing or retaining, should have a minimum batter of 8 inches. To provide a good guide, place a peg into the bank, in the case of a 4-foot-high *retaining* wall, 8 inches in front of the vertical stake at each end of the wall. Stretch a taut line between the two pegs and, with the aid of a straight edge placed between the two lines, that is, the one at the top and the one at the base, you will have the batter measurement. The right amount of tilt to each stone will give the correct slope throughout the entire length of the wall. In the case of a *free-standing* wall, stretch a line at ground level to mark the front of the base on either side, and place a vertical stake at both corners, at each end of the wall, to the required height. Join the top of each stake with a cross-member, and on this mark 8 inches back, either side, and fix a taut line (as shown opposite).

Plants are placed in the crevices either during construction or after the wall has been built. The wall must be built with the soil compost firmly packed between the stones. In the case of the free-standing wall, there should be a good core of soil compost, at least 12 inches thick, to support a wide range of alpines. A free-standing wall is subject to drought, but a retaining wall is very seldom deficient in moisture.

It is not necessary for all the stones to be dressed or squared, but if they are it makes building much easier. Use the largest stones at the base to achieve stability. Avoid having vertical joints one above the other, and endeavour to bond the stone as each layer proceeds. Dry walls, like rock gardens, seem to attract rats and mice. It is therefore important to ram the compost firmly into all crevices, and subsequently to top dress where any settlement has taken place. Any signs of vermin will then quickly be noticed, and the appropriate bait in a drain tile should eliminate them.

The more vigorous plants are really unsuitable for walls. I suggest the following:

Acantholimon glumaceum
Aethionema warleyensis 'Warley Rose'
Androsace lanuginosa
Calamintha alpina
Campanula portenschlagiana

This dry stone retaining wall pictures *Penstemon davidsonii* and *Geranium subcaulescens*.

205

Helianthemum nummularium 'Wisley Pink'.

Cytisus ardoini
Cytisus × *beanii*
Cytisus kewensis
Dianthus deltoides
Dianthus hybrid 'Crossways'
Dianthus hybrid 'Elf'
Dianthus hybrid 'Mars'
Dianthus hybrid 'Spark'
Erinus alpinus
Erodium 'Merstham Pink'
Geranium dalmaticum
Gypsophila fratensis
Gypsophila repens
Gypsophila 'Rosy Veil'
Haberlea rhodopensis
Helianthemum nummularium varieties
Hippocrepis comosa 'E. R. Janes'
Hypericum coris
Hypericum nummularium
Hypericum polyphyllum
Hypericum reptans
Lewisia cotyledon
Linum capitatum
Lithospermum diffusum 'Heavenly Blue'
Morisia hypogaea

In the foreground is *Phlox douglasii*, in the background *Saxifraga bathoniensis*.

Penstemon newberryi rupicola
Penstemon scouleri
Penstemon 'Six Hills'
Phlox stolonifera 'Blue Ridge'
Phlox subulata 'Apple Blossom'
Phlox subulata ' G. F. Wilson'
Phlox subulata 'Moerheimii'
Phlox subulata 'Temiscaming'
Ramonda myconi
Saxifraga aizoon
Saxifraga moschata (all varieties)
Saxifraga 'Tumbling Waters'
Veronica rupestris

Rock gardens

The idea of building a rock garden is often prompted by the availability of a bank or slope, which does make the job of capturing that elusive, all-important quality of 'belonging', or 'naturalness', much easier, as we shall see. A slope or bank is not essential, of course. Many fine rock gardens have been built on flat sites, and the way to do this will be discussed later.

Before embarking on the construction of a rock garden, a careful study of a small rock outcrop in Wales, the Lake District or north-west Scotland is very helpful. It is there for all to see, and is clearly very much easier to understand than a list of the basic rules of construction. It is not suggested, or indeed desirable, that you attempt to copy any example from the wild, but it is easier to achieve the right effect if you have looked at, and thought about, the placement of stone in a natural example. A rock garden should always integrate with its surroundings to achieve the harmony that every garden should possess. The stone should look stately, dignified, and above all as though it were just a glimpse of an immense bed of rock under the soil. It should, moreover, give this impression without a single plant having being planted. In achieving this the main considerations are, first, that one large stone is more effective than several smaller ones, and second, that the stone should be a suitable stratified rock – either sandstone or limestone. Granite, Portland stone, marble, slate and bricks are not suitable.

Local stone is more acceptable, both aesthetically and, because transport costs are high, much cheaper, than imported stone. There is no point in buying a Westmoreland limestone if

207

you live in Kent where Kentish ragstone (sandstone) is readily available. Ensure that the stone is hard; there are soft sandstones and limestones which are seriously affected by hard weather, causing them to disintegrate. The stones should weigh no less than 2 hundredweight.

Where there is sufficient space, endeavour to site the rock garden well away from the house, with a south-west aspect if possible, and a background of trees, conifers and shrubs. An informal pond and bog garden, designed as an integral part of the rock garden, are particularly attractive (see drawing). If this is not wanted, broad drifts of grass between the outcrops are pleasing to the eye and give useful access for top dressing, weeding and replanting when required.

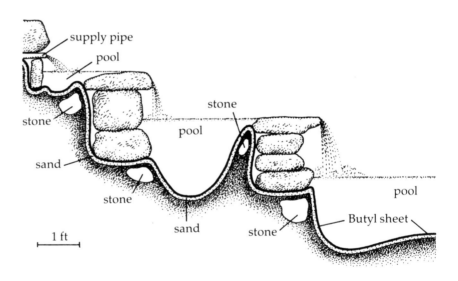

A small winch, long levers (tree stakes would do) and a measuring stick for ascertaining depths of stone are essential items when building. The first job is to peg out the site into three rectangles, (see diagram), with the largest rectangle at the rear. The stones will be laid beginning at the front, that is, in the smallest rectangle, which on a sloping site will be at the base and on a flat site will at the front. Before starting, however, it is essential to understand how the stones should be laid. Sandstone and limestone were formed in water under great pressure, creating beds of solid rock. As a result of the earth's subsequent crust movement the beds of rock were

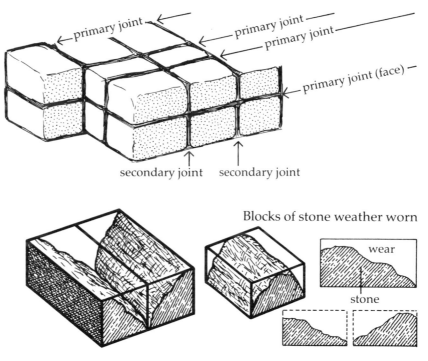

primary joint
primary joint
primary joint
primary joint (face)

secondary joint   secondary joint

Blocks of stone weather worn

wear

stone

fractured horizontally and vertically. These fissures are useful when blasting in the quarry, and they determine the sizes of the individual pieces of stone. When building a rock garden, imagine a cube of stone as each piece is laid. Exposed to the elements the stone will of course wear, the softer parts being eroded by wind, frost and water; but for building purposes be very mindful of the complete cube. The vertical fissures (called secondary joints) should run from top to bottom, the horizontal fissures (the primary joints) should, naturally, run hori-

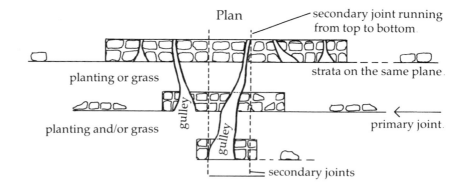

Plan   secondary joint running from top to bottom.

planting or grass   strata on the same plane.

planting and/or grass   gulley   gulley   primary joint.

secondary joints

zontally. The cardinal rule is that no stones should intrude on the primary or secondary joints. As each stone is laid, ensure the base is buried, that is, that the lowest edge is hidden, to give the impression that it is coming out of the ground naturally. The next rule is that the strata should run in the same direction, and on the same plane; they should also be continuous, although there may be wide gaps.

The secondary joints should extend from the top stratum to the bottom stratum, and should run at right angles to the horizontal lines of stratification. It would be quite wrong to bond the stone as in brickwork. The stones should fall within a rectangle, and each outcrop should relate and correspond to each other as if, before erosion, the whole formed a bed of stone.

It is useful to select the largest stones for the bottom stratum, and then choose or match (marking with chalk) those that have similar wear. These, used together, can form useful crevices for planting. To form a gulley, leave out a stone; if this is repeated as each stratum is built, the gulley will extend from top to bottom, giving the impression of water erosion. Worn stones are useful in terminating a stratum. All stones should be laid with a slight tilt backwards into the ground; this will direct rainwater into crevices, which, of course, are ideal planting positions.

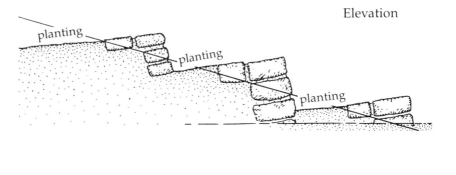

Elevation

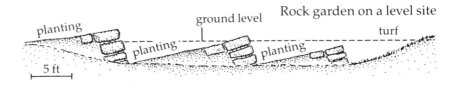

Rock garden on a level site

Different aspects are especially useful if a variety of plants is to be grown. The main aspect should ideally be south-west, but a north face formed by a rock return is the perfect spot for those plants, such as *Haberlea rhodopensis, Ramonda myconi* and some dwarf rhododendrons, which dislike the sun.

When building on a flat site the same main rules apply. The best effect is to excavate a depth of soil to about 2 feet, and if the stone is 2 feet above surrounding ground level a 4-foot bluff can be achieved. Drainage could be a problem on some soils, and if there is no satisfactory outlet it is best to build in the way suggested in the diagram below, which is not as low below ground level that suggested in the diagram opposite. (The pond, of course, need not be included.) The commonest error when building is to try to get too much height. A 4-foot maximum bluff is very effective in a meduim-sized garden. Another common mistake is to use too much stone. It is not necessary to have masses of stones; a few large ones are more effective. Leave plenty of gaps because these can be filled with splendid colourful drifts of one particular variety of plant. A continuous face of rock is not very effective, but is easily built. If the stone is fresh, the colour can be toned down by painting it with a manure solution on completion.

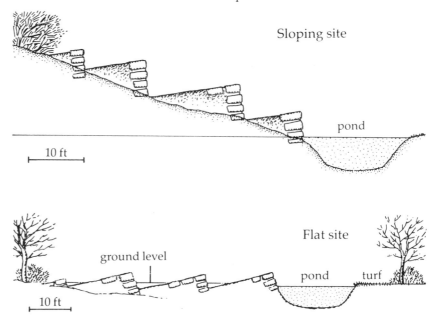

Sloping site

pond

10 ft

Flat site

ground level

pond   turf

10 ft

As building proceeds, a prepared compost of 7 parts (by volume) loam, 4 parts peat and 3 parts grit should be rammed firmly around each stone. This compost can be used to form the planting beds and crevices. Where sharp drainage or an acid compost is required, this can be arranged when all the rock has been placed and the delightful task of deciding what to plant and where begins.

It would be quite impossible to cover such a large subject as alpines in a book of this size, and all I can do is list some of my favourites. Membership of the Alpine Garden Society and the Royal Horticultural Society, who have a magnificent rock garden at Wisley, is strongly recommended. Some alpines suitable for a rock garden which I find particularly appealing, and which are quite easy to grow, are as follows. Recipes for the recommended soil mixtures are given after the list.

Acantholimon glumaceum (lime mixture)
Aethionema warleyensis 'Warley Rose' (general soil mixture)
Androsace sarmentosa (general soil mixture)
Androsace primuloides (general soil mixture)
Anemone pulsatilla varieties (general soil mixture)
Aphyllanthes monspeliensis (general soil mixture)
Arnebia echioides (general soil mixture)
Campanula carpatica (general soil mixture)
Campanula cochleariifolia (general soil mixture)
Campanula collina (general soil mixture)
Campanula garganica (general soil mixture)
Campanula glomerata (lime mixture)
Campanula pulla (general soil mixture)
Campanula pulloides (leaf mixture)
Campanula turbinata (general soil mixture)
Ceratostigma plumbaginoides (general soil mixture)
Cytisus ardoini (general soil mixture)
Cytisus × *beanii* (general soil mixture)
Cytisus kewensis (general soil mixture)
Cytisus procumbens (general soil mixture)
Daphne blagayana (lime mixture)
Daphne cneorum (lime mixture)
Dianthus deltoides (lime mixture)
Dianthus 'Whitehills' (lime mixture)
Dryas octopetala (general soil mixture)
Erinus alpinus (general soil mixture)
Genista lydia (general soil mixture)
Genista sagittalis (general soil mixture)
Gentiana acaulis (general soil mixture)
Gentiana asclepiadea (peat mixture)
Gentiana hascombensis (peat mixture)
Gentiana septemfida (peat mixture)
Gentiana sino-ornata (peat mixture)
Gentiana verna (peat mixture)
Geranium dalmaticum (lime mixture)
Geranium sanguineum Lancastriense (lime mixture)

A shingle top dressing
suppresses weeds,
conserves moisture and
provides a cool root run.

Polygonum affine 'Donald
Lowndes' has 9 inch
spikes of pink flowers
from August to October,
and bronze and crimson
tinted foliage during the
winter months.

Globularia cordifolia (lime mixture)
Gypsophila repens (lime mixture)
Gypsophila fratensis (lime mixture)
Haberlea rhodopensis (peat mixture)
Hypericum olympicum (general soil mixture)
Hypericum polyphyllum (general soil mixture)
Jeffersonia dubia (peat mixture)
Linum flavum (general soil mixture)
Linum narbonense (general soil mixture)
Linum perenne (general soil mixture)
Lithospermum diffusum 'Heavenly Blue' and 'Grace Ward'
(general soil mixture)
Nierembergia rivularis (general soil mixture)
Oenothera speciosa (general soil mixture)
Omphalodes cappadocica (general soil mixture)
Phlox adsurgens (peat mixture)
Phlox douglasii varieties (general soil mixture)
Phlox stolonifera (general soil mixture)
Phlox subulata varieties (general soil mixture)
Polygonum affine (general soil mixture)
Potentilla × *tonguei* (general soil mixture)
Primula denticulata (general soil mixture)
Primula frondosa (general soil mixture)
Primula nutans (leaf mixture)

213

Primula rosea (leaf mixture)
Primula spectabilis (lime mixture)
Primula veitchii (leaf mixture)
Ramonda myconi (peat mixture)
Rhododendron 'Bric-à-Brac' (peat mixture)
Rhododendron 'Elizabeth' (peat mixture)
Rhododendron 'Ethel' (peat mixture)
Rhododendron impeditum (peat mixture)
Rhododendron 'Jenny' (peat mixture)
Rhododendron leucaspis (peat mixture)
Rhododendron 'Treasure' (peat mixture)
Roscoea cautleoides (leaf mixture)
Saxifraga irvingii (very sharp mixture)
Saxifraga jenkinsae (very sharp mixture)
Saxifraga longifolia 'Tumbling Waters' (lime mixture)
Saxifraga 'Stormonth' and other mossy varieties such as
'Apple Blossom', 'Wenlock Peach' (general soil mixture)
Sempervivum tectorum varieties (lime or very sharp mixture)
Silene alpestris (general soil mixture)
Sisyrinchium bermudianum (general soil mixture)
Thymus serpyllum varieties (general soil mixture)
Tiarella cordifolia (leaf mixture)
Veronica fruticans (very sharp mixture)
Veronica kellereri (general soil mixture)

Bulbs (see Chapter 9) are also particularly good on rock gardens.

Alpine composts

General soil mixture: 7 parts loam, 4 parts peat, 3 parts coarse sand or grit (⅛ inch).

Peat mixture: 7 parts peat, 4 parts coarse sand or grit (⅛ inch), 3 parts loam. Rotten bracken and conifer needles are excellent substitutes for the peat.

Leaf mixture: 7 parts leaf mould, 4 parts coarse sand or grit (⅛ inch), 3 parts loam.

Lime mixture: 7 parts loam, 2 parts peat, 3 parts coarse sand or grit (⅛ inch), 2 parts mortar rubble.

Very sharp mixture: 2 parts general soil mixture, 3 parts washed shingle (⅛ inch).

This fully planted rock 'outcrop' shows the alignment of the horizontal and vertical joints between the rocks.

CHAPTER 13

Water and bog gardens

The presence of water in a garden gives a wonderful opportunity of embarking on the pleasant task of cultivating aquatic and moisture-loving plants.

The character and extent of your water garden will obviously be governed by the amount of space available. Those fortunate enough to have a natural pond or stream can plant and develop it in such a way that it will become a major feature in the overall design. Any alterations to a stream or small river must, of course, be very carefully considered if the risk of winter flooding is to be avoided; nevertheless the possibility of diverting it to supply a pond, bog garden, primula ditch or series of pools cascading gently through a rock garden is exciting and worth investigation. Most gardens do not have natural water, but this need not preclude the making of a bog garden which, if it is well proportioned in relation to the size of the garden, sited in the sun and tastefully planted, will bring the coolness and peace which water always imparts, whether it is static or in the form of some magnificent fountain display. Very few plants will survive fast running water (and this includes water lilies); apart from this it is the depth of water and the amount of sunlight which chiefly determine the type of planting. One of the delights of a pool is reflection; but this is lost if the pool is overplanted. Constraint is a difficulty as far as the enthusiast is concerned, but a pool is most effective if two-thirds of its surface is free of plants.

A pool can be either formal or informal. A formal pool could be the focal point in a lawn, terrace or sunken garden. It will be square, rectangular, oval, circular or a symmetrical design in a combination of these shapes. It can be raised above ground level, or level with the ground. I prefer a flat design, where the water is a few inches below ground level, with a simple surround of York stone or a border of hard engineering bricks set in a fine lawn. An informal pool will be irregular in shape,

Opposite:
A well-established pool epitomizing good planting and illustrating the value of reflection.

217

and can be enhanced by association with a bog garden or garden. The planting of bog plants can be much more extensive around an informal pool than by a formal pool. They should be on the north or east side to ensure maximum reflection and warmth from sunlight.

The actual construction of a pool is not difficult; it can be made with concrete, puddled clay, fibreglass or a ready-made pool liner. The puddled clay method is not completely satisfactory, and I advise against it except for those who have a very heavy clay soil. The concrete pool must be made correctly, or it will leak, and this is difficult to rectify. If it does leak, once the initial disappointment and despair is overcome line the pool with a mixture of 2 parts sand and 1 part Pudlo to a thickness of ⅜ inch.

Concrete-lined pools

Having decided on the size and shape of your pool, excavate to allow a 6-inch concrete thickness for both floor and walls. A depth of 2½ to 3 feet is ideal. Having firmed the soil and floor, line the hole with a 500-gauge polythene sheet. Using fresh cement (this is very important), make the concrete by mixing 1 part cement to 4 parts ¾-inch ballast. When mixing, add a waterproofing agent such as Pudlo or Medusa. Observe the manufacturer's instructions strictly, and avoid getting the concrete too wet. Lay the floor first to a depth of 6 inches, using a rammer to consolidate the concrete, and smooth off with a plasterer's trowel. Having levelled off the floor, fix into position a 1-inch-thick timber shuttering, secured to battens and suitably braced top and bottom to keep it in place. Before putting in the concrete for the walls, make sure the bottom is clean and the edge of the floor slab roughened to achieve a good key. Ideally, the walls should be constructed on the same day as the floor is laid. Damp, mild weather is the best time for concreting. Avoid frosty weather, and on a hot day cover the concrete with damp sacks to prevent it from drying too quickly. When constructing a concrete pool, it is most important to have the top level, both to minimize the amount of concrete showing, and to avoid an overspill at one end.

After a week, fill the pool with water and leave it for six months, after which period impurities from the concrete, harmful to fish and plants, will be minimal. This may seem a long time, but in practice it works out reasonably well. Ideally, make the pool in October (just the right time for concreting), and leave it until April–May, which is the best time for planting aquatics. A filter system connected with a fountain or waterfall may be installed (see diagram). Fish should not be introduced until the plants are growing and established, otherwise the new growth will be eaten as it appears. During the winter, float pieces of timber in the water to relieve the pressure of expanding ice on the concrete walls. A pond 12 feet by 8 feet could accommodate an old wooden door as an excellent precaution against damage. Do not break thick ice around the edges, because the shock to fish is detrimental.

Butyl-sheet-lined pools

The method I prefer for making both formal and informal pools is by the use of a butyl sheet, provided that certain plants are not planted in the immediate vicinity. Bamboos, which are excellent waterside plants, have a very tough root system, and the butyl sheet will be punctured and ruined if they are planted closer than 6 feet away. Large willow species, including the weeping willows which are so often planted in association with water, are a particular threat. They are much too big for small gardens anyway, quickly outgrowing their station. The roots are particularly invasive, extending 100 feet or more. On one occasion willow roots were found to have spread under the entire bottom of a very large pool, about 120 by 80 feet. The butyl liner was extensively damaged, and had to be replaced after removal of the willow tree.

A butyl sheet can be made to any size and shape; it is durable, and if laid properly will survive twenty years or more. I do not consider 500-gauge polythene liners on their own to be worth the effort of excavation and subsequent planting, because they rarely last more than five years. 'To buy cheap is to buy twice' is a most appropriate adage in this instance.

Once the excavation has been made, remove sharp stones and line the whole excavation. If the pool is to be saucer-shaped, put in a 1-inch layer of sand. If the sides are too steep, make a layer of thick cardboard, newspapers, sacking, old carpet or similar material to prevent the liner from being damaged against the surround when the weight of the water presses on it.

Before the pool is filled a filter system could be installed along with a fountain or waterfall to keep the water reasonably clear. This system is one which I used for the ponds in the Barbican Arts Centre conservatory, where I was responsible for the layout and planting. It has been very satisfactory in both pools (one lined with concrete and the other with a butyl liner). Lay 2-inch-diameter rigid PVC pipes at about 18-inch intervals throughout the entire floor area, either as a grid or

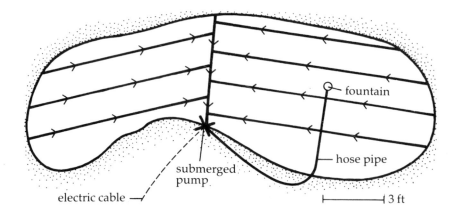

in a herringbone pattern (see diagram). Each pipe end should be capped. Holes should be drilled in the pipes 6 inches apart at the ends furthest from the submerged pump, graduated to 24 inches apart near the pump. Connect the fountain or waterfall to the submerged pump by hose-pipe. Over the whole pipe layout place a layer of ⅜-inch washed shingle, which should be 2 inches above the pipes (see diagrams).

With the pump running continuously, a filter barrier is formed on the surface of the shingle. Water passes through the shingle into the pipes and is then pumped to the fountain and returned to the pond. This system reduces algae growth and keeps the water remarkably clean and oxygenated.

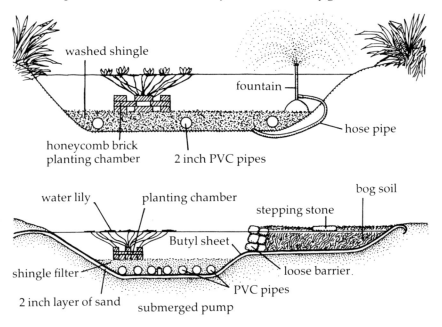

Fibreglass-lined pools

There are numerous shapes and sizes of ready-made fibreglass pool linings which are tough and durable, but if one of these is chosen it must be properly installed by excavating a hole large enough to accommodate it. It is best to lay it on a 1-inch bed of sand, carefully level the edges with a spirit level, and pack some bricks as an underpinning to guard against tilting while you backfill with soil. If it is not level there will be an overflow at one end and unwanted edges visible at the other. Before filling it with water, check again to ensure that the pool is level, because ramming the back-filling of soil firmly into place does tend to lift the pool out of position.

Planting-containers, plastic baskets, turf placed upside down to form walls, and bricks laid in a honeycomb fashion all make useful ways of holding soil in position for planting. Small containers and baskets are adequate for small pools, but larger pools should, of course, have bigger planting positions. The depths of the containers should vary depending on the plants (see list of recommended plants for planting depths).

Where there is insufficient space for a pool, or if the cost of construction is prohibitive, a few water lilies and other aquatics can be grown in one or more tubs (half wine-barrels) or tanks sunk into the ground. They must have sunshine to be successful. The edges can be planted with a few suitable marginal plants to complete a very interesting and attractive feature for very little expenditure.

Algae in a hot summer can be a most difficult problem, particularly in shallow pools. The Barbican lakes, which are only about 15 inches deep, developed the typical green pea soup appearance during hot weather. Chemical control is not satisfactory, and is by no means permanent; furthermore the fish population, which is so essential in providing the biological control of midges and mosquitoes, are at risk when potassium permanganate or copper sulphate are used. Because of the algae's photosynthesis process, daytime oxygen levels are high, but because of oxygen demands via respiration, the oxygen level at night falls dramatically, which is extremely stressful for the fish. To overcome this problem it is necessary to pump air into the deepest section of the pool. Install an electric pump, linked to a pipe with drilled holes graduated from 6 inches apart to 24 inches apart (near the pump) laid at the bottom of the pool. By means of a time-switch from midnight to 7 a.m., pump air through the pipe; the fish will quickly discover the lifeline and remain in its vicinity. This is only necessary during the hot summer months when algal growth is at its peak.

Bog gardens

A bog garden is a natural extension of an informal pool or stream. I have a particular fondness for moisture-loving plants, the majority of which are very handsome in both leaf and flower. They are shown off to their best advantage in a natural setting. The sides of a stream, pond or ditch are excellent positions provided there is plenty of sunshine. In the average garden, where natural water does not exist, a 'natural' setting can be made. Excavate the area to be set aside for a bog garden to a depth of 15 inches, preferably on the north side of an informal pool. There are many advantages in laying the bog garden at the time an informal pool is made. The liner may be either a 500-gauge polythene sheet, or the better-quality and more expensive butyl sheet. Lay the liner on a 1-inch-thick bed of sand. Between the bog garden and pool build a loose wall of pieces of rock about 6 to 9 inches in diameter, to form a rough barrier, which will allow water to seep through to moisten the bog garden soil (see diagram). Over the sheeting, fill the area with a mixture of equal parts of loam, peat and well-rotted compost or decayed farmyard manure or spent

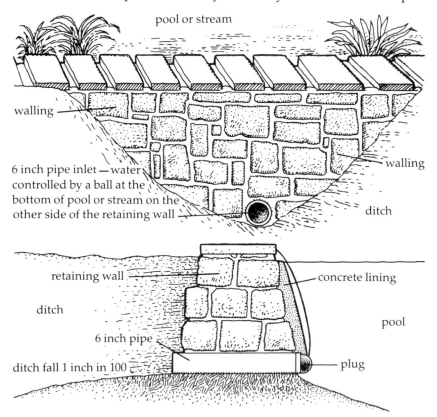

mushroom manure (a good rich soil is wanted for bog plants) to 4 to 6 inches above the water level.

Stepping-stones through the bog garden are an attractive feature and provide access for early weeding (later the growth is so lush that all weeds are suppressed), and for dead-heading spent flowers if the seed is not required.

Another attractive possibility is a primula ditch. I suggest that it should be 10 to 30 metres long, with a depth starting at 15 inches and falling to 30 inches; a fall of 1 in 100 is sufficient to supply water as and when necessary. A good selection of primulas to plant on the banks is as follows: *Primula rosea, P. pulverulenta, P. florindae, P. aurantiaca, P. beesiana, P. burmanica, P. helodoxa, P. japonica, P. secundiflora* and *P. sikkimensis*. These can be most attractive throughout May and June. All that is necessary regarding maintenance is weeding and removing old flower heads if the seed is not wanted (primula seed soon loses its viability; sow immediately after collection). Lift the plants, divide and replant as and when necessary. Top dress with a sifted leaf mould each spring. The banks need not, of course, be devoted entirely to primulas, but may be used to grow a variety of bog plants.

There is a considerable range of aquatics and bog plants, and here I am able to mention only a few of the best.

Bog garden plants

Aconitum napellus bicolor. Strong 3-foot spikes bear light blue and white flowers in July-August. *A.n.* 'Bressingham Spire', an excellent bog plant, has violet-blue flowers. The roots of *Aconitum napellus* (monkshood) are extremely poisonous to both humans and livestock.

Acorus calamus 'Variegatus' **(variegated sweet flag).** This plant will grow in very wet bog or a few inches of water, and is recommended for its iris-like, variegated foliage. A fine plant, 3 feet high.

Aruncus sylvester **(goat's beard).** A fine, imposing plant with lovely, 4-foot, creamy-white plumes of flower in June. *A.s.* 'Kneffi' is a less vigorous but equally attractive plant, 30 inches high.

Arundinaria murieliae **(bamboo).** This is one of the best bamboo species in cultivation. It should be sheltered from wind, and is ideal in a moist but not waterlogged soil. It will grow to 9 feet high by about 6 feet wide.

***Butomus umbellatus* (flowering rush)**. An exceptionally beautiful plant, which in July-August forms lovely umbels of pink flowers on 2- to 3-foot stems. This is a magnificent plant for growing in 12 inches of water or a wet bog.

***Calla palustris* (bog arum)**. A lovely plant with small white arum flowers and attractive, heart-shaped leaves. 9 inches high. It is suitable for a wet bog, and at the water's edge.

***Caltha palustris* (kingcup)**. This is excellent for the wet bog or under 12 inches of water. There are lovely yellow flowers in April, 12 inches high. *C.p.* 'Flore Pleno' is the double form.

***Chusquea couleou* (bamboo)**. This is a magnificent bamboo which grows up to 18 feet high. It is difficult to acquire, but is well worth having in a large bog garden.

***Eupatorium purpureum* (Joe-Pye-weed)**. A very effective bog plant with heads of purple-lilac flowers in autumn, growing to 4 feet or more.

***Filipendula hexapetala* 'Flore Pleno' (dropwort)**. From delightful ferny leaves, 24 inches high, come stems of flat heads of ivory-white blossoms opening in June-July. A good bog plant.

Gunnera manicata. This is a huge plant which looks rather like rhubarb. It must have winter protection of a covering of bracken or straw. It is a splendid plant where there is space for it at the edge of water. It grows 8 feet high by 10 feet wide, and the leaves are often 6 feet across. Therefore only suitable for the large pond!

***Hemerocallis* (day lily)**. There is an immense range of hybrids – lovely, hardy plants which thrive in moist soil, growing up to 3 feet high and flowering in July-August. Varieties well worth growing include:

    H. 'Black Prince'. Ruby-purple.
    H. 'Conspicua'. Coppery orange.
    H. 'Hyperion'. Canary yellow.
    H. 'Margaret Perry'. Tangerine-yellow.
    H. 'Marie Ballard. Salmon-apricot.
    H. 'Saladin'. Bronze-red.

Hosta. This is a genus grown chiefly for its very handsome foliage. Recommended species include:

Gunnera manicata is a plant for the larger garden and best situated by the edge of a pond or stream.

H. albo-marginata 'Thomas Hogg'. White-edged, mid-green leaves.

H. fortunei. Lilac-mauve flowers, 18 inches high, appear from July to September.

H.f. gigantea is an impressive plant, 3 feet high.

H. glauca. Blue-green leaves, 9 inches wide and 12 inches long.

H. lancifolia. Dark green, glossy leaves.

H. l. 'Aurea'. Golden-green leaves.

H. ventricosa. Big, oval, glaucous leaves with deep blue flowers on 3-foot stems.

Iris kaempferi **(clematis-flowered Japanese iris).** There are numerous varieties of this lovely bog iris. The flowers, which have three large petals, are exceptionally beautiful in June. Although they thrive in boggy conditions, they will not tolerate standing in water, or an alkaline soil.

Iris sibirica. A lovely waterside plant, of which there are many hybrids, flowering in June and July. 'Caesar', 'Emperor', 'Perry's Pygmy', 'Snow Queen' and 'Mrs Saunders' are all good varieties.

Kirengeshoma palmata. This is a hardy Japanese plant that flourishes in a moist soil, and grows 3 feet high. It has attractive foliage and pretty, waxy, bell-shaped flowers in August – an ideal bog plant.

Ligularia clivorum. This splendid, stately plant has broad, heart-shaped leaves and orange flowers growing to a height of 4 to 5 feet. Outstanding varieties are 'Orange Queen' and 'Othello'.

Lysichitum americanum. A superb bog plant with huge, broad leaves, 24 inches or more in length. But before any leaves appear, in April, lovely large yellow spathes are produced.

Lysichitum camschatcense. This is similar to *L. americanum*, but it has white spathes instead of yellow.

Lysimachia clethroides. A 3-foot-high plant with white flower spikes, July-September.

Lythrum salicaria **(purple loosestrife).** There are several varieties, all about 4 feet high, bearing slender spikes of flower in

Lysichitum americanum.

225

June and July. 'The Beacon' (rosy red). 'Lady Sackville', (deep pink) and 'Robert' (a dwarf pink) are recommended

Lythrum virgatum. This is shorter and less vigorous than *L. salicaria*, growing to about 30 inches. Good varieties are 'Rose Queen' (rosy pink) and 'The Rocket' (a darker pink).

Peltiphyllum peltatum. This has large round leaves, about 12 inches in diameter, pink flowers on 12–15-inch stems, and thick rhizomes on the soil surface. It is an interesting plant, but not very showy.

Phyllostachys flexuosa **(bamboo).** This is a lovely bamboo, up to 10 feet high and 6 feet wide.

Phyllostachys nigra **(black bamboo).** Another graceful bamboo, with black stems up to 15 feet tall and 8 feet wide. The varieties 'Boryana', 'Henonsis' and 'Puntata' are all splendid bog plants.

Phyllostachys viridis. This is a splendid bamboo growing up to 15 feet by 10 feet wide.

Primula. A particularly beautiful genus containing many species and varieties that flourish in boggy conditions. No water-side should be without them.

The following are recommended:

P. aurantiaca. Candelabra stems, deep orange flowers, May-June. 12 inches.
P. beesiana. Purple flowers, May-June, 18 inches.
P. bulleyana. Orange flowers, May-June, 18 inches.
P. chronantha. White flowers, May-June, 18 inches.
P. chungensis. Pale orange flowers, June, 12 inches.
P. cockburniana. Orange flowers, June, 18 inches.
P. florindae. Yellow flowers, July-August, 24 inches plus.
P. helodoxa. Yellow flowers, June-July, 24 inches plus.
P. japonica. Many forms and varieties, May-June, 12-18 inches.
P. pulverulenta. 'Bartley Strain'. Many shades of colour, reds, pinks, May-June.
P. rosea. Crimson flowers, April-May, 6-9 inches.
P. secundiflora. Rose-red, June, 12 inches.

Primula bulleyana.

Osmunda regalis (**royal fern**). This beautiful fern flourishes at the pool edge, and grows up to 5 feet high.

Rheum palmatum. A handsome large rhubarb, with spikes of creamy-white flowers, 6 feet high. There is also an attractive purplish-red foliage form, *R.p.* 'Atropurpureum'.

Sidalcea (**Greek mallow**). Excellent in boggy conditions, this attractive plant has pink flowers, July-August. Varieties are numerous. A few of the best are listed in the chapter on herbaceous border plants.

Thalictrum adiantifolium. This has lovely foliage, up to 4 feet high. The flowers are insignificant.

Trollius. This is a truly splendid bog plant. There are many varieties which are worth growing; 'Alabaster', 'Canary Bird', 'Orange Glow', 'Golden Monarch', 'Lemon Queen' and 'Orange Princess' are just a few of the best.

Water plants

Aponogeton distachyus (**water hawthorn**). A beautiful floating aquatic which has narrow, dark green leaves and small, white, scented flowers, water depth 18–30 inches.

Butomus umbellatus. (See under Bog garden plants.) Quite happy in 12 inches of water.

Calla palustris (See under Bog garden plants.) Quite happy in water up to 12 inches deep.

Hottonia palustris (**water violet**). This makes masses of finely divided, submerged foliage with upright spikes of pale lilac flowers. It will grow in water up to 18 inches deep.

Iris laevigata. This is a lovely Japanese iris which thrives in 2 to 3 inches of water. Very attractive, pale blue flowers are produced in June, 2 feet high.

Nymphaea (**water lilies**). This is the biggest and most showy genus of aquatic plants. There are a considerable number of hybrids of great beauty, and making a choice is simply a matter of selecting those you like from those that are available. I particularly like the following:

Nymphea 'Sunrise'.

'Chromatella'. Yellow. Water depth 1½–2½ feet.

'Escarboucle'. Red. Water depth 2–6 feet.
'James Brydon'. Red. Water depth 1½–3 feet.
'Purpurata'. Red. Water depth 1–2 feet.
'Rosea'. Rose. Water depth 2–4 feet.
'Sulphurea'. Yellow. Water depth 1–2 feet.
'William B. Shaw'. Pink/red. Water depth 1–2 feet.

Pygmaea hybrids
'Alba'. White. Water depth under 12 inches.
'Helvola'. Yellow, water depth under 12 inches.

***Pontederia cordata* (pickerel weed).** This has lovely blue flowers, July-August, with attractive foliage, 18 inches high. Happy in up to 12 inches of water.

***Sagittaria sagittifolia* (arrowhead).** A good bog plant, and quite at home in up to 12 inches of water. The leaves are arrowhead-shaped, and attractive white flowers are produced, July-August.

***Scirpus tabernaemontani zebrinus*.** A most attractive plant, resembling a bulrush. The stems have wide cream bands, making a striking variegated effect. Height 3 feet. It is happy in a wet bog or shallow water, and is a fine plant for any water garden.

No room for a pool is no excuse for no pool at all! but this pool in a half barrel would probably be even more effective if sunk into the ground.

Glossary of specific names

acaulis stemless
adpressus closely pressed
adsurgens ascending
aestivus summer, summer-flowering
aizoon evergreen
albus white
albo-marginatus white-edged
alpestris alpine
alpicola dwelling in high mountains
altissimus very tall
amabilis lovable
amoenus lovely
amplexicaulis with leaves embracing stems
angustifolius narrow-leaved
aquifolius with pointed leaves
arboreus tree-like
argenteus silvery
argutus sharp-toothed
argyrophyllus silver-leaved
armatus armed with thorns
aurantiacus orange
aureus golden yellow
azurea pale blue
baccatus berried
barbatus bearded
bifolia two-leaved
blandus attractive
borealis northern
buxifolius having box-like leaves

brachyphylla short-leaved
caesius blue-grey
caespitosus growing in tufts
calcaratus spurred
calcareus lime-loving
campestris of the fields
candicans white
canescens becoming hoary white
capillaris hair-like
capitatus closely clustered
cardinalis scarlet
cardiophyllus having heart-shaped leaves
carneus flesh-pink
chinensis from China
chrysanthus golden-flowered
ciliatus edged with fine hairs, like an eyelid
cinereus ash-grey
cirrhosus tendrilled
citrinus lemon-yellow
coccineus scarlet
coelestis heavenly, blue
collinus growing on hills
communis common
comosus hairy
confertus crowded together
contortus involved
cordatus heart-shaped
coronarius crown-like, wreath-like
crassifolius thick-leaved

crinitus long-haired
crispus curly
cruentus blood-red
cyaneus dark blue
dasycarpum hairy-fruited
dealbatus washed with white
dens-canis dog-toothed, in the shape of a dog's tooth
diffusus spread out
dixhyllus two-leaved
diversifolius with leaves of more than one kind
dolabrata axe-shaped
dumosus with a bushy habit
eburneus ivory-coloured
elatus tall
elegans elegant
erectus with an upright habit
eximius excellent
farinosus mealy, covered with powder
fastigiatus upright
femina female
filifolius having thread-like leaves
flabellatus fan-shaped
flavus golden-yellow
flore pleno double-flowered
floribundus many-flowered
formosus finely formed
fragrans scented
frigidus growing in cold regions
frutescens becoming shrubby
fulgens glowing
fulvus tawny
glaber hairless
glaucus blue-grey
globosus ball-shaped
glomeratus clustered into a head
glutinosus sticky
gracilipes slender-stalked
gramineus grass-leaved
grandiflorus large-flowered

grandis large
graveolens strong-smelling
hederifolius having leaves like ivy
helodoxa marsh-glory
hirsutus hairy
hispidus clothed with stiff hairs
hyemalis winter-flowering
ilicifolius holly-leaved
imbricatus overlapping
incanus hoary, or grey
incumbens prostrate
inodorus scentless
insignis remarkable
integrifolius whole-leaved, not broken at the edges
involucrata having a collection of bracts round a cluster of flowers
isophyllus equal-leaved
japonicus from Japan
junceus rush-like
lacteus milky
lactiflorus white-flowered
laevigatus smooth
lanceolatus lance-shaped
latifolius broad-leaved
laurifolius with laurel-like leaves
laxiflorus with loosely arranged flowers
litoralis of the sea-shore
longiflorus long-flowered
longifolius long-leaved
lucidus shining
luteus yellow
macrocarpus with large fruit
macrophyllus large-leaved
maculatus spotted
magnificus splendid
maritimus of the seaside
mas male
medius medium-sized
microphyllus small-leaved

millefolium thousand-leaved
minimus smallest
minor, minus small
minutus very small
mollis soft, tender
montanus of the mountains
mucronatus musk-scented
multicaulis many-stemmed
muralis of walls
mutatus changed
nanus dwarf
nemorosus of woodland
niger black
nitidus glossy, polished
nivalis of snowy places
nobilis excellent
nutans with nodding flowers
obtusatus blunted
odoratus sweet-scented
officinalis medicinal
oppositifolius having the
    leaves set opposite each
    other
pallidus pale
palmatus divided like a hand
palustris of the marsh
paniculatus with loose,
    branching flowers
parviflorus small-flowered
patulus outspread
pauciflorus few-flowered
pectinatus comb-like
peduncularis stalked
perennis perennial
petiolaris having a long
    petiole, or leaf stalk
petraeus growing among rocks
playtypetalus broad-petalled
plicatus folded
plumosus feathery
polyphyllus many-leaved
polyrrhizus having many roots
populifolius with poplar-like
    leaves
praecox early-flowering

procerus tall
procumbens prostrate
procurrens spreading
pubescens covered with soft
    hairs
pulchellus dainty
pulcherrimus beautiful
pullus dark-coloured
pumilio dwarf
punctatus dotted
pungens having piercing
    thorns or pointed leaves
puniceus reddish
pusillus dwarf
racemosus with individually
    stalked, spirally arranged
    flowers
radicans rooting easily
ramosus having many
    branches
recurvus downward-curving
reflexus bent back
repandus having leaves with
    wavy edges
repens creeping
retans creeping flat
reticutalus net-like
riparius of river banks
rivularis of brook-sides
roseus rosy-pink
rotundifolius round-leaved
ruber red
rufus reddish
rugosus wrinkled
rupestris of rocky places
rupicola living among rocks
sagittatus arrowhead-shaped
salicifolius having willow-like
    leaves
sanguineus blood-red
sarmentosus having many
    runners
scaber rough to touch
secundiflorus having flowers
    turned to the same side

semperflorens ever-flowering
sempervirens evergreen
serotinus autumn-flowering
serpyllifolius having leaves like thyme
sessilifolius without stalks
siliquastrum having pods with a partition between the seeds
speciosus handsome
spectabilis notable
sphaerocephalus round-headed
spicatus spiked, spiky
spinosus thorny
splendens brilliant
squarrosus rough
stenophylla narrow-leaved
stellatus star-like
striatus streaked
strictus drawn together
sylvaticus growing in woods
sylvestris growing wild
tardus slow in growth
tenax tough
tenellus delicate
tetraptera having four wings, or winged seed pods
tinctorius used in dyeing
tinus obscure
tomentosus densely hairy
triandrus having three stamens

triflora three-flowered
trifoliatus three-leaved, having leaves arranged in threes
tristis sad
turbinatus inversely conical
umbellatus having flowers in umbels
umbrosus shade-loving
uniflorus one-flowered
vagans widely distributed
venosus having many veins
venustrum pleasing
vernus spring, spring-flowering
versicolor of a changeable colour
verticillatus having whorled leaves
vestitus clothed, usually with hairs
virgatus of twiggy habit
virginalis pure white
vitifolium having vine-like leaves
viridiflorus green-flowered
viridis green
volubile twining
vulgaris common

Index to Plants